CHANGING ADOLESCENCE

Social trends and mental health

Edited by Ann Hagell

Nuffield

D0263983

First published in Great Britain in 2012 by

The Policy Press
University of Bristol
Fourth Floor
Beacon House
Queen's Road
Bristol BS8 1QU, UK

t: +44 (0)117 331 4054
f: +44 (0)117 331 4093
tpp-info@bristol.ac.uk
www.policypress.co.uk

North American office:
The Policy Press
c/o The University of Chicago Press
1427 East 60th Street
Chicago, IL 60637, USA
t: +1 773 702 7700
f: +1 773-702-9756
sales@press.uchicago.edu
www.press.uchicago.edu

© The Policy Press 2012

British Library Cataloguing in Publication Data
A catalogue record for this book is available from the British Library.

Library of Congress Cataloging-in-Publication Data
A catalog record for this book has been requested.

ISBN 978 1 44730 103 5 paperback
ISBN 978 1 44730 104 2 hardcover

The right of Ann Hagell to be identified as editor of this work has been asserted
by her in accordance with the Copyright, Designs and Patents Act 1988.

Cover design by The Policy Press
Front cover: image kindly supplied by
istock.com
Printed and bound in Great Britain by
Henry Ling, Dorchester.
The Policy Press uses environmentally
responsible print partners.

MIX
Paper from
responsible sources
FSC® C013985

Contents

List of tables and figures

Tables

Figures

Acronyms and abbreviations

ADHD	Attention deficit hyperactivity disorder
A-level	Advanced-level British secondary school public examination (two-year course)
BCS70	1970 British Birth Cohort Study
BHPS	British Household Panel Survey
DSM-III	Diagnostic and Statistical Manual of Mental Disorders, 3rd edition
DSM-IV	Diagnostic and Statistical Manual of Mental Disorders, 4th edition
EPPI-Centre	Evidence for Policy and Practice Information and Co-ordinating Centre
ESYTC	Edinburgh Study of Youth Transitions and Crime
ESPAD	European School Survey Project on Alcohol and Other Drugs
EU	European Union
EURYDICE	Information on Education Systems and Policies in Europe
Foundation	The Nuffield Foundation
GCSE	General Certificate of Secondary Education (taken at 16 years)
GHQ	General Health Questionnaire (and GHQ-12, an abbreviated version)
HBSC	Health Behaviour of School-aged Children survey
HPA axis	Hypothalamic-pituitary-adrenal axis
MORI	Market and Opinion Research International Ltd
MTO	Moving to Opportunity
MTUS	Multinational Time Use Study
NEET	Not in education, employment or training
Ofsted	Office for Standards in Education, Children's Services and Skills
ONS	Office for National Statistics
SALSUS	Scottish Schools Adolescent Lifestyle and Substance Use Survey
SDDU	Smoking, Drinking and Drug Use Survey
SHEU	Schools Health Education Unit
RELACHS	Research with East London Adolescents; Community Health Survey
UK	United Kingdom
UNICEF	United Nations Children's Fund
USA	United States of America
WHO	World Health Organization

Notes on contributors

Judith Aldridge is senior lecturer in the Centre for Criminology and Criminal Justice at the University of Manchester, UK. Her research spans aspects of drug use and drug dealing, including drug dealing within street gangs, and the sales and use of both illegal and legal psychostimulants. She has co-authored a number of books including the recent *Illegal leisure revisited* (Routledge, 2011), documenting the drug journeys of a cohort of 14-year-olds in the early 1990s into adulthood, and *Dancing on drugs* (Free Association Books, 2001).

Stephan Collishaw is senior lecturer in developmental psychopathology in the Child and Adolescent Psychiatry section, Department for Psychological Medicine and Neurology, and a member of the Medical Research Council (MRC) Centre for Neuropsychiatric Genetics and Genomics, Cardiff University School of Medicine, UK. He was awarded a DPhil in psychology from the University of Sussex in 2003.

Sarah Curtis is professor of health and risk at Durham University. She is internationally recognised for her research in geographies of health and has published widely in this field. She is co-director for the Institute of Hazard Risk and Resilience and also carries out multi-disciplinary health research through the Wolfson Research Institute at Durham. She has been senior editor, medical geography, for the *Journal Social Science and Medicine* from 2003-12.

Shari Daya was awarded a PhD in geography at Durham University, UK, in 2007. She is lecturer in human geography in the Department of Environmental and Geographical Science at the University of Cape Town, South Africa.

Michael Donmall is reader in health sciences, and director of the National Drug Evidence Centre within the School of Community-based Medicine, at the University of Manchester, UK. He served on the government's Advisory Council on the Misuse of Drugs for many years, and is the originator of the UK National Drug Treatment Monitoring Systems and treatment demand indicator expert at the European Monitoring Centre on Drugs and Drug Addiction representing the UK. He has published widely on all aspects of drug use and treatment.

Sara Fuller is a research associate in the Department of Geography at Durham University, UK. She joined the department in 2008 following completion of her doctoral research at the University of Sheffield that explored environmental protests in relation to large-scale infrastructure projects in Central and Eastern Europe. Her current research focuses on concepts and practices of justice and democracy in the field of the environment. Prior to her PhD, Sara worked as a researcher at the Centre for Sustainable Development, University of Westminster, exploring the interfaces between social exclusion and the environment.

Maurice Galton is best known for a series of classroom studies (Observational and Classroom Learning Evaluation, ORACLE), which began in the mid-1970s and continued with a replication study two decades later. He is emeritus professor at the Faculty of Education, at the University of Leicester, UK, and currently senior research fellow at the Centre for Commonwealth Education in the University of Cambridge, UK.

Frances Gardner is professor of child and family psychology in the Department of Social Policy and Intervention, University of Oxford, UK. She has been director and deputy director of the graduate programme in Evidence-based Social Intervention at Oxford since 2003, and is co-director of the Centre for Evidence-based Intervention. Her research focuses on risk factors for anti-social behaviour in young people, particularly the influence of early parenting style. She conducts randomised trials of parenting interventions in the UK and US, and systematic reviews and longitudinal studies, including with AIDS-affected children, in South Africa. She serves on scientific boards including the National Academy of Parenting Practitioners; SFI, Danish National Centre for Social Research; and the United Nations Office on Drugs and Crime (UNODC) Expert Panel on family skills training.

John Gray is professor of education at the University of Cambridge, UK, and served as the first dean of research in its newly converged Faculty of Education. Prior to joining the faculty he was director of research at Homerton College, Cambridge (1994-2001) and professor of education at the University of Sheffield (1987-93). He has been a visiting professor at the London Institute of Education and was elected a Fellow of the British Academy in 2000.

J. Ignacio Giménez-Nadal works in the field of time use. He has focused on the study of the determinants of time allocation decisions of individuals, with an emphasis on child care, adult care and leisure. He obtained his PhD in economics at the University of Zaragoza (Spain) in 2010 and is currently based in the Economic Analysis Department of the University of Zaragoza. He is also research assistant at the Centre for Time Use Research, University of Oxford, UK.

Ann Hagell ran the Nuffield Foundation initiative on time trends in adolescent mental health, which completed in 2011. She is a chartered psychologist with a specific interest in at-risk adolescents and has undertaken social policy research in both the UK and the USA. Ann undertook her PhD at the Institute of Psychiatry in London, and has written widely on various aspects of adolescent life, including three previous books. She has also been editor-in-chief of the *Journal of Adolescence* since 2000.

Yasmin Khatib is research associate at University College London Medical School, UK, in the Faculty of Medical Sciences, and was formerly research fellow at the Centre for Psychiatry in the Wolfson Institute of Preventive Medicine, Barts and the London School of Medicine and Dentistry.

Robert MacDonald is professor of sociology in the School of Social Sciences and Law at the University of Teesside, UK, where he co-founded the BSc (Hons) Youth Studies programme, the first of its type in the UK. He teaches across undergraduate and postgraduate programmes in sociology, criminology and youth studies, and is deputy director of the Social Futures Institute.

Colleen McLaughlin is deputy head of the Faculty of Education at the University of Cambridge, UK. Her current responsibilities include being director of International Initiatives as well as directing the therapeutic counsellor training and SUPER (Schools–University Partnerships for Educational Research) initiative. She edited the *Journal for Pastoral Care in Education* for 10 years and is now an editor of the *Educational Action Research* journal.

Barbara Maughan is professor of developmental epidemiology at the Medical Research Council (MRC) Social, Genetic and Developmental Psychiatry Centre, King's College London Institute of Psychiatry, UK. Her research focuses on family, social and environmental risk factors for children's emotional and behavioural development, and the long-term consequences of childhood difficulties. She specialises in longitudinal research and has utilised data from all of the UK's major birth cohort studies – the 1946, 1958 and 1970 national birth cohorts, the Avon Longitudinal Study of Parents and Children and the Millennium Cohort Study.

Petra Meier studied psychology at the University of Heidelberg in Germany, before completing an MSc by research in child health (University of Hertfordshire) and a PhD in epidemiology and health sciences (University of Manchester). She joined the University of Sheffield in 2006 where she is now professor of public health and deputy director of the Section of Public Health in the School of Health and Related Research.

Tim Millar is senior research fellow and deputy director of the National Drug Evidence Centre at the University of Manchester, UK. His research includes work to estimate the prevalence of opioid and crack cocaine use and work examining intervention effects on drug-related morbidity, mortality and crime.

Rachel Pain is professor in the Department of Geography at Durham University, UK, and co-director of the Centre for Social Justice and Community Action. Her research focuses on urban life and well-being; fear, violence and community safety; everyday geopolitics and the war on terror; the safekeeping of young refugees and asylum seekers; critical perspectives on gender, old age, youth and intergenerational relations; and participatory action research.

Stephen C. Peck received his BA in psychology from California State University, Long Beach in 1985; his MA in experimental social psychology from the University of Montana, Missoula in 1990; and his PhD in personality psychology from the University of Michigan, Ann Arbor, in 1995. He is research investigator at the Achievement Research Lab, Research Center for Group Dynamics, Institute for Social Research, University of Michigan, USA.

Catherine Rothon received her doctorate in sociology from the University of Oxford in 2005. She has undertaken additional training in epidemiology at the London School of Hygiene and Tropical Medicine (MSc, 2008). She is Medical Research Council (MRC) Special Training Fellow in Health Services and the Health of Public Research at the Wolfson Institute of Preventive Medicine, Barts and the London School of Medicine and Dentistry, Queen Mary, University of London.

Seija Sandberg has specialist's qualifications in child and adolescent psychiatry both in Finland and in the UK. She is honorary senior lecturer at the Mental Health Sciences Unit at University College London, and is docent (reader) at the University of Turku, Finland. Since leaving her consultant post in London in 2009 she has been working privately at Eira Hospital in Helsinki.

Karen Schepman received her PhD in child psychiatry from the Institute of Psychiatry, King's College London, in 2005. She is research associate in the Department of Psychological Medicine and Neurology and the Medical Research Council (MRC) Centre for Neuropsychiatric Genetics and Genomics, Cardiff University School of Medicine.

Jacqueline Scott is professor of empirical sociology in the Faculty of Politics, Psychology, Sociology and International Studies, and a fellow of Queens' College Cambridge. She trained at the University of Michigan, Ann Arbor, where she received her PhD in 1987 and joined the Faculty in 1994. Her recent edited books include the 2004 *The Blackwell companion to sociology of families* (with Judy Treas and Martin Richards; John Wiley & Sons), the 2005 Sage *Benchmark series on quantitative sociology* (with Yu Xie) and the 2008 *Women and employment: Changing lives and new challenges* (with Shirley Dex and Heather Joshi; Edward Elgar).

Stephen Stansfeld is professor of psychiatry and centre lead for psychiatry at the Wolfson Institute of Preventive Medicine, Barts and the London School of Medicine and Dentistry. He is currently principal investigator in the RANCH and RELACHS studies and was previously co-director of the Whitehall II Study. He also works as a consultant psychiatrist in psychiatric rehabilitation. He has published widely on the effects of the physical and social environment on mental health.

Jennifer Symonds completed her DPhil in education at the University of Cambridge in 2010. She is a postdoctoral research fellow at the Helsinki Collegium for Advanced Studies, University of Helsinki, Finland. Jennifer also works freelance as an educational researcher and consultant and has recently managed a UK national project on school transition for the Paul Hamlyn Foundation. She is currently working on the Pathways to Adulthood international postdoctoral fellowship programme, funded by the Jacobs Foundation and the Academy of Finland.

Sharon Witherspoon is deputy director of the Nuffield Foundation, where she leads the Foundation's research in social science and social policy. Before she joined the Foundation in 1996, she was a senior researcher at the Policy Studies Institute and the National Centre for Social Research (formerly Social and Community Planning Research). Sharon is a member of the Strategic Forum for the Social Sciences, housed at the British Academy, and various other strategic bodies supporting rigorous social science research. She was awarded an honorary MBE for services to social science in 2008, and the British Academy President's Medal in 2011.

Nicole Zarrett received her MS and PhD in developmental science at the University of Michigan in 2006. After earning her degree she completed a postdoctoral fellowship at the Institute for Applied Research in Youth Development, Tufts University, USA. She is currently an assistant professor in the Psychology Department at the University of South Carolina, USA.

Acknowledgements

Each of the chapters in this volume draws on work funded by a programme that I led for the Nuffield Foundation, called 'Changing Adolescence'. A number of experts working in the field took part in the programme, many of whom are co-authors to the chapters that follow, and my first acknowledgement is to all of them for their contribution.

I am also grateful to the external Commissioning Group who advised on the selection of the studies and the overall direction of the work. Members included Professor Sir Michael Rutter (Chair), Professor Andrew Pickles, Professor Robert Sampson, Anne Sofer, Dr Hilary Steedman, Professor Sir David Watson, Sharon Witherspoon and Professor Dieter Wolke. I owe special thanks to Professor Rutter for his continued encouragement for the work and the time he gave to critiquing and discussing the research findings throughout the course of the programme, and to Sharon Witherspoon for her support on behalf of the Foundation. Dr Jennifer Symonds provided excellent research assistance in the final stages of drawing the work together, and I was also helped enormously by the many people who acted as anonymous peer reviewers for us at various stages of the work.

A number of people have assisted with the administration of the programme and the preparation of this volume, in particular Rocio Lale Montes, Frances Bright, Bernadine Chelvanayagam, Velda Hinds, Sarah Jenkins and Rakinder Reehal. In all its work, the Foundation is very lucky in drawing on a wide circle of critical friends for input; on this occasion I am particularly indebted to Professor Barbara Maughan, Dr John Coleman, Renuka Jeyarajah Dent and Dr Simon Dupont for many useful conversations and debates.

Although the work was funded by the Foundation, the views in the publication do not necessarily reflect the Foundation's views.

Ann Hagell
January 2012

Foreword

Professor Sir Michael Rutter

This important volume very usefully brings together the concepts and findings that are relevant with respect to time trends in the mental health of young people. It is important, however, to note at the outset that, because of publication delays in the data sets used, almost all the findings apply to the time period *before* the current worldwide financial crisis and, therefore, before the present Coalition government. Undoubtedly, this will mean that the time trends reported here will not reflect the huge recent rise in youth unemployment or the increase in inflation. The implication is that the book's attention to the social context of both particular behaviours and time trends mean that the findings are likely to be even more important in the years ahead as young people have to cope with a worsening economic situation. The broad principles outlined in the various chapters are likely to hold, but it will be increasingly important to monitor changes over the long term in order to understand better the complex interrelationships between individual development and social trends.

The volume starts with an overview of the evidence on time trends with respect to the level of behavioural and emotional problems in young people. Careful attention is paid to crucial methodological issues but it is concluded that, over the last three or four decades, there has been a rise in emotional and behavioural problems, although it may have levelled off. The rise has not been as great as some media reports appear to have suggested, but it is nevertheless enough to be a cause for concern. The chapter on substance use similarly shows a rise, in that case rather greater, in substance use – both recreational and harmful. It is difficult to build links between these findings and those on emotional and behavioural problems, but it would be very surprising if there were no interconnections.

It is perhaps surprising that none of the chapters deals systematically with the need to use research strategies (such as those exemplified by so-called 'natural experiments') to test environmental mediation causal hypotheses (see Rutter, 2007). That reflects the fact that psychosocial researchers have rather neglected this issue, and more particularly, the data sets that needed to be used for this volume also ignored the need. Of course, it is the case that the 'natural experiments' that could be used to test environmental mediation causal hypotheses mainly apply to individual causes rather than time trends. Nevertheless, they can apply to time trends (Rutter and Smith, 1995) as shown by the evidence that neither the MMR (measles, mumps or rubella) vaccine nor thimerosal account for the worldwide rise in the diagnosis of autism. In this case the 'natural experiments' arose because Japan ceased using the MMR vaccine at a time when the rest of the world continued its use, and Scandinavia ceased using thimerosal preservatives in its vaccines at a time when they were widely used in the rest of the world. The international comparison design was good and their findings were decisive but, unfortunately, there are no obvious equivalents in relation to the putative causal influences considered here. However, the strategy should be available through different time trends in different countries (as, for example, with marriage and cohabitation).

Some reviewers (or critics) may be concerned that, given the huge national (and international) investment in genetic and biological research, this gets little or no mention here. However, the genetic findings on individual genes, despite the 'hype', have been surprisingly unimpressive (see Rutter, in press). Moreover, quantitative genetic evidence clearly points to the great importance of environmental causal factors because they account for so much of population variance (see Academy of Medical Sciences, 2007). In addition, there are the major policy implications stemming from social science research through its value in tackling causal connections (see British Academy, 2010). There need be no apology for a focus on possible environmental influences on time trends. Genetic factors as such are scarcely likely to be responsible for time trends because the gene pool cannot change so quickly. On the other hand, the old-fashioned subdivision of disorders into those due to genes and those due to the environment is no longer tenable. Perhaps, therefore, it would have been useful to pay rather more attention to gene–environment interdependence. Even when genetic influences are relatively strong, environmental solutions may constitute the best way forward. Thus, height has a very high heritability but, despite this, the average height rose by some 10 centimetres over the first half of the last century. Improved nutrition undoubtedly played a major role in this increase.

The chapters focusing on parenting, school influences, stress, the community and time usage bring out many important findings. Often these serve to downplay the supposed importance of deterioration in these domains as causes of a rise in youth problems. The authors are careful to emphasise the substantial limitations in measurement of the possible influences but, nevertheless, it is clear that many popularly held views fail to receive support. Rather than be dispirited by this, everyone needs to view the findings as a challenge. If the answers do not seem to be where so many people thought they would be found, where do they lie? One really important conclusion is that we must beware of relying on overall mean levels to tell the complete story. The analysis of subgroups clearly brings out the importance of considering the different experiences of particular subgroups of young people.

Some of the chapters end with a plea for more and better epidemiological studies. Maybe they are needed, but perhaps the greater need is for a better design of such studies to provide data in a form that is useful for tackling causal inferences. That constitutes a major challenge for social science and it is crucial that researchers rise to that challenge. The chapters here provide many useful leads on what needs to be done and it is to be hoped that researchers, policy makers and practitioners will read the book carefully in order to decide how best to move the field forward. Ann Hagell, Sharon Witherspoon and the other authors are to be warmly congratulated in putting together this very thoughtful set of essays.

ONE

Introduction

Ann Hagell

Background

Adolescents' lives are shaped by the social context in which they live. A number of key social institutions structure and dominate their lives, such as those of education, family and part-time employment. It is an intensely social time of life; friends, peers, classmates, parents, extended family, teachers and neighbourhood groups are all critical. Pressures and expectations arise from several directions at once, and although we are more healthy, wealthy and comfortable than at any time in the past, British teenagers are undoubtedly subject to a range of stresses.

The general well-being of British adolescents has been the topic of considerable debate in recent years, but *are* today's young people any more stressed than previous generations? Are they any more depressed or anxious? Do we have useful and robust evidence on this? If so, what might have changed about the social context that might be particularly salient for their lives?

Indeed, evidence *has* suggested that the current level of behavioural and emotional problems in teenagers is higher than in the past. Our work in this area began in 2004 with the publication of a study funded by the Nuffield Foundation, which provided specific evidence on time trends across 1974, 1986 and 1999. Undertaken by Barbara Maughan, Stephan Collishaw, Robert Goodman and Andrew Pickles, the comparison of large-scale surveys of 15/16-year-olds at each point in time showed rises for problems such as depression, anxiety and conduct disorder (Collishaw et al, 2004). In fact, addition of a fourth wave of data collection from 2004 suggested that by this time the time trends may have been levelling off, providing cause for guarded optimism. As Stephan Collishaw's chapter in this volume shows, this still, however, leaves young people of today with a general level of emotional and behavioural problems that is significantly higher than it was for 16-year-olds living through the 1970s and 1980s. And it still leaves us with questions about why this might be the case. That is what this volume is about.

Some key terms

For the purposes of exploring the research in this area of young people and social change, we have taken a deliberately broad definition of adolescence. Generally we mean it to include the second decade of life. This encompasses the last year of primary school and the preparation to move into secondary education. At the higher end it includes the move to further or higher education, or the beginning of employment. We have also used the term 'young people', and we mean this as interchangeable with our definition of 'adolescence'. Some more formal definitions of 'youth' take an age range that goes up to the mid-20s or even higher, but the lower end of these ranges tend to be in the mid- to late teens, and we wanted to make sure we included at the very least all children at secondary school. A warning, however – it is possible to find a number of papers with 'adolescence' in the title that all address rather different age groups. In this area in particular, there is always a need to be explicit about samples and to make sure that like is being compared with like. And, as the essays in this volume will make clear, we do not regard adolescence as a homogeneous life stage, but see all sorts of ways of sub-dividing groups, by age and also by 'pathway' and by socioeconomic status.

How to refer to the geographical setting for this work has also been somewhat problematic. At the outset our intention was to take a look at 'British adolescents', or, for some purposes, 'United Kingdom (UK) adolescents' particularly with a view (if possible) to comparing them to their counterparts in other European or North American countries. However, very few research studies take 'British' or 'the UK' as their sampling frame, and this applies equally to official statistics given the vagaries of the British administrative and political boundaries. Most commonly the information contained in the following pages refers, strictly speaking, to 'English and Welsh adolescents', but this is a rather clumsy way to denote the groups of interest. Unless there is good information to suggest that Scottish or Northern Irish young people are significantly different, we have tended to stick to British, but the reader will note that we do chop and change a little in the text, depending on the original research samples from which findings are drawn. The aim is to be as accurate as possible without reducing readability.

Nuffield Foundation Changing Adolescence Programme

The Nuffield Foundation Changing Adolescence Programme was a portfolio of research on time trends in adolescent mental health, focusing on various aspects of social change and adolescent experiences in order to reveal some of the changes in adolescents' lives today. The programme brought together the Foundation's long-standing interests in young people, social institutions, mental health and educational transitions. Six research reviews were funded, taking different areas of social change and interrogating the evidence for links with emotional and behavioural problems in young people. The aim was to contribute to policy and practice debates in ways that could potentially improve outcomes for young people.

In this volume, we begin by outlining our main 'outcome' measure – changes in young people's emotional and behavioural problems. The remainder of the volume presents a series of essays that draw on the research we funded and build on it, and that begin the process of thinking about what the implications might be. We take a particular look at the evidence on stress – have their lives become more stressful over our period of interest? We then take a rather selective look at two specific social institutions important to young people (school and families), followed by one key area where much social change has happened (use of alcohol and drugs), and we then explore some aspects of the broader social context in which they live (neighbourhoods and peers).

We would be the first to admit that this represents a rather idiosyncratic collection of questions and topics. It is a collision of the interests we brought to the topic, the strengths and weaknesses of the field, the resource limitations and the availability (or otherwise) of experts to work with us. The result should be regarded as illustrative of some of the relevant topics, rather than an exhaustive account of all aspects of social change. We are particularly indebted to the researchers who undertook the original scoping work for us, and in Appendix I we indicate the Foundation-funded work that we have drawn on. Some of this is starting to be published by the research teams themselves, and what we present here is the Foundation's particular 'take' on that work, rather than a formal summary of the reviews themselves. What we hope is that the programme as a whole refocuses some attention on the interesting issue of the implications of social change for young people's experiences, and encourages others to take up these issues further.

Changing context for adolescence in the UK, 1975-2005

If we turned the clock back to the mid-1970s, the start of our period of interest, what would life look like? Overviews of social change for UK society across this period do exist, and referral to, for example, Office for National Statistics (ONS) trend documents (for example, the ONS *Social Change* publication series), will provide more detailed information, although it is sometimes a challenge to pull out statistics that are relevant for our particular age group of interest. There are occasional publications in the ONS series that do focus on young people, although this includes younger children as well as adolescents (for example, ONS, 1994, 2002). Some elements of social change over recent decades are included in the compilations of *Key data on adolescence* (most recent edition, Coleman, Brooks and Threadgold, 2011), although the series is not specifically focused on time trends. Two particularly helpful recent overviews of social change specifically in relation to adolescence are also available: Coleman (2011) and Furlong and Cartmel (2007). Finally, an international perspective is given in a publication from the American Society for Research in Adolescence entitled *The changing adolescent experience* (Mortimer and Larson, 2002a).

Broad overviews highlight that the last three decades of the 20th century were a time of relative political stability in the UK. As far as impacts on children might be concerned, both positive and negative trends can be identified. Despite recurring economic recession, this was a period of rising living standards and expanding consumer power and acquisition. International standards on the rights of children, such as the United Nations (UN) Convention on the Rights of the Child 1989, reflected widespread concern about the need to protect children in a variety of different settings. Other developments of potential benefit to children within the UK across this period included the introduction of the minimum wage in the late 1990s, and political changes that brought a Children's Commissioner and a Minister for Children (Bradshaw and Keung, 2011). However, child poverty rose during the beginning of our period before levelling out or falling by the 2000s (depending on which indicators are used).

Throughout these 30 years, from the mid-1970s to the mid-2000s, five main sets of changes are of particular significance to adolescence, and frame their experiences as described in the following chapters. More detail on all of these will arise throughout the text, and at this stage the intention is to provide a broad-brush perspective:

- *Expansion in the higher educational system* The collapse of the youth labour market through the 1980s has been widely documented (Furlong and Cartmel, 2007; Côté and Bynner, 2008), as has the accompanying expansion of the education system (Symonds and Hagell, 2011). The proportion of 16-year-olds heading directly into employment approximately halved between 1988 and 2004, and the proportion of 16-year-olds in full-time education rose across the same period (Furlong and Cartmel, 2007). This is an important context for all of the chapters in this volume, but particularly those relating to time use and educational transitions.

- *Changes in living arrangements* The average age of leaving home in the UK has been estimated to be around 23 years old (Iacovou, 2001), and this has risen in recent decades (ONS, 2009). This serves as an index for a number of important changes, such as the continued role of parents in everyday life, changes in financial support and arrangements, context for peer relations etc. The link between leaving home and establishing new family relationships weakened across our period of study, and more young people left home to go into higher education (Holdsworth, 2000; Berrington et al, 2009). This forms part of the background particularly for the chapters on relationships with parents, and also time use in the 16-18 year groups.

- *Extension of adolescence* As a result of the trends in staying on in education, leaving home later and delayed financial independence, there has been much written about the elongation of transition to adulthood, and many have noted the emergence of multiple, non-linear pathways to adult living (Furlong and Cartmel, 2007; Côté and Bynner, 2008; Coleman, 2011). This cuts across all of the chapters in this book and is a key part of the story of social change.

- *Changes to family structure* The proportion of children living in homes headed by a lone parent rose from approximately 12 per cent in the early 1980s to 20 per cent by 2001 (ONS, 2002), and across our time period adolescents increasingly lived in a wider variety of family structures as a result of changes in cohabitation, marriage and re-marriage. It has been estimated that in Europe 25 per cent of young people now live through the divorce of their parents (Coleman, 2011), leading to an increase in experiences of reconstituted families: stepfamilies, extended families, and so on. Coleman points out three likely implications – more stress (we return to this in Chapter Three), shifts in beliefs about relationships and marriage including separation of parenthood from marriage and new challenges for parenting of teenagers within these new and reconstituted family patterns (Coleman, 2011).

- *Changes in sexual behaviour, relationship patterns* The average age of puberty in the UK fell in the 100 years to 1970, but in fact by the period that the programme focused on, the fall had levelled out. Across this period the median age of menarche in British teenagers was around 13 years (Whincup et al, 2001). Any decrease is estimated to be in the order of a few months. Similar findings have arisen in USA samples (Anderson et al, 2003). However, it is possible that the age at which children began their first sexual relationships, and the nature of those relationships, may have changed. This crops up in the chapter on stress, and is important in considering peers and neighbourhoods.
- *Globalisation* Young people are subject to a much wider range of information about the wider world than they were three decades previously, fuelled in part by explosion in new media and communication structures and information technology. Awareness of what is going on well beyond the boundaries of the local area is now the norm, and with it has come the sense that we are part of a much larger society.
- *Demographic shifts* In the UK, the proportion of the population made up by young people under the age of 16 has not changed a great deal since the 1970s – it still stands at approximately 20 per cent (ONS, 2002). However, there have been demographic shifts in the proportions of young people from minority ethnic groups, now representing around 12 per cent of children in Great Britain (ONS, 2002). Important aspects of these changes include a growth in young people in mixed-race groups, and the potentially changing nature of ethnic identity as a result.

Overarching questions and themes

Although there was no doubt that society had changed over the years that Collishaw et al's study covered, there was little concrete information available to us about time trends in some of the key areas where social institutions were shaping the lives of young people. One of the first aims of the programme was to interrogate the existing literature to firm up what we know – and do not know – about social change for this age group over this period. In each of the areas where we funded reviews, we also wanted to know how good the evidence was that each of these areas of life (parenting, education, peers etc) were related to emotional and behaviour outcomes for young people. That is, was there anything more than just correlational evidence that these domains of life mattered in some way?

The focus was clear and the questions were simple, although the tasks of pulling together and interrogating the evidence proved more challenging than anticipated. We were clear that we wanted to know specifically about adolescence, about social change and about social institutions and how they shape lives. Everything in the programme was viewed through the lenses of time trends. The underlying question is, is there any evidence that social change was responsible for the rise in emotional and behavioural problems that Stephan Collishaw demonstrates in the next chapter?

TWO

Time trends in young people's emotional and behavioural problems, 1975-2005

Stephan Collishaw

Introduction

Trends in child and adolescent mental health can be seen as a barometer of the success of society's efforts to improve children's well-being and life chances. Improving the mental health of children was identified as a key strategic target in *The Children's Plan* (DCSF, 2007a). In this context, evidence of long-term deterioration in the mental health and behavioural adjustment of young people (Rutter and Smith, 1995; Maughan et al, 2005), and unfavourable comparisons with child well-being in other countries (UNICEF, 2007), has provoked significant concern among policy makers and health professionals in the UK (see, for example, Layard and Dunn, 2009).

Child and adolescent mental health problems are common and often have long-lasting and far-reaching consequences for children's lives. Large, well-designed epidemiological studies demonstrate that at any one time approximately one in ten of Britain's 5- to 16-year-olds suffers from a clinically impairing psychiatric disorder (Meltzer et al, 2000; Green et al, 2005). Depression, anxiety, conduct disorder and attention deficit hyperactivity disorders (ADHDs) are all common, with wide-ranging associated functional impairments. They affect children and adolescents' educational progress, relationships with friends, family life and physical health.

The focus of this report is on trends in adolescent mental health (although comparisons are drawn where relevant with what is known about trends in younger children's mental health). The reason for this focus is that adolescence is an important risk period for the onset of mental health problems. The prevalence of many mental health

Figure 2.1: ICD-10 Depression diagnoses by child age and gender, 1999 and 2004, British Child and Adolescent Mental Health Surveys

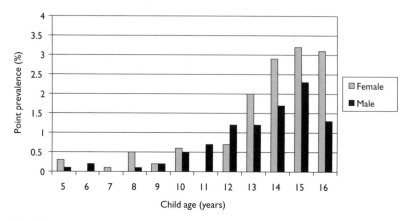

Data from the ONS British Child and Adolescent Mental Health Surveys 1999 and 2004 downloaded from the UK data archive; data for years combined using sample weights.

problems, including depression and anxiety, increases sharply during adolescence (see Figure 2.1).

Moreover long-term prospective follow-up studies highlight strong continuities between adolescent and adult mental health. More than half of all early adult psychiatric disease is preceded by mental illness before the age of 18 (Kim-Cohen et al, 2003); conversely, adolescents with anxiety or depression are at substantially increased risk for adult psychiatric illness. Adolescent depression, for example, is highly recurrent, with 50-70 per cent showing future episodes of depression in adulthood (Lewinsohn et al, 1998). Depression is associated with significant morbidity and mortality, and suicide is the second or third leading cause of death among adolescents (Thapar et al, 2010).

Adolescence is also an important risk period with respect to behavioural disorders such as conduct disorder, oppositional defiant disorder and substance misuse. Notwithstanding a natural developmental course which sees a decline in physical aggression after around age two to four years (Tremblay, 2010), there is evidence that adolescence sees a sharp rise in the prevalence of more broadly defined conduct problems (for example, lying, stealing, disobedience, relational aggression, serious violence, etc). There is a peak in the age–crime curve in mid-late adolescence, widely replicated in many countries and communities (Hirschi and Gottfredson, 1983; Gottfredson and Hirschi, 1990; Fabio et al, 2006). Although anti-social behaviour may for many individuals be limited to adolescence, with the worst outcomes seen in those with early onset and lifecourse persistent problems (Moffitt, 1993), evidence highlights that adolescent conduct problems also carry substantial long-term risk. For example, a 40-year follow-up has highlighted lifelong impairments across multiple social and health outcomes (Colman et al, 2009). The immediate and long-term economic and social costs for society as a whole are also considerable (Scott et al, 2001).

The aim of this chapter is to set out evidence on time trends in adolescent emotional and behavioural problems. The primary focus is on changes in prevalence in the UK, but parallels are drawn with adolescent mental health trends in other high-income countries. In addition to long-term change going back 30-40 years, evidence on recent trends over the past decade is reviewed. Where possible the chapter addresses whether trends in problems have affected girls and boys similarly or differently, and how far they generalise across young people from different social and family backgrounds. The chapter also examines whether observed trends are specific to adolescents or also extend to children and adults.

As noted by Rutter and Smith (1995), studies of trends in youth mental health face major methodological problems. The first major challenge comes from the need to compare like-with-like – both in terms of the characteristics of samples and measures of mental health. A second important issue is that data from good robust samples of the population are required to make sure that we are not simply looking at special groups. For example, many young people with depression do not go to the doctor for help, and those who do may differ in important ways. The third major challenge relates to possible changes in the way mental health problems are reported – even when identical instruments are compared across time. It is possible that people have come to interpret particular questions differently, or they may now be more willing to disclose feelings of depression or instances of anti-social behaviour. No single data source is able to avoid all problems, and thus this chapter brings together a diverse set of relevant evidence – including data about changes in service use, diagnosis and treatment, official records of suicide and crime and repeat epidemiological studies using symptom screens.

Trends in adolescent emotional problems

There has been a steep increase in adolescent service use for depression and anxiety, including help-seeking from general practitioners (GPs), diagnosis and hospitalisation in many high-income countries over the past 30 years (Sourander et al, 2004; Smith et al, 2008; Tick et al, 2008;

Collishaw, 2009; Kosidou et al, 2010). For example, in the USA the number of visits to doctors by children and adolescents during which depression was reported more than doubled from 1.4 million in 1995-96 to 3.2 million in 2001-02 (Ma et al, 2005). Despite recent concerns about use of anti-depressant medication in juvenile populations (FDA, 2004; Whittington et al, 2004), past decades have witnessed substantial increases in anti-depressant prescription up to the present day, including in the UK (Vitiello et al, 2006; Hsia and MacLennan, 2009). As an aside, it is striking that despite these changes still only 20 per cent of children and adolescents with a mental health disorder in the UK in 1999 accessed specialised mental health services over an 18-month follow-up (Ford et al, 2003).

Increases in service use may in part reflect changes in the population prevalence of anxiety and depression, but alternative explanations are also possible. First, changes in public awareness may have led to increased help-seeking by young people themselves or via parents and school professionals. Second, changes in diagnosis and prescribing could also reflect changes in clinical recognition, diagnostic practice and treatment availability. Evidence from unselected epidemiological samples is therefore needed to properly assess whether or not the population prevalence of adolescent depression/anxiety has increased.

Initial concerns about rising rates of depressive disorder were prompted by comparisons of lifetime rates and age at onset of affective disorders between different birth cohorts in large representative investigations in the USA (for example, the Epidemiological Catchment Area Study and National Comorbidity Survey) and elsewhere (Cross-National Collaborative Group, 1992). A consistent finding has been that lifetime rates of depression and anxiety are highest in more recent birth cohorts (Robins and Regier, 1991; Cross-National Collaborative Group, 1992; Kessler et al, 2005). Given the shorter at-risk periods for younger age groups this is the reverse of what might be expected. For example, lifetime rates of depression have been reported to be three to four times higher in those aged 18-29 compared with those aged 60+ (Kessler et al, 2005). However, caution is needed in interpreting these findings as they are based on retrospective reports. Age is confounded with length of recall period, and older people may have greater difficulty remembering episodes of depression that for them occurred decades ago. In addition, there may be systematic differences in the biases that affect the reporting of mental illness; perhaps younger generations are less reluctant to reveal mental health difficulties. Third, studies such as this only include survivors, and do not take account of the fact that depression is associated with earlier mortality (Cuijpers and Smit, 2002).

In contrast, a meta-analysis combining data from 26 epidemiological studies of child and adolescent mental health carried out between 1965 and 1999 found no evidence of any increase in childhood or adolescent depressive disorder (Costello et al, 2006). This study had two major advantages over the preceding studies – first, it pooled information from unselected general population samples; and second, all studies involved concurrent assessments of depression in juvenile populations rather than relying on adult retrospective reports. Nevertheless, the meta-analysis was complicated by differences between studies in diagnostic definitions of depression, methods of assessment, sampling etc. Efforts were made to control for these factors statistically. However, this does not fully address the wide variability in estimated prevalence rates from one study to the next. For example, rates of depression for adolescent girls born between 1977 and 1984 varied from 1-2 per cent (see, for example, Olsson and von Knorring, 1999; Doi et al, 2001; Steinhausen and Winkler-Metzler, 2003) to 10-26 per cent (see, for example, Oldehinkel et al, 1999; Fergusson and Horwood, 2001). It is likely that any systematic change in prevalence of depression would be hard to detect across studies that vary so substantially in their basic prevalence estimates.

Other relevant evidence comes from monitoring of suicide mortality. The outcome here is in principle unambiguous. Depression is a primary risk factor for suicide, and unlike most mental health outcomes, suicide data are collected annually in many countries including the UK. Suicide statistics show substantial change in prevalence among adolescents and young adults over the past 50 years. First, there was a sustained and substantial rise in recorded suicide in many countries during the second half of the 20th century (Mittendorfer-Rutz and Wasserman, 2004). Second, the rise in suicide has not been continuous or sustained to the present day – many countries saw a levelling-off in the increase in suicide during the 1990s and some have seen a reversal in suicide trends since. In the UK, for example, suicide rates among young men peaked in the UK at 18.1 deaths per 100,000 in 1999 and have since fallen to their lowest levels for 20 years (ONS, 2008; see Figure 2.2). What do these data tell us about trends in adolescent emotional problems? Although changes in the population prevalence of depression may well result in changes in suicide, considerable caution is needed in extrapolating from rare events such as suicide to trends in more common problems such as anxiety or depression. First, suicide trends partly reflect changes in recording. There is evidence of under-recording of suicides, and misclassification due to a variety of factors. Some of these (for example, social stigma) have themselves altered over time, and there is evidence of greater under-recording in the past. However, this effect only partially explains increases in suicide over the second half of the 20th century (Mohler and Earls, 2001). Second, suicide rates are influenced by a host of complex factors including the availability and lethality of different methods of suicide, survival rates due to improvements in medical treatment of suicide attempters and changes in rates of proximal and distal psychosocial risk factors linked with suicide. This might include changes in prevalence of depression, but other factors are also likely to be important (for example, substance misuse, child maltreatment, unemployment). Third, it is interesting to note that rates of self-harm requiring hospital treatment increased in Australia over the same period that saw falls in completed youth suicide (Eckersley, 2010) even though at the individual level both are closely linked with depressive disorder. Finally, an interesting, but thus far unresolved, debate is whether the recent reductions in suicide rates are a result of increased anti-depressant medication (Isacsson et al, 2010).

Figure 2.2: Suicide and undetermined deaths of 15- to 24-year-olds in the UK, 1971-2006

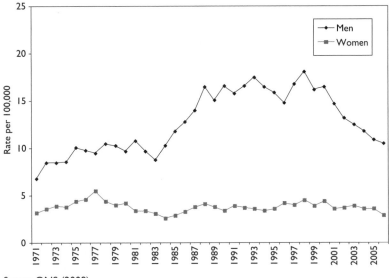

Source: ONS (2008)

The most direct evidence about trends in adolescent emotional problems comes from repeated epidemiological studies in the UK, USA and Europe conducted from the 1970s onwards. A number of general population studies have used the same questions to screen young people for symptoms of anxiety and depression. Some limitations are a focus on symptoms rather than clinically defined disorders, and that studies only provide information about prevalence at different snapshots in time rather than year-on-year trends.

Even so, on the whole, studies provide strong support for the notion that adolescent emotional problems have become more prevalent over the past 30 years (Collishaw et al, 2004, 2010; Fichter et al, 2004; Sourander et al, 2004; Sigfusdottir et al, 2008; Tick et al, 2008; Sweeting et al, 2009; Kosidou et al, 2010).

For instance, in the UK a comparison of parent-reported symptoms (depressed mood, worry, fearfulness) across 15/16-year-olds in 1974 (the National Child Development Study), 1986 (the 1970 British Cohort Study, BCS70) and 1999 (the British Child and Adolescent Mental Health Survey at www.cls.ioe.ac.uk) showed no change in rates of problems between 1974 and 1986, followed by a marked increase in emotional problems between 1986 and 1999 (Collishaw et al, 2004). Evidence from youth self-reports points to a similar conclusion. A comparison of three Scottish studies assessed in 1987, 1999 and 2006 showed a major increase in problem scores (as reported using the General Health Questionnaire [GHQ]; see Sweeting et al, 2009). A study comparing English teenagers in 2006 (sampled from the Health Survey for England) and in 1986 (BCS70) confirmed an increase in symptoms of anxiety/depression (assessed using the GHQ-12 and Malaise Inventory; see Collishaw et al, 2010). These studies also undertook more detailed analyses of whether patterns of change differed by overall problem severity and by type of symptoms (Sweeting et al, 2009; Collishaw et al, 2010).

Importantly, both studies found that increases in emotional problems were not confined to those with relatively low-level difficulties. In fact, increases were more marked for those with more severe problem levels. In one study increases in problems was evident across the full range of symptoms assessed (Sweeting et al, 2009). In the other the increase was specific to a subset of items (worry, irritability, fatigue, sleep disturbance and feeling stressed; see Collishaw et al, 2010). All three UK epidemiological studies point to a worrying and dramatic increase in prevalence of youth emotional problems. The proportion of parents reporting high problem scores increased by 70 per cent between 1986 and 1999 (Collishaw et al, 2004), the proportion of young people meeting established GHQ 'case criteria' almost doubled for Scottish boys and more than doubled for Scottish girls between 1987 and 2006 (Sweeting et al, 2009), while the proportion of adolescents endorsing five or more symptoms of anxiety or depression doubled from 7 per cent to 15 per cent in the latest English study (Collishaw et al, 2010). Finally, short-term comparisons of emotional problem screens and depressive and anxiety disorders in the 1999 and 2004 British Child and Adolescent Mental Health Surveys demonstrate that upward trends in prevalence have levelled off or begun to reverse (Green et al, 2005; Maughan et al, 2008). However, rates remain at historically high levels (Collishaw et al, 2010).

Evidence from other European countries is broadly consistent, with most studies showing long-term increases in self-reported emotional problems. Studies in Sweden, Iceland, Norway, Finland, the Netherlands and Greece all found increased self-reported adolescent symptoms of depression and anxiety since the late 1980s (Fichter et al, 2004; Sourander et al, 2004, 2008; Sigfusdottir et al, 2008; Tick et al, 2008; Kosidou et al, 2010) as well as increased sleep-onset difficulties (Pallesen et al, 2008), and increases in somatic complaints (Santalahti et al, 2005). Tick et al (2007a) also report long-term increases in parent-reported emotional problems in the Netherlands, but this finding is not replicated in Scandinavia (Sourander et al, 2004). Evidence from the USA suggests a somewhat different pattern of trends over the past three or four decades, with parent and teacher-reported emotional problems increasing between the mid-1970s and late 1980s (Achenbach et al, 2002a, 2003), followed by improvements in parent, teacher and youth-rated mental health up to 1999 (Achenbach et al, 2002a, 2002b, 2003).

There is relatively little information on earlier trends and about trends among younger children, but available data are consistent with the UK in showing no evidence of change in emotional problems during the 1970s/1980s in Scandinavia and the Netherlands (Verhulst et al, 1997; Wangby et al, 2005). Evidence on trends in emotional problems in younger children is inconsistent. One study of eight-year-olds in Finland found increased self-reported depressive symptoms between 1989 and 2005, but no changes in parent-reported problems (Sourander et al, 2008), while another study of parent-reported problems in pre-school children in the Netherlands found evidence of improved mental health between 1989 and 2003 (Tick et al, 2007b).

There have also been long-term increases in adult self-reported emotional problems and service use for depression (Olfson et al, 2002; Ferri et al, 2003; Compton et al, 2006), although historical increases appear to be greater among younger than for older adults (Kosidou et al, 2010). A recent study tested links between trends in adult and adolescent trends, and it found that historical increases in parents' emotional problems may have contributed to, but do not fully explain, trends in offspring adolescent problems (Schepman et al, 2011).

Summary

Self-reported emotional problems in adolescents increased substantially between the mid-1980s and late 1990s in the UK and other European countries. Parent-report data are partially consistent. Increases in rates of problems followed periods of stability in the UK, the Netherlands and Sweden during the 1970s/1980s. The UK has seen a recent plateauing of trends (Maughan et al, 2008).

There is also evidence for country-specific trends in youth emotional problems – for example, a decline in rates of emotional problems in the USA during the 1990s. It is not yet clear whether secular change in emotional problems are specific to adolescents. Adult trends in depression and anxiety are broadly consistent, but only a few studies have examined trends in pre-adolescent children's emotional adjustment (Tick et al, 2007b; Sourander et al, 2008). Finally, there is little or no evidence about trends in emotional problems from lower-income countries.

Trends in conduct problems and delinquency

Trends in recorded and victim-reported crime

Information about trends in UK crime comes from two main sources – offences recorded by the police and victim surveys. Victim surveys are often seen as more reliable indicators of crime trends because they are less affected by changes in official recording. However, both sources paint a consistent picture, with rates of crime approximately doubling between 1981 and 1995 in the UK, followed by a consistent fall in recorded and victim-reported crime up to 2010 (Home Office, 2010; see Figure 2.3). Crime rates are now close to those in 1981. Although the general increase and decrease has been seen for most forms of crime over this period, the extent of change has varied. The biggest increases and decreases were seen for victim-reported vehicle-related theft and for violence; the smallest increase and decrease for domestic burglary.

Overall levels of offending vary considerably between countries. For example, most recent estimates of homicide rates were 0.5-2.0 per 100,000 in the majority of Western European countries (1.2 per 100,000 in England and Wales) (Coleman et al, 2011) to around 5 per 100,000 in the USA and as high as 20-60 per 100,000 in parts of Central America and Southern Africa (UNODC, 2011). However, crime trends are broadly similar across many high-income nations. As in the UK, crime figures peaked in the early/mid-1990s after prolonged periods of increase, and have since fallen substantially across the European Union (EU), in Canada, in the USA and in Australia (International Crime Victimization Survey, see van Dijk et al, 2008). The most extensive information relates to trends in crime in the USA. Crime rates increased by 350 per cent between 1960 and 1990, with increases in violence, homicide and property crime. As in the UK, the 1990s then saw a marked reduction in all forms of crime (van Dijk et al, 2008; FBI, 2009).

Self-reported offending

One difficulty is that both officially recorded crime and victim-reported crime provide indexes of the total burden of criminal activity rather than prevalence statistics for the numbers of offenders in the population. It is particularly difficult to estimate trends in the proportion of offenders within particular age or gender groups. Surveys assessing self-reported offending therefore provide a valuable complement. Data from the Youth Lifestyle Surveys point to increased male and female juvenile offending between 1992-99 in the UK (East and Campbell, 1999), while data from the Offending, Crime and Justice Survey and a Market and Opinion Research International (MORI) survey indicates little change in rates of offending by adolescents and young adults since the late 1990s (Maughan et al, 2005; Home Office, 2008). Reasons for the discrepancies of these data with official criminal statistics remain unexplained.

Conduct problems

Recent years have also seen increased concern about youth anti-social behaviour, whether or not this is categorised as criminal offending. Epidemiological data indicates that adolescent conduct problems (for example, lying, disobedience, aggression, bullying) are far more prevalent than criminal offending, but also reach a peak prevalence during adolescence (Moffitt, 1993). Collishaw et al (2004) compared to the prevalence of parent-reported conduct problems in three national UK cohorts of 15/16-year-olds assessed in 1974, 1986 and 1999. There was a substantial increase in adolescent conduct problems over this 25-year period (see Figure 2.4), with similar increases for boys and girls, and for young people from socially advantaged and disadvantaged homes. The most recent available evidence from the UK indicates a small drop in conduct problems between 1999 and 2004 (Maughan et al, 2008; Nuffield Foundation, 2009a).

Figure 2.3: Indexed trends in reported and recorded crime, 1981-2009/10 (1981=100)

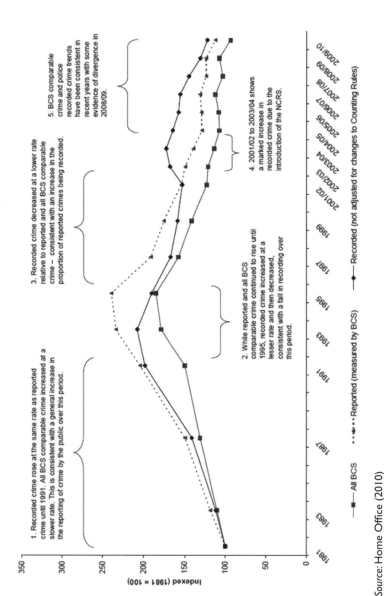

Source: Home Office (2010)

Rising rates of anti-social behaviour were largely confined to non-aggressive behaviours (lying, stealing, disobedience) with little change in parent-reported aggression. However, consequences for long-term outcomes appear far from benign. Longitudinal analyses for the first two cohorts demonstrated similarly high levels of adverse adult outcomes for subgroups of adolescents with conduct problems. Adult functioning was assessed using 10 indicators such as unemployment, homelessness, poor physical and mental health, problem drinking and divorce. Odds for pervasive adult psychosocial dysfunction (that is, four or more such problems) were elevated three- to four-fold in both cohorts for those with adolescent conduct problems. The fact that conduct problems were as predictive of adult problems in both cohorts argues against the notion that trends over time merely reflect changes in parental reporting (see Figure 2.4).

Questionnaire-based studies of trends in conduct problems in other countries are relatively limited. The evidence that there is highlights an increase in parent, teacher and youth rated conduct problems in the USA between the 1970s and 1980s, followed by a fall in the 1990s (Achenbach et al, 2002b, 2003). Wangby et al (2005) found evidence for a small increase in conduct problems in Swedish adolescent girls between 1970 and 1996. Studies in the Netherlands have found evidence for small increases in parent-rated but not self-rated conduct problems in adolescents in the Netherlands since the early 1990s (Tick et al, 2007a, 2008). Other studies focusing on younger children have found no changes in rates of conduct problems either in primary school

Figure 2.4: Trends in parent-rated conduct problems over four nationally representative UK cohorts of youth (aged 15-16 years)

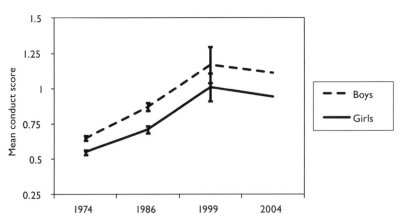

Source: Adapted from Collishaw et al (2004)
Reproduced with permission from Wiley Publishing

children (McArdle et al, 2003; Sourander et al, 2004; Santalahti et al, 2005) or among pre-schoolers (Tick et al, 2007b).

Summary

Police-recorded and victim-reported crime, as well as self- and parent-reported youth conduct problems, all point to rising rates of youth anti-social behaviour during the 1970s, 1980s and early 1990s in the UK. There was a peak in crime in the early 1990s, and rates have since fallen substantially. Trends in conduct problems have also levelled off and perhaps begun to reverse over the past decade, although the prevalence of conduct problems in the UK remains at high levels compared to the 1970s or early 1980s. Broadly speaking, trends in crime have been similar across many developed countries, with the exception that a peak in crime rates was observed somewhat earlier in the USA.

There is, however, some evidence that trends in anti-social behaviour have been more marked in the UK than in other European countries, and that they have been more apparent for adolescents than for younger children. However, these are tentative conclusions given how little available data there is.

Trends in attention deficit hyperactivity disorder

Community studies have found little or no change in the prevalence of ADHD symptoms (Achenbach et al, 2003; Collishaw et al, 2004, 2010; Sourander et al, 2004) despite the marked increase in recognition, diagnosis and treatment of ADHD in clinical practice since the 1980s in the UK (Hsia and MacLennan, 2009), the USA (Olfson et al, 2003; Toh, 2006) and Europe (Wong et al, 2004; Atladottir et al, 2007). This specificity (that is, rising rates of emotional and conduct problems but not hyperactive behaviour) is important because it provides strong evidence against the view that there has simply been a systematic change in reporting. In other words, parents and young people today are not simply more open about reporting undesirable behaviour than in the past; something is changing.

Demographic differences in adolescent mental health trends

An important issue is the extent to which trends in adolescent emotional and behavioural problems are similar or different between different population subgroups. Comparison of population means can obscure important variation in trends for different groups. For example, the average increase in life expectancy obscures the fact that gains have been greater for men than for women, and for socially advantaged than disadvantaged groups (Singh and Siahpush, 2006). Some of the most deprived areas of the UK have in fact seen a fall in life expectancy (CSDH, 2008).

So, in relation to mental health it is plausible that increasing social inequalities might in fact have resulted in improvements in mental health for some groups but deterioration in others. Identifying specific subgroups of young people who are more or less affected by changes in mental health, or alternatively noting that trends apply to all groups of young people can also help narrow down potential explanations for secular change.

Do trends differ for boys and girls?

Many, but not all, studies suggest that trends in adolescent emotional and conduct problems differ for boys and girls. Such findings are important because they suggest that boys and girls may be differentially susceptible to the kinds of environmental risk factors that have changed over time. Most contemporaneous studies comparing self-reported symptoms have found that increases in emotional problems are more pronounced for girls (West and Sweeting, 2003; Fichter et al, 2004; Sigfusdottir et al, 2008; Tick et al, 2008; Collishaw et al, 2010). However, other studies using parent reports find parallel trends (Achenbach et al, 2003; Collishaw et al, 2004; Tick et al, 2007a). To make matters more complicated, trends in completed suicide show the exact opposite, with major rises and falls in male suicide, but little or no change for young women (see Figure 2.2). This again highlights the likelihood that the factors responsible for trends in suicide and common emotional problems are not identical. Turning to trends in anti-social behaviour, it has been suggested that the gender gap in delinquency has been closing over past decades, reflecting in part increases in female violent crime. However, more detailed analyses of USA data from various sources (arrest statistics, victim surveys and self-reports) suggests that this may be due to changes in police practice resulting in girls' arrest proneness, for example, increased policing of domestic violence, or reduced tolerance of female violence (Steffensmeier et al, 2005). In addition, parent-reported conduct problems in the UK (Collishaw et al, 2004) and elsewhere (Achenbach et al, 2003; Tick et al, 2007a) show parallel trends for boys and girls.

Do trends differ for advantaged and disadvantaged families?

Few studies have tested whether trends in emotional and conduct problems differ between deprived and affluent families. There is little evidence for differential trends between socially advantaged and disadvantaged teenagers. However, it is clear that deterioration in mental health is not confined to the most socioeconomically deprived groups (see, for example, Collishaw et al, 2004, 2010; Sweeting et al, 2009). Young people from high socioeconomic status families showed increases in rates of problems that were at least as large as for adolescents from low socioeconomic status backgrounds. One of the biggest social changes affecting young people is in the types and complexity of family structure. Many more young people today grow up in single- and stepfamily households. In addition, there is also evidence for increasing deprivation among single-parent families relative to other family types (Collishaw et al, 2007). Given the strong association between family structure and conduct problems in most epidemiological studies it is noteworthy that increasing rates of conduct problems are not accounted for by changes in family type (Collishaw et al, 2007) – critically, rising rates of conduct problems over the last 25 years of the 20th century were observed equally for all family types.

Finally, studies to date have been under-powered to assess whether trends have differed for specific minority ethnic groups. However, evidence suggests that overall trends in conduct and emotional problems have been largely unaffected by changes in the ethnic composition of the population (Collishaw et al, 2004, 2010; Tick et al, 2008).

Real change or change in reporting?

Even the best designed studies using comparable representative epidemiological samples and identical measures of mental health face the critical question of whether observed changes in *reported* mental health problems reflect real change in population mental health. Horwitz and Wakefield (2007) have argued that what has been interpreted as an 'epidemic of depression' can be explained by changes in the conceptualisation of depression. In their view, diagnostic systems changed with the publication of the *Diagnostic and Statistical Manual of Mental Disorders* (DSM)-III in 1980 and now take little account of whether symptoms reflect normal reactions to external stressors. They argue that everyday emotions such as sadness have been 'medicalised', so that these are now interpreted as symptoms of depression. Changes in attitudes towards child emotional and behavioural problems also raise the question of whether informants' openness about reporting of mental health problems has changed. For all these reasons it might be argued that trends in adolescent mental health merely reflect a systematic shift in the way that adolescents or their parents interpret and complete mental health symptom checklists.

There are no easy solutions for dealing with this issue, but one way would be by providing evidence of external validation. An increase in adolescent mental health problems would be expected to result in immediate and long-term observable functional impairment (Robins, 2001; Collishaw et al, 2004), but few studies have the necessary data to test this. As already discussed, one exception comes from analyses of two British birth cohorts assessed in adolescence and adulthood (Collishaw et al, 2004). These showed that conduct problems in adolescence predicted adult psychosocial difficulties equally strongly for cohorts assessed in adolescence in the 1970s and in the 1980s. The increase in prevalence of conduct problems over this period was not merely artefactual, but accompanied by observable and equivalent later psychosocial impairment.

Other evidence also points to the likelihood of real changes in adolescent mental health. As noted, trends appear to be specific to particular forms of emotional and behavioural problems. For example, trends in youth emotional problems are more marked for some symptoms than others (Collishaw et al, 2010), trends in conduct problems are most evident for non-aggressive problems (Collishaw et al, 2004) and parent-reported symptoms of adolescent hyperactivity/ inattention have not changed over the past 30 years in spite of marked changes in media attention and public awareness (Collishaw et al, 2004, 2010). This suggests that there has not been a general tendency for informants to report more mental health problems in epidemiological studies per se. Changes in public awareness may have only limited effects on informants' reports of problems, and the findings are also inconsistent with a general shift due to changes in willingness to report problems.

Conclusion

Although there are some important exceptions (see, for example, Costello et al, 2006), there is now a variety of evidence – officially recorded suicide and crime, victim surveys of crime, mental health service utilisation and treatment, retrospective reports of lifetime mental disorder and contemporaneous epidemiological surveys of parent- and self-reported symptoms – that shows long-term and substantial change in rates of adolescent emotional and conduct problems. The 1970s,

1980s and 1990s saw substantial increases in youth problems in many high-income nations. Some evidence shows a levelling off or decline in problem levels over the past 10-15 years, but rates of common emotional and conduct problems remain at historically high levels. It is important to remember that the specific patterns of change may vary across countries. In the UK, the general pattern of change across psychosocial indicators suggests that rates of emotional and conduct problems remain at historically high levels. Understanding the reasons behind these long-term trends is the aim for the remaining chapters of this book.

THREE

Stress and mental health in adolescence: interrelationship and time trends

Ann Hagell, Seija Sandberg and Robert MacDonald

Introduction

'Stress' is a term often used in the broader media and public debates about the changing experiences of adolescents in our society. Indeed, it has sometimes been thought of as a defining characteristic of the adolescent life stage, as part of the classic formulation of the classic 'storm and stress' hypothesis (Hall, 1904). It is also occasionally suggested that young people's lives today are more stressful than they used to be. From our perspective, with a focus on adolescent mental health trends, if this is true then it is potentially important.

But *are* young people's lives more stressful? How can we tell? What do we mean by stress? Of all the topics in this volume, this one probably caused the most internal debate and interrogation within the Changing Adolescence Programme. It is a difficult topic to pin down, as the term is vague and used in a very imprecise way. However, it is such common shorthand for people's concerns about adolescents that it seemed a mistake to ignore it. Our main aim for this review was thus to consider what we might mean by stress, to explore what concerns we might have about adolescent stress in particular, to examine what evidence there might be in relation to whether there had been a trend for stress to increase, and to see if there was evidence that stress was related to trends in mental health symptoms.

Underpinning this chapter is a detailed search for relevant evidence undertaken by Seija Sandberg and Robert MacDonald for the Nuffield Foundation. They searched scientific journals in the fields of psychiatry, psychology, sociology, general medicine and epidemiology, looking for empirical studies, systematic reviews and other reports. They also searched for textbook chapters and selected monographs, government and other survey reports, and official statistics. Keywords included stress, life events, chronic stress, psychological stress, adolescence/adolescents, psychopathology (or psychological symptoms or psychological disorder), mental health, longitudinal studies and time/secular trends in adolescent stress. Additional checks were made for literature on adolescent anxiety and worries. The main focus was on literature published since the early 1970s, and the searches produced vast numbers (well over 100,000) of citations, although in fact there were very few results specifically relating to time/secular trends.

In addition to the formal searching, Sandberg and MacDonald explored sociological and qualitatively based research on young people that included reference to aspects of their psychological health, in part guided by communication with UK youth researchers.[1] This literature tends not to deal directly with the links between stress and social change, but it does provide a wider sociological context for the discussion.

In this chapter we draw on Sandberg and MacDonald's searches, and on other reviews and commentaries, and highlight some of the key emerging themes.

What do we mean by 'stress'?

We all know what stress feels like, but the term is notoriously ill-defined. It covers a range of experiences, from minor irritation to nervous breakdown. It usually refers to the feeling experienced when a person perceives that demands of the situation exceed the personal and social resources available. In this way, the lay definition emphasises subjective feelings, the fact that stress is negative and that reactions depend on how well someone can cope. However, all of these are themselves very difficult to make concrete, or to measure. Before asking whether stress is on the increase, we need a clearer understanding of the concept of stress.

Early definitions of stress referred to an autonomic, biological response to a threat to the individual (Selye, 1936). The *physiological part of stress* relates to what is now known as the hypothalamic-pituitary-adrenal (HPA) axis, all parts of the brain and hormone system that regulate various body responses such as mood and anxiety. Cortisol is part of this system; a chemical produced in the adrenal glands, it sets the 'flight/fight' response to external stressors. The physical stress response works as a dynamic feedback loop, with various checks and balances intended to help the body to respond to the threat, and also to regain equilibrium. The body thus gears up to protect itself (and in this sense stress is positive), and also limits its own response to stressful situations. This is important, as the equilibrium can be unbalanced and damaged by certain experiences, and lack of balance has negative consequences, as we shall see. However, it is also important to note that the responses to acute stressors and to chronic adversities seem to be quite different. For example, in a recent review, McCrory et al (2010) summarised the effects of adversity in terms of the dysregulation of the cortisol response, which includes lower baseline cortisol levels, which is quite different from that found with acute stressors. This is a reminder, of course, that studies of laboratory stress cannot necessarily be generalised to naturalistic circumstances.

While these systems may provide the biological basis for stress, current definitions are more than just biological, and it is obvious that there are clear interactions between the mental state and the nervous and immune systems of humans. Thus, you cannot be stressed by something unless *you interpret it as a threat*. In the 1970s and 1980s, psychologists wove cognitions into the original biological stress models, including, for example, Lazarus' cognitive appraisal model (Lazarus and Folkman, 1984), where what one thinks about stress and coping ('Do I have the resources to deal with this?') is an important part of the model. As researchers have pointed out, one of the implications of these kinds of models is that both differences in levels of exposure to 'objective' stress, and differences in *interpretation* of stress, may matter for pathways between stress and outcomes (see, for example, Chen and Hanson, 2005), and both will be important when we think about time trends. Changes over time could concern either changes in the rates of objectively recorded stressful events, or they could relate to changes over time in the *perception* of stress.

Models of stress that include both physiological processes and perceptions of threats have been called 'transactional models', but it has proved difficult to understand and measure the transactional part, the actual interaction between physiology and perception (Grant et al, 2003). In fact measurement tends to concentrate on 'objective' checklists to measure stressful life events, which means that we miss an important part of the picture.

It might be easier if we could assume that certain events are usually perceived as stressful, a sort of half-way stage that consists of 'normally threatening', where only exceptional people would not perceive the event to be a stressor. The construct of 'contextual threat' was developed to deal with this notion; it is defined as the level of psychological threat that a particular negative experience would cause to most teenagers of the same age, sex and life situation, and is thus essentially norm-referenced (Goodyer et al, 1985; Monck and Dobbs 1985; Sandberg et al, 1993). Contextual threat takes into account the person's life situation, the nature of the stressor and their reaction to it.

So we have a model about stress that involves biological, cognitive and psychological processes, where stress is appraised or experienced in different ways by different people. One further challenge that bedevils much of the literature on stress is that much of what we might ordinarily refer to as stress is actually better conceptualised and measured as *the consequences of stress* such as depression, anxiety or behavioural ways of coping. We need to be clear where the lines are drawn between stress and mental health symptoms, and not confuse the two, or the discussion becomes tautological. This is not to dismiss the importance of the effects of stress, but to ensure that we have as precise a way as possible to distinguish between the experience of stress and the consequences of it. Grant and colleagues suggest that 'By examining the components of the stress process separately, greater precision may be obtained in understanding developmental differences and their effects' (Grant et al, 2003, p 449). At the very least we need to be clear which parts of the model we are trying to measure. In this way, Grant et al (2003, p 450) argues, 'stress research' can be defined as the study of 'the role of cognitive, behavioural, social and biological processes in relation to stressful experiences at various developmental stages'. This is a useful starting point for this chapter, although it is rather broad and all-inclusive.

Finally, it is important in our conceptualisation of stress to note the extraordinary range in the types of things that can be included as *stressors*, including the distinction between acute versus chronic stressors. There are, for example, clear distinctions between severe life events (such as divorce, changing school, an accident, a bereavement) and chronic adversities (such as disability, or abuse) (Allen et al, 2008). Stressors might be very immediate and close-by (for example, poor lighting in the classroom, examinations, parental arguing) or more distant, and harder to pin down (risk of financial instability relating to the economic climate, threat of global warming). Past, present and perceived future risk factors can operate cumulatively on each other, and be moderated by perceptions of any of the past, present or future supportive resources. It is most unlikely that our responses to all these kinds of stressors will be the same and indeed, as mentioned earlier, there is evidence that the underlying physiological events are quite different for sudden events versus longer-term adversity.

The three key components of the stress concept we have identified thus include the physiological stress response, the individual's perception of a threat and details about the stressor being faced. It is crucial to remember, however, that challenges are normal and adaptive, and that stress is not defined as a necessarily negative construct. It may indeed play a part in developing resilience (Elder, 1974; Rutter, 1985). Therefore, in thinking about stressors we need to remember that there is such a thing as *positive stress*. The traditional view of stress as a significant discrepancy between the demands of a situation and the organism's capacity to respond, resulting in detrimental consequences, implies that all stress is harmful. However, throughout life, including adolescence, some stress may be positive. Mild stressors are often benign and sometimes even promote adaptation, as people change in response to their environment. Studies have been consistent in showing that, in some circumstances, stress experiences may be protective, exerting an immunising or even 'steeling effect' (Rutter, 1983). Steeling effects refer to the fact that negative experiences, as well as challenges and transitions, are a normal part of life that all people have to learn to cope with. Challenge is an essential ingredient for human development.

Measurement issues

Given what we have established about the range and variety in definitions of stress, it is no surprise that measurement has provided some challenges. As a result, researchers tend to focus on different parts of the construct.

Assessing stressors, mainly in the form of life events, has been by far the most common approach. This is usually through simple checklist-based assessment tools using a pre-defined catalogue of life events, known or hypothesised to be stressful or to have particular consequences, which are rated on occurrence over a specified time period (usually the previous year). Reflecting the variety of stressors we described earlier, measurement can include acute events (moving home, divorce) and chronic stressors (long-term poverty, bullying) or daily hassles (arguments). They can be common events that most people experience at some time (such as changing school), or they can be unusual and dramatic (such as death of a parent). Perhaps as a result of the muddle of different types of experiences, and an overlap between them (if you experience an acute event such as divorce, you will probably also experience some long-term chronic stress as well from the build-up of poor relations for several years before the event) it is not surprising that simply summing scores of items such as these have proved of little value in the attempts to clarify how stress contributes to the risk of mental health problems in young people.

However, there have been methodological developments over recent years, with the use of more detailed and systematic interview-based assessments that attempt to combine a quantification of the experience as rated objectively, and also a subjective appraisal by the individual affected by the experience (Dohrenwend, 2006). In the UK, these include, for example, the Camberwell Family Interview (Brown and Rutter, 1966), the LEDS (Life Events and Difficulties measure, see Brown and Harris, 1978), and, specific for children, the Psychosocial Assessment of Childhood Experiences (PACE) (Glen et al, 1993; Sandberg et al, 1993, 2000). North American examples include the Stressful Life Events Schedule (SLES) for children and adolescents (Williamson et al, 2003).

Various problems remain with measurement. First, as Grant et al identified in their review of 500 stress studies with children and adolescents, there is still enormous variety in which instruments people use, making comparisons across studies very difficult (Grant et al, 2003). Because the construct is so broad, and the range of stressors so wide, there can be a lack of comparability between studies that sound as if they are addressing the same topic. There may also have been less attention than necessary paid to the possible reporting and non-reporting of stress; qualitative research suggests that the potential under-reporting of stress and associated psychological problems may be socially patterned, particularly by gender and social class (Webster et al, 2004; MacDonald and Marsh, 2005). Finally, measurements have tended (with some exceptions) to ignore positive as well as negative aspects of life events, and indeed positive and negative aspects of stress.

In addition, existing measurement approaches tend to be based on a static model of stress development. Like most other aspects of cause and effect in adolescent development, there is probably potential for a more dynamic model of the process, as the transition to adulthood includes a process of becoming more resilient. It is possible to imagine, for example, a pathway that starts with exposure to a stressor, goes through a round of initial reactions, results in a feeling of competence as one starts to cope, and finally ends with a positive self-evaluation and confidence that one could cope again. Or alternatively, the path could end in peaks and troughs of coping and non-coping, involving periods of depression and anxiety. At what point in this cycle would measurement be appropriate?

Finally, measurement of the biological substrates of stress also brings challenges; this often relies on tests of salivary cortisol, which are then aligned with measures of self-reported stress. In some cases (see, for example, Gunnar et al, 2009) measures also include cardiac activity.

Actually getting accurate measurements can be tricky; salivary assays are useful as they can be taken at home and are relatively non-invasive, but they can be vulnerable, for example, to use of cotton materials for collection (Shirtcliff et al, 2001), and interpretation of the findings can also be challenging, as not enough is yet known about how the endocrinological and other biological systems work in interaction with the environment.

Measurement has thus been largely restricted to rating of stressors and to the internal, biological stress response. More recent work has tried to bridge part of this gap. With that in mind, we move on to an overview of what we know about stress during the adolescent years.

Particular stressors in adolescence

Adolescents face some particular and unique stressors, many arising from the move to more independence and autonomy. These include stresses of puberty and physiological change; the family and home; school, education and work transitions; and challenges from relations with their peer groups. Change is stressful, and adolescence is defined by change. Much of this is normal, and although there is not a vast literature describing adolescent experiences of stress, this topic has not been ignored; researchers including Compas (Compas et al, 1993, Compas, 1995), Seiffge-Krenke (1995) and Aneshensel and Gore (1991) have documented both stress arising from normal, common challenges, and stress arising from unusual events that might happen during this age period.

Puberty and physiological change are, of course, part and parcel of the experiences of this age group. Swift bodily changes are likely to be stressful in themselves, but the timing of puberty relative to peer norms is also a factor – particularly early maturation which may be related to more substance use and problem behaviours (van Jaarsveld et al, 2007). Interestingly, however, much research on stress and puberty has tended to focus on the role of the former in predicting pubertal timing, rather than the reverse effects (Susman et al, 2003). Stressors related to the family and home and negotiation of new independence are also prominent, including battles over rules and boundaries and extent of autonomy, and negotiating the effects of divorce, although most adolescents report good family relationships (Coleman, 2011). The challenges of school, examinations and school and work transitions peak in adolescence; the stresses will vary depending on whether young people are immersed in high-achieving expectations or are being excluded and marginalised by educational failure. The increasing prominence and importance of peer groups for this age group also brings stressors, including managing intergroup relations, the challenges of establishing identity and establishing social hierarchies and relationships, handling romantic relationships and break-ups and responding to pressures to behave in different ways. Finally there may be aspects of the broader social context that are particularly salient in the teens – the impact of poverty and high-risk neighbourhoods, and issues to do with minority youth (Gonzales et al, 2005), which may expose youth to chronic adversities and cumulative stressors. Stressful and unpredictable negative life events occur more often to young people in low versus high socioeconomic status contexts, and the way the stressors are interpreted can also vary, so that the world can seem a more threatening place (Chen and Hanson, 2005).

Not everyone will experience all, or even any, of these as stressful, and the general consensus is that the old model of adolescence being defined by 'storm and stress' is outdated and generally not true (Arnett, 1999). But these are the types of challenges most adolescents will face at some point, and it may be as much the pile-up of life events at a time of ongoing transition (or of chronic adversity) that provides the real stressors in adolescence.

What do adolescents themselves report as being the stressors in their lives? This has not received a great deal of rigorous attention in the academic literature although it is the focus of acres of web and press comment. Researchers have asked adolescents to report the things that they worry about in open-ended surveys, interviews, focus group discussions and in diary entries. For example, an Evidence for Policy and Practice Information and Co-ordinating (EPPI)-Centre systematic review of adolescents' perceptions of mental health (Harden et al, 2001) identified 12 studies where young people reported their views on the things that were stressful to them (Gallagher et al, 1992; Aggleton et al, 1995; HEA, 1995; Derbyshire, 1996; Friedli and Scheerzer, 1996; Gallagher and Millar, 1996; Bowen, 1997; Gordon and Grant, 1997; Armstrong et al, 1998; Balding et al, 1998; Tolley et al, 1998; Scott Porter Research and Marketing Ltd, 2000). The sources of stress most commonly reported by adolescents across studies were (in order): things to do with school, friendships and peer relationships, family and material resources, and lack of things to do/no job opportunities. In contrast to commonly held notions of adolescence being a time of great concern about sexual relationships and life changes, only a couple of the studies reviewed by Harden et al (2001) identified romantic relationships, life transitions and health behaviours to be a felt concern. A study published after the EPPI-Centre review (Cairns and Lloyd, 2005) found similarly that the most frequently reported stressors for 16-year-old respondents in the Young Life and Times Survey in Northern Ireland were: schoolwork/exams (69 per cent), family problems (9 per cent) and financial problems/work (9 per cent). Lesser reported problems (like in the review) were: being under pressure (6 per cent), life in general/ worrying (3 per cent), problems with friends (2 per cent), relationship problems (1 per cent) and health problems (1 per cent).

A recent cross-sectional picture of adolescents' worries in England was provided by the 2009/10 Ofsted (Office for Standards in Education, Children's Services and Skills) Tellus survey of a nationally representative sample of 253,755 Year 6, 8 and 10 pupils from 3,699 schools. Adolescents selected up to three worries from a list. The most commonly selected worry across ages 10 to 16 was school work and examinations (51 per cent), followed by career choice, friendships and physical appearance (Chamberlain et al, 2010). Pressure of school work was also included in the Health Behaviour of School-aged Children surveys, where approximately half of UK-based 13-year-olds and two thirds of 15-year-olds reported that they felt pressurised by school work in the latest wave (Currie et al, 2008).

The difficulty with the work on worries is that the lists muddle up particular features of adolescence (such as school work and exams) with general features of life (such as 'being healthy') and actual events (such as 'being bullied'). As we suggested earlier, these different categories of worry should be treated as conceptually distinct and are likely to have different effects. The questions and lists presented to the respondents can also be very vague; what does it mean to feel 'pressurised by schoolwork'? Are experiences of disengagement and failure more or less stressful than experiences of academic pressure and success? Worry is often assumed to be a proxy for stress, but are there some conceptual differences? It would seem that this is where the literature is probably its most diffuse and imprecise.

Stress reactions in adolescence

Evidence is emerging that adolescents may respond differently to stress because of the hormonal flux and brain development that are a feature of the second decade. At puberty, the secretion of sex hormones in the brain promotes rapid changes in physical growth as well as a tendency for mood alteration. In studies of rodents, these sex steroids are shown to directly influence HPA axis activity (McCormick and Mathews, 2007) and studies of humans have found moderate associations between pubertal maturation and HPA axis activity (Gunnar et al, 2009). In comparison to children, adolescents are found to have a greater average cortisol response in relation to the stressor of performance (that is, public speaking), and greater HPA activity and cortisol response for the stressor of peer rejection (Stroud et al, 2009). They have also been found to exhibit a greater cortisol response to stressors with increasing age (Gunnar et al, 2009). These findings suggest that only some aspects of the stress response system are more sensitive in older adolescents, and perhaps only in response to certain stressors (Spear, 2009).

However, the inverse pattern occurs for self-reported stress. Adolescents participating in Gunnar et al's (2009) laboratory tests report *less* perceived stress across age groups, despite having higher cortisol responses. This shows a disassociation between actual and perceived stress. Following the same pattern of perceived stress, Northern Irish teenagers aged over 16 reported worrying significantly less frequently than their younger counterparts (Gallagher and Millar, 1998). To add more complication, this pattern may be gender-specific. In London, the HABITS study measured stress perceptions of 5,229 adolescents over five years (aged 11 to 16). Boys were found to have no significant change in average levels of perceived stress, whereas girls' perceptions increased linearly across time (van Jaarsveld et al, 2007). Stress was higher for girls than boys on average at each time point.

Raised reactivity may serve a developmental purpose, heightening the young person's awareness of the outside world and perhaps in some way aiding the move to more independence and self-reliance. In this respect, perceiving stress differently might be important too. The possibility that adolescents react differently to stress is not directly relevant to understanding time trends, of course. However, if social change has particularly exacerbated the specific stresses of adolescence, or certain subgroups of at-risk adolescents, then this may be relevant.

Stress and mental health: causal links in adolescence?

What is the evidence that stress is related to mental health symptoms? Although there is more to stress than just life events, for various reasons research has generally concentrated on the role of life events in leading to symptoms, that is, a focus on the stressors.

Looking first at the *evidence for associations*, we certainly know that these two go hand in hand; large-scale robust studies have clearly demonstrated over many years that experience of more stressors in adolescence is associated with more symptoms of depression (Ge et al, 1994; Goodyer et al, 2000; Jose and Ratcliffe, 2004; Sandberg and Rutter, 2008), with suicidal ideation/attempts (King et al, 2001) and also with anxiety problems (Allen et al, 2008). Prospective associations (across time, with earlier life events associated with later mental health symptoms) have also been demonstrated for adolescents, particularly for more extreme and overwhelming stressors such as kidnapping, war, earthquake and serious assault, which have been shown to result in post-traumatic stress disorder (PTSD) (Yule and Smith, 2008). Prospective associations are also demonstrated for more normal adolescent stressors and depression (Monroe et al, 1999; Hankin et al, 2007; Parry-Langdon, 2008), and stressors and anxiety (Allen et al, 2008).

The associations go both ways. Teenagers' own emotional and behavioural problems can also give rise to stressors that further compound their existing problems (Williamson et al, 1995, 1998), or have an adverse effect on their future mental health and negative life experiences in adult life (Robins, 1966). Champion et al's (1995) 20-year follow-up of London school children demonstrated that mental health problems at age 10 (especially conduct problems but, to a lesser extent, emotional difficulties) were associated with a more than doubling in the risk of both negative life events and chronic stressors in adult life (see also Fergusson et al, 2000; Winograd et al, 2008). In Colman et al (2009), a 40-year follow-up of a national UK cohort study of over 3,500 adolescents, teacher ratings at 13 and 15 years of age identified adolescents with severe or mild conduct problems, showing them significantly more likely to have adverse adult outcomes involving poor mental health, family life and relationship problems, and educational and economic difficulties, compared with those with no teenage conduct problems.

There are clearly links between stress and mental health outcomes, but do we know how they are connected? This has been subject of several recent reviews, including Grant et al (2003, 2006), and Sandberg and Rutter (2008). We should also note that reviews generally consider both child and adolescent stress together; we have not seen a review just on *adolescent* stress and mental health. There is quite a challenge inherent in picking out the specific messages about the adolescent age group. Researchers have focused on three types of possible causal links: physiological, psychological and family.

We looked earlier at the evidence about how the biology of stress might work (Gunnar et al, 2009). We know that prolonged stress, with its underlying *physiological* implications, might lead directly to illness and disease. Prolonged stress seems to have implications for immune response, development of somatic symptoms, lower levels of energy and potentially depression as a direct result of biological processes. In the case of adolescents, this might help us to consider how young people with troubled childhoods might be particularly vulnerable. However, despite the intuitive appeal of these biological models, it has not been as easy as might have been imagined to map out the pathways and to understand how elevated and depressed levels of different hormones actually have an effect. There is an emerging science of looking for biological and genetic markers, but the way in which these actually play a causal role in linking vulnerable childhoods, adolescent life events and later outcomes is still largely uncharted territory.

Other causal links might include individual *psychological processes*, and how these may be particularly important for adolescents who are learning how to handle stressful life events. For example, research has looked at the role of 'rumination' as the mediator between stressful events and depression (Jose and Huntsinger, 2005). Rumination – repeatedly going over preoccupying thoughts – seems particularly salient for adolescent girls, who do more of it. It tends to be a maladaptive coping strategy, as it amplifies the effects of the stressful event (Nolen-Hoeksema et al, 2008). Co-rumination has also been the topic of study, the tendency for dyads or groups of adolescent girls to discuss and emphasise stressful events together, which may be good for friendship but bad for emotional adjustment (Rose et al, 2007). Again, there is a particular relevance for adolescence, with the importance of social groups and peer influence. It may be an important part of understanding why some groups of girls may be more prone to examination stress. Indeed, understanding this kind of social process may help us to understand how institutional changes in, for instance, how classes are organised in schools, can be made to provide protection or even improve coping.

Another risk mechanism, again especially to explain the emergence of higher rates of depression among females from adolescence onwards, is the cognitive vulnerability-transactional stress model, introduced by Hankin and Abrahamson (2001). This transactional model involving bidirectional effects between puberty-related biological changes and the timing of puberty, negative affect, cognitive styles and 'social' life events, posits a causal chain leading to higher rate of depression in girls. It argues that negative affect resulting from an adverse life event is more likely to be perpetuated by a tendency towards a negative cognitive style (for example, blaming oneself). This is more common in girls than boys, and promotes depression, which in turn promotes self-generated negative interpersonal life events, and these then help to keep the chain going. In addition, Silberg et al (1999) provided evidence for stronger genetic heritability and genetic mediation in girls than boys, which might also be part of the explanation for increased depression in girls over adolescence.

Not surprisingly, given that adolescents generally live in families, a considerable amount of research has focused on the role played by *family processes*. As we have seen already, family processes are a clear source of stressors in adolescence, through events such as divorce and marital conflict, and parental mental health problems. Families are usually part of early chronic adversity, which is linked to rises in later stressful life events, and may well increase vulnerability to such events (Brown and Harris, 1986; Sandberg et al, 1993, 2000; Rojo et al, 2006). Parents with their own mental health or substance use related problems can struggle when faced with the needs of their adolescent children, and their own problems can bring on more stresses for the family in general (Rutter, 1989; Adrian and Hammen, 1993; Murray and Cooper, 1997; Minde et al, 2003; Riggins-Caspers et al, 2003; Ellenbogen and Hodgins, 2004). Studies of adults with a childhood history of abuse have implicated long-term dysfunction of the body's biological stress response systems, and it has been proposed that that these effects underlie the symptoms of PTSD and other stress-related conditions (McEwen, 2000; Grossman et al, 2003; Shea et al, 2004). Likewise, dysregulation of the stress systems has been suggested as the possible link between exposure to major traumatic events such as childhood sexual abuse, for example, and mental health problems in adolescence (Carrion et al, 2002).

But the question here is whether family processes are more than just a source of stress – it is whether they are also part of the process by which stressors (*any* stressors – they could be from outside the family) are translated into mental health outcome. For example, it has been suggested that experience of childhood abuse and/or neglect may sensitise individuals to the effects of acute life events at a later stage. Thus, in a study of depression in adolescents (Harkness et al, 2006), the researchers found that in teenagers with a history of childhood abuse and/or neglect, life events with a lower level of threat were more likely to provoke depression than in those without similar adverse early experiences. Family processes might 'sensitise' adolescents. Traumatic childhood experiences may result in altered cognitive sets or styles of emotional and cognitive processing (Dodge et al, 1995; Overmier and Murison, 2005).

As well as evidence on links through physiological, psychological and social processes, researchers have also suggested that more problems arise when *acute and chronic stressors occur together* (Goodyer et al, 1990, 1997; Sandberg et al, 1993, 1998). In fact, studies suggest that the link between stressors and mental health outcomes frequently depend on *chain events* (Kim, 2005; Grant et al, 2006). Examples of this can also be found in qualitative, sociological work in the UK and elsewhere, such as research on young adults who resort to the use of 'poverty drugs' such as heroin as a way of coping with social exclusion but which further compound social exclusion (MacDonald and Marsh, 2002; Allen, 2007), and Savelsberg and Martin-Giles (2008) reported similar spirals of stressors and outcomes among the young homeless.

Finally, as we have already noted, it is important to acknowledge that there is such a thing as *positive stress*. The traditional view of stress as a significant discrepancy between the demands of a situation and the organism's capacity to respond, resulting in detrimental consequences, implies that all stress is harmful. However, as far as adolescents are concerned, the opposite is sometimes true. Mild stressors are often benign and sometimes even promote adaptation. Studies have been consistent in showing that, in some circumstances, stress experiences may be protective, exerting an immunising or even 'steeling' effect (Rutter, 1983). Steeling effects reflect the fact that negative experiences, as well as challenges and transitions, are a normal part of life that all people have to learn to cope with. While some individuals succumb following stress, others survive relatively unscathed, or even strengthened, following severely adverse experiences (Rutter, 2005, 2006a).

This leads us on to a brief mention of the constructs of coping and resilience. How well the individual views their own *coping* resources and how well they then deploy them has an impact on the effect of the stressor on them (see, for example, Compas et al, 1993, 2001). The links between stress and mental health might be exacerbated if coping ceases to be effective. The majority of studies in this field have reported 'engagement coping' and 'problem-focused coping' to be associated with better psychological adjustment. Conversely, 'disengagement coping' and 'emotion-focused coping' – including social withdrawal or resigned acceptance, or wishful thinking and self-blame – have generally been shown to be associated with poor adjustment. Although both boys and girls increase their emotion-focused coping during early adolescence, their actual coping methods differ from one another (Compas et al, 1993, 2001). Girls tend to increase the use of emotionally attentive or ruminative coping strategies whereas boys increase the use of emotion-distraction coping.

Resilience is also relevant to understanding the links between stress and mental health. It is generally considered to be a basic human adaptational system (Masten, 2001), and according to Masten and Powell (2003), determining whether someone is resilient requires making two judgements: first, that 'the person is doing OK', and second, that the person has experienced significant risks or adversity that could undermine the successful negotiation of age-salient developmental tasks. Resilience has been associated with a supportive marriage or relationship with a significant other, educational achievement in community college, participation in a church community and service in the military (Werner and Smith, 1992).

Resilience does not refer to an individual trait, and it does not assume that the same processes will apply to all individuals, all stresses and all outcomes, or indeed to all phases in a person's life (Rutter, 2006a, 2006b). The focus, therefore, is not on a single quality of the individual, or on fixed variables, but rather on coping processes – coping incorporating both physiological and psychological mechanisms. Delayed recovery sometimes stems from life changes (turning points) later on. However, resilience is not unlimited as it may be constrained by biological programming in early life, or from damaging effects of stress on neural structures – and, at extreme levels of stress, even the most salient protective factors may lose their impact (D'Imperio et al, 2000).

In conclusion, there is good evidence that acutely negative life events (stressors) are related both cross-sectionally and longitudinally with mental health outcomes for adolescents. Effects are strongest for extremely negative life events leading to PTSD, and for chronic or continued bad events and adversities. Evidence on the mediators that translate stressful events into outcomes is beginning to accumulate but is not yet definitive. There are strong indications that family relationships play a role in translating experiences into outcomes for young people, perhaps by sensitising children to the effects of acute life events. Evidence on moderators is also beginning to emerge. Gender is clearly part of the picture; boys and girls respond differently by using different strategies to different effects. There is some evidence of specificity of effect – between very serious events and PTSD for example – but not much beyond that. Some of the evidence on causal pathways suggests particular sensitivities in adolescence – the importance of social groups and peer influence, and the fact that uncontrollable and social-evaluative elements of stressors have special significance for outcomes. On the other hand, there is plenty we do not yet know. For example, the physiological research is at an early stage (as with adolescent brain development studies) and needs more clarification. The emphasis has been on biological substrates, stressors, reports of 'worries' and on coping strategies. These are only part of the whole 'stress' model.

If adolescents have been experiencing more stress, there is enough evidence to suggest that we could expect this to be related to rising

Sweeting, 2003, p 399). There is a problem, however, in establishing a research method that reflects the subjective interpretive elements of 'stress' but still allows us to compare like with like over time.

Rutter and Smith (1995), in their comprehensive review of time trends in psychosocial disorders, identified some other important changes in adolescent life transitions and in the pattern of stressors facing them in the decades since the Second World War. These involved changes in *family structure* through increased rate of divorces and remarriages, potentially affecting family life and relationships. Indeed, divorce has gone up. Again, this is a topic addressed by another review in this volume, and the trends are tracked in Chapter Five. More children certainly experience the stressor of divorce, and it seems unlikely that a single child escapes without at least temporary stress as a result. However, as we will see in the parenting chapter, research has suggested that the divorce event itself tends not to be the main stressor; the stressor comes from family conflict and family relationships, from prolonged chronic problems rather than from single life events (Fergusson et al, 1992; McMahon et al, 2003; Cuffe et al, 2005). As the parenting chapter shows, there is no evidence that parent–adolescent relations have got worse over this time; in fact they seem to have improved, and the increased warmth and authoritative parenting that is documented in that review could in fact help young people weather stressful storms.

Similarly, while the challenges of *peer relations, identity development* and *sensitivity about appearance* are often listed as stressors in the surveys mentioned, it is very difficult to identify any objective record of increased stressors in these domains. Where data are presented, they are often only for a few years (for example, reports of worries in the Schools Health Education Unit survey by Balding et al, 1998) and cannot really be described as time trends. Our searches did not uncover any long-term comparative data on these topics. It is interesting to note that the effects of some of the other social changes we have noted, such as the increased amounts of time spent in educational environments in the 16-18 period, and the collapse of the youth labour market, mean that it is possible that adolescents live in more age-segregated environments and spend more time with their peers than previously. It has been noted recently that 'the modern social organization of adolescent lives highlights peers' (Moody et al, 2010, p 324). Peer relations may thus have more salience and more intensity, and this may be a stressor for some adolescents, but this is purely a hypothesis.

One domain where the increase in peer pressures might be important is in relation to pressure to use drugs. As we saw in Chapter Seven on substance use, more widespread availability and use of both alcohol and other types of drugs was a distinctive feature of the last half of the 20th century. Decisions about whether or not to use substances are forced on young people in ways that they were not in earlier decades prior to, for example, the 1960s. This might provoke some stress. In addition, there are, of course, physiological effects of drugs that may be related to the physiological aspects of the stress process; drugs may create feelings of stress and anxiety (see Chapter Seven in this volume on substance use). The relationship between drug use and stress in adolescence is not well researched, but raises some interesting questions. Similarly, peer pressures in relation to sexual behaviour may be relevant to understanding trends in adolescent stress. Age at first intercourse dropped in the decades leading up to the 1990s, with increased proportions of girls reporting first intercourse before 16 years (Wellings et al, 2001). This may imply that some of this pressure is occurring at an age when individuals may be less psychologically equipped to cope with the experience.

The possibility that stressors have increased as a result of *other aspects of 'modern life'* has been debated at some length in the literature on the sociology of youth; for example, the youth of today face, it is suggested, increased risks and uncertainties created by the more complicated, protracted and apparently more choice-driven transitions to adulthood (see, for example, Furlong and Cartmel, 2007). However, the majority of this work relates to early adulthood; transitions such as labour market entry, leaving the parental home and parenthood are not normative experiences of adolescence any more. The choices for adolescents tend to be focused around examinations, colleges and training. Indeed these are potentially either overwhelming, or excluding, but whether they have got more stressful is moot. It is possible that the promises for better opportunities for equal success for everyone conveyed by the global media, for instance, create even greater disillusionment (and more stress) for adolescents to whom the road to success just seems filled with obstacles, but Sandberg and MacDonald's review did not reveal any good evidence on this. Also, we could argue that the concept is too negatively oriented – what about positive developments such as cheaper clothes and electronic goods available, the positive benefits of increased participation in education, more funding for some aspects of training and so on? Surely there are elements that *reduce* stress for some youth in comparison to the 1970s?

Finally, it is worth providing a cross-link at this stage to Collishaw's chapter in this volume (Chapter Two) on time trends in mental health problems, which referred to the data on rates of *suicide* in young people. Analysis of trends in suicide of young people aged 15-19 in the World Health Organization (WHO) European region from 1979 to 1996 showed increases for male adolescent suicide even though adult trends showed different patterns (Rutz and Wasserman, 2004). Suicide is not a direct correlate of stress, but research tends to show that it is frequently precipitated by acute stress of one kind or another.

As well as looking for increases in stressors, we could also look for absence of stressors that used to be present. The assumptions in this field that things are getting worse seem to be so pervasive that the null hypothesis is never even raised, let alone tested. We could hypothesise, for example, that adolescents are much less exposed to family bereavement than they used to be, as a result of major advances in medicine and early intervention. There is less corporal punishment in most of the environments they inhabit, and estimates of child abuse suggest rates have fallen since, for example, the early 1990s (Finkelhor and Jones, 2006). We could hypothesise that widely implemented bullying interventions should have made secondary schools safer environments than they were in, for example, the 1960s and 1970s.

It is extraordinary, given the widespread discussions about increases in adolescent stress, that there is such a complete absence of underlying data on increases in stressors and experiences of stress, apart from in relation to very extreme events such as suicide. More focused reanalysis of some of the larger, repeated surveys may allow us to get some kind of grip on whether stressors have risen, but it seems more likely we are going to have to look to future studies to (a) tighten up models and definitions, (b) broaden sources of information and think more imaginatively about measurement, and (c) focus on time trends.

Conclusion

In summary, stress is a very broad term. It sounds important and intuitive, but it can be used in a multitude of different ways. Hard to pin down, it implies a large set of interrelated constructs. Work addressing our particular questions about adolescent stress has only really just begun. The area suffers a little from conceptual woolliness; in particular, commentators tend to use the evidence of rising levels of anxiety and depression as evidence that stress has risen, but as discussed earlier, this confuses mental health and stress and creates a tautology. The life events literature, while more robust with respect to conceptualisation and measurement, does not seem to tell us much about whether the pattern of events in adolescent lives differs to that in adult lives, nor much about how it differs for different subgroups of young people. The worries literature seems impossibly imprecise. Both rely heavily on self-report. The biological literature is potentially very interesting, but is only a small part of the story. But we do have some indicators that (a) stress is a particularly salient construct in adolescence, and (b) it is clearly related to mental health outcomes.

What we do not know is whether it is on the increase. Despite widespread assumptions, there are no good, repeated surveys of adolescent stressors in the UK over the last three decades that might give us a fully rounded picture of even how much 'objective' stress they are being subjected to, quite apart from any trends in how they might respond and the quality of the coping they can bring to bear. Much of the material we explored simply bought into the zeitgeist without really challenging it. We need to encourage a tougher minded approach to the topic, and a more explicitly developmental perspective that does justice to what we know about the context and challenges of adolescent lives.

Note

[1] The authors would like to note that they are indebted to Bob Coles (University of York), Professors Andy Furlong and Patrick West (University of Glasgow), Professor Ken Roberts (University of Liverpool) and Professor Rachel Thomson (The Open University).

FOUR

Trends in adolescent time use in the United Kingdom

Ann Hagell, Stephen C. Peck, Nicole Zarrett,
J. Ignacio Giménez-Nadal and Jennifer Symonds

Introduction

Asking how young people's use of time in the UK has changed over recent decades is an important, but deceptively simple, question. How we use our time is both a measurement of direct change, and is also an index of more subtle, underlying shifts in social values and preoccupations, so it is crucial to our task of looking at social change. Understanding *what* young people are doing and *who* they are doing it with is an important anchor for understanding the social patterning of interactions that are part of the transition to adulthood for young people.

The way that children and young people use their time involves both elements that are structurally arranged by the legal and statutory frameworks within which they order their days (compulsory attendance at education, for example), and elements of 'free' (and therefore more clearly 'chosen') time. Patterns of time use thus reflect both how we as a society shape our time, and how we decide to spend some of it ourselves. As Professor Robert Sampson challenged us early on in our work, understanding time use helps us see how we as a society have chosen (implicitly or explicitly) to structure the transition from adolescence to adulthood.

How we spend our time is such a crucial question that it formed a central part of the work of the Changing Adolescence Programme. We funded a team led by Professor Leon Feinstein who was then at the Institute of Education, working with Karen Robson and Annik Sorhaindo in London, and Dr Stephen Peck and Professor Jacqueline Eccles at the University of Michigan, USA. This chapter draws on the work that they did in setting out the key constructs and identifying previous work on the topic. As a result of the findings of the review,

the Foundation also supported an exercise in mining the existing UK Time Use Surveys for useful data that would fill in some of the gaps, and help pose more sharply certain questions. This chapter synthesises the main messages from both the review, and from the additional analyses, as well as drawing on a wider reading of the relevant literature. Fuller versions of the work on which it draws are available from Dr Stephen Peck (for the review), or from the Foundation (for the data analysis).

There is a growing literature on time use, and many countries now have regular Time Use Surveys. The literature on time use is beginning to suggest various ways in which it might matter for positive youth development. This poses an interesting question about whether there have been significant changes in time use that may be related to changes in emotional and behavioural outcomes.

What do we mean by 'time use' and how is it researched?

A wide variety of different kinds of research can be brought under the heading of 'time use'. Some of this falls under the heading of adolescent leisure activities (see, for example, Trainor et al, 2009) or organised youth activities (see, for example, Larson et al, 2004) and after-school programmes (see, for example, Durlak and Weissberg, 2007). There is also the rather separate world of general time use research, often arising out of the activities of the International Association for Time Use Research and its conferences and publications, where there has been some limited work specifically on adolescent time use in recent years (see, for example, Chenu, 2003; Zuzanek and Mannell, 2003). Another rather separate literature has arisen on time use and media use, often concerning the impact of different types of new media on young people's lifestyles and leisure (see, for example, Griffiths, 2005). Finally, a long established world of sociological analyses of adolescent leisure brings a rather different perspective with an interest in social structures and inequalities (see, for example, Furlong and Cartmel, 2007).

All these ways of thinking about time use have different things to offer, and consider time use in different ways, some of which are more directly relevant to our own underlying questions than others. Researchers in leisure studies distinguish between constructive organised activities and passive leisure. Sport psychologists distinguish between competitive team-based and individual non-competitive activities. Somewhat more broadly, research in education distinguishes among extracurricular, co-curricular and academic activities. Developmental psychologists distinguish between time that is supervised by adults versus unsupervised activities, structured versus unstructured time, in-school and out-of-school activities, and pro-social and anti-social activities. Researchers have also developed classification schemes for activities based on aspects such as the time and place in which the activity occurs (school versus community-based after-school programmes); who and how many are participating (solo activities, activities primarily with peers, activities with one's family); the intent of the activity (to teach skills or provide opportunities for play); and the content domain itself (music, reading, sport, work, watching television, hanging out). It is these sorts of issues that we want to examine in assessing how different groups of UK adolescents may have changed the way they spent their time over the past 30 years, and whether this might suggest any fruitful lines of inquiry in comparing adolescent experiences and socialisation in the UK compared to those of adolescents elsewhere.

In doing so, we note that while there is something seductive about time use statistics – they are overtly quantitative, representing a concrete index of social behaviour in a world where we have few such indices, with all the variables conveniently sharing the same denominator – using time use data presents severe challenges, even at a descriptive level (see Fisher et al, 2009). A key concern of the Feinstein review was the extent to which time use data provides salient information on the experiences of young people. Time use data are necessarily distal in terms of experience. A child may be classified as in school for a certain number of hours but by itself this tells us little or nothing about the actual experience of the child, whether they are learning, happy or engaged, for example. This is an important challenge for the interpretation and meaningfulness of time use data. On another instance, although analysing averages for an entire sample gives a type of indicator of whole population involvement in a certain activity and may be useful in an epidemiological sense or when tracking trends, at another level it may tell us little about the lives of individuals or groups. This is always true, not just of time use data, but there are risks to over-emphasis on the average (Peck et al, 2008a). For example, averages do not take into account the proportion of people who actually engage in the activity; there is a difference, for example, between the percentage of engagement in the activity for the whole age group (which might, for example, have dropped) and the average time spent in the activity for those people who actually did it to any extent at all (where, for example, fewer people might be doing it for longer). So while it may be important to show that young people today on average spend less time in physical activity, it may not help us understand why that is so, or who in particular it applies to.

For this reason, as well as exploring differences in time use across the population of young people, we also need to look at participation rates, and at averages for different subgroups of young people. Time use varies by social group, by level of income, by geographical location, by age and gender and educational status, and these are just the most obvious subgroups. Some of what we will find in this chapter looks at this issue in conjunction with other evidence in order to suggest fruitful areas for investigation to understand more about how looking at time use could illuminate social change and adolescent outcomes. And although it is beyond the scope of this chapter, it is also undoubtedly essential to look at qualitative information about changes in the meaning of activities for people if we are to understand patterns and their implications.

A separate, but crucial issue is that almost all time use data are based on self-report. There is some innovation around different ways of asking the question (see, for example, experience sampling methods in Box 4.1), but very little time use research depends on observational data or sources of information other than the main actor. This raises familiar questions about the validity and meaning of the reports, particularly if we are asking the same questions of different cohorts, at different points in history.

Even constructing the categories with which to examine patterns in time use for an age group is not straightforward. People can do several things at the same time, they can vary how they do activities depending on their company at the time, and they can pass off an activity as one thing when it is really another. What counts as one activity at one time may mean something very different a few years later. Methods and coding systems for studying time use vary throughout the literature. We summarise some of these in Boxes 4.1 and 4.2.

Box 4.1: Methods used in adolescent time use research

- Questionnaire or interview measures of involvement in specified activities over given periods; dichotomous indicators of involvement (yes/no) versus continuous scales of the amount of time spent doing the activity.
- Time use diaries, where respondents routinely write down what they were doing at pre-specified time points during the day or week.
- Experience sampling methods. Respondents are signalled via a bleeper or mobile telephone to record their experiences at different times.

Box 4.2: Ways of analysing time use data

(see Fisher and Gershuny, 2009):

- Categories: often a large number of individual items are reduced to categories such as sleep time and non-sleep time, school time and out-of-school time, family time, etc. These might be mutually exclusive or they might imply overlapping time use episodes – you can do two things at once, of course.
- Changes in the average time spent in certain activities within a 24-hour period, for the sample as a whole (*total mean*).
- Changes in the proportion of the sample who are taking part in any given activity within a 24-hour period (*participation rate*).
- Changes in the average time spent doing certain activities in a 24-hour period, but only for those who took part in it (that is, excluding those who did not do the activity – participation *mean*).
- It is also possible to look at time as a *proportion* of all time (50 per cent of time spent sleeping).

A couple of additional points. First, it is obvious that time use data operate as a type of index or indirect measure of what is going on in young people's lives, rather than always being a precise reflection of their actual experiences at that moment. This means that while time use data may not be very good as a measure of psychological features, they may be useful in potentially enabling us to examine how young people experience social institutions. For example, the social category 'being in school' may mean being in classrooms in structured activity overseen by a teacher or it may mean being in a study hall with little or no structure or even just hanging around on campus or in a schoolyard with peers. Using time data to understand how the different parts of the day fit together, and who is doing what with whom, might help us to think more concretely about how adolescent development (both social and cognitive) could potentially be affected.

The second point is even more fundamental for our examination on adolescent well-being. Previously, most time use research has often blocked together age groups in ways that do not make a great deal of sense to developmental scientists. The most common of these seems to be use of a single 16-25 year age group. Although at a stretch we could label this age group as 'emerging adulthood' (Arnett, 2004), the differences in time use between the top and bottom ends of this age range are likely to be huge. They certainly do not all qualify as 'adolescent', and simply looking at the different roles of statutory social institutions (like compulsory schooling) shows how big the differences will be. On the other hand, it is also not uncommon to find age groupings that include both children and adolescents, from early childhood up to age 15 or 16 years. Again, this seems unhelpful for the issue of time use, and ignores the development of autonomy and independence that characterise adolescence and which are likely to have a big impact on the adolescent trajectories we wish to understand.

What matters about time use?

In their review of the literature, Feinstein's research team identified a number of different ways in which time use might have a role to play in emotional and behavioural outcomes for young people:

- Positive or negative reinforcement of *behaviour*: elements of the activity might provide positive feedback, reward engagement, develop self-efficacy (Bandura, 1997), or, conversely, could produce boredom or agitation.
- Cognitive and other *skill gains*. Things might be learned, including cognitive functioning, interpersonal competence, initiative, leadership skills.
- Development of *identity*, and a sense of 'mattering' (Larson, 2000; Eccles and Templeton, 2002). For many young people, identity is closely bound up with their place in their social worlds.
- Broader issues of *socialisation*, including the importance of developmentally appropriate supports – time use can be thought of as part of this. In the review they undertook for the Foundation, the review team suggested that it is useful to think of time use in the context of a 'person–environment fit' (see also Feinstein et al, 2006). This theory has been influential in child development, stressing that a match is needed between the basic developmental needs of young people, and the structures and frameworks provided for them (what Eccles calls 'setting features', see Eccles and Gootman, 2002 – contexts should be sensitive to exactly what it is that young people need at that point in their lives). If there is a poor match, outcomes for children will be less good. For example, adolescents have a need to establish competence, autonomy and belongingness (Ryan and Deci, 2000), and different settings may enable or hinder this.
- If spending time in some activities is more beneficial (or harmful) than others, and if access to opportunities is shaped by structural issues such as socioeconomic resources, then youth activities may be part of the transmission of *inequality* (Feinstein et al, 2006).

In particular, research has shown that the following characteristics of activities seem to be helpful for positive outcomes for young people:

- Activities that help enhance competence, autonomy and relatedness (Ryan and Deci, 2000), or focus on developing a particular skill.
- Activities that provide relevant opportunities for adolescents to participate meaningfully in social groups and institutions.
- Activities that allow experience of appropriate levels of supervision and support, and that transmit coherent values about behaviours and goals.
- Supervised and structured activities, which offer opportunity for structured engagement with peers and adults.
- Activities undertaken with a certain level of intensity; more than transient participation (Mahoney et al, 2003; Zaff et al, 2003), possibly because this may contribute particularly to the development of a new skill (Larson et al, 2006).

A useful shorthand for these kinds of features is *constructive activities*, and examples include school and community-based activities, organised out-of-school activities and volunteering. Research reviewed by the Feinstein team suggested descriptively that young people who participate in constructive activities tend to have higher self-concepts and better psychological health (Larson and Kleiber, 1993; Kivel, 1998; Eccles and Barber, 1999; Barber et al, 2001), higher rates of civic engagement (Youniss et al, 1999) and lower rates of criminality, drug use and feelings of loneliness (McNeal, 1995; Mahoney and Cairns, 1997; Eccles and Barber, 1999; Yin et al, 1999; Mahoney, 2000; Marsh and Kleitman, 2002), compared with non-participants. Participation has also been linked to greater social competencies like learning to work with others and leadership skills (Dubas and Snider, 1993; Patrick et al, 1999; Eccles and Templeton, 2002). There may be particular advantages for low-income and low-achieving students (Mahoney, 2000; Eccles and Templeton, 2002; Mahoney et al, 2005; Peck et al, 2008b). Very few of these examples map directly on to our construct of mental health problems (specifically anxiety, depression and conduct disorder) but, with regard to conduct disorder at least, features such as criminality and drug use are likely to be correlated.

A focus on 'constructive activities' thus seems important but care has to be exercised in making links between a particular activity and these broader claims. Conclusions about the role of sport demonstrate this. Feinstein et al's search for relevant literature revealed that in the USA sport has been associated with positive outcomes such as lower use of cigarettes, marijuana, cocaine and 'other drugs' (Page et al, 1998), lower rates of depression and lower incidence of suicidal behaviour (Barber et al, 2001; Gore et al, 2001), skills such as taking initiative (Duda and Ntounumis, 2005; Larson et al, 2006) and such values as responsibility, conformity, persistence, risk-taking, courage and self-control (Kleiber and Kirshnit, 1991) and emotion regulation (Larson et al, 2006). On the other hand, again in the USA intense sport participation has also been linked with adolescents' higher engagement in risk behaviours including greater use of smokeless tobacco, steroids, alcohol and adolescents' binge drinking and getting drunk (Rainey et al, 1996; Winnail et al, 1997; Eccles and Barber, 1999; Garry and Morrissey, 2000), greater exposure to risk-taking peers (Eccles and Barber, 1999), and, at times, to impediments in pro-social development (Shields and Bredemeier, 2001).

This may be where we need to be much more focused on particular subgroups. Peck et al (2008b) demonstrated that adolescent sport participation was associated with heavy drinking in early adulthood only for those sport participants who were also characterised by an adolescent history of drug use and externalising behaviour. It is likely too that factors other than the activity itself (in this case sports) are important – such as who it is done with, under what supervision and how it relates to other activities and social networks.

Feinstein et al also evaluated research on *unconstructive activities*: unstructured activities lacking imposed challenge, structure or opportunities for skill-building (Larson and Kleiber, 1993; Kleiber and Powell, 2005), falling more into the 'hanging out' category. This is sometimes viewed as 'wasted' time, although it is likely too that a certain amount of unconstructed relaxing time is needed by young people (as with all of us) both in the context of the many challenges young people are facing (cf Larson and Seepersad, 2003) and perhaps because it starts a move to self-structured as compared to 'other' structured time. But what the research tends to show is that, for example, time spent in unsupervised, unstructured youth centres without adult supervision or support for positive group activities is predictive of increases in adolescents' risk and delinquent behaviours (Mahoney et al, 2004; Feinstein et al, 2006; Robson and Feinstein, 2007).

These findings may be influenced by *selection biases*. For example, at-risk young people seeking out risky activities may only participate in activities and engagements that provide escape from adult control and opportunities to act out externalising behaviour, and then the absence of adult supervision, advice and scaffolding may exacerbate prior difficulties. Different groups of young people may self-select into sport, or into unsupervised youth groups, and by doing so may increase the likelihood that they associate with similar peers who reinforce pre-existing tendencies (see, for example, Dishion et al, 1999). We simply cannot be sure about causality.

So it is clear that in time use studies, the data are a tool or measurement device, but should not be mistaken for a direct insight into explanatory mechanism. As with all data, they are more or less useful to answer particular questions, and they are only as good as the questions they allow us to ask – and answer. But there may be two particularly important issues that time use data allow to consider and that have perhaps been more neglected in considerations of adolescent mental health and well-being.

The first is using time data to give us more information about what actually happens in social institutions that we know are important. As we have noted, Eccles has urged us to look not just at the patterning of activities, but also at the interaction between individual characteristics and key features about the activity (Is it supervised? Do you do it on your own or does it involve other people?), as any positive impact of different activities is likely to be in part through the extent to which they meet an individual's developmental needs for certain kinds of structures. Time use research has been much less focused on non-discretionary time, and it is here that we might be able to address the more sociological questions about how young people's time use reflects how they engage in social structures such as education and work, and indeed how those experiences are structured very differently for different types of young people. For instance, it seems unlikely that being in education is the same socialising experience for a young person in a sixth form school, with a highly structured curriculum, and a high number of contact hours, as for someone doing different kinds of qualifications in a further education college with only a few contact hours each week. In theory time use data could allow us to unpick the socially and developmentally relevant features of participation in even 'statutory' social institutions, and begin to ask whether UK institutions are structured to help those who might be most likely to experience challenges in making the transition to adulthood. So using time use data to understand compulsory social structures, and not just those discretionary or leisure activities that young people choose to do, is relatively neglected in the broader literature.

A second set of questions that may be important for understanding adolescent development may also be formulated more concretely using time use data. Early work by Jacqueline Eccles pointed out the importance of the overall activity pattern, in that the balance of choosing one activity rather than another at any given time might be important (Eccles, 1983). This leads us to consider patterns of time use across activities, and the balance between them. Some researchers have begun to examine the influence of participation intensity across multiple activities using pattern-centred techniques to examine how young people who participate in different combinations of constructive and unconstructive activities vary on indicators of functioning (Shanahan and Flaherty, 2001; Bartko and Eccles, 2003; Zarrett, 2007; Zarrett et al, 2007; Peck et al, 2008b). Lots of unstructured time spent with peers may pose risks if that is all you do, but may be helpful if you combine it with certain other sorts of constructive activities too. Having a balance between different types of experiences, and one that varies as young people mature, may be an important predictor of mental health and behavioural outcomes. Of course, even if these data help us pose descriptively more precise and concrete hypotheses/ questions, the difficulty then lies in finding a way to research the selection processes, which reflect the interaction between the young people and the activities they choose.

What does existing research tell us about trends in young people's time use?

Having considered some of the ways in which time use might be studied and how it might be important, we move on now to ask what we know about the ways in which time use is changing. What sort of evidence do we have to date? There is a growing and important literature on adult time use (see, for example, Gershuny, 2000), but the Feinstein review team concluded that published, peer-reviewed data on trends in adolescent time use in the UK are sparse. There are, however, some international studies that may provide pointers, and which might reveal some apparently common trends in time use in Western countries, and occasionally suggest differences or areas for future exploration. But these findings should at this stage be regarded as preliminary given issues of comparability in methods and measurement.

We can consider a range of categories of activities.

School and school-related learning

Education of one sort or another takes up a significant proportion of adolescent time in industrialised nations, and indeed is the main way that young people are compelled to spend time (now that very few work full time before age 18). Most children in England (approximately three quarters) are located in the state system, which consists largely of comprehensive schools, with a small number of grammar schools, secondary modern schools, middle schools and schools for children with special needs. At the time of writing, a new type of school, the 'academy', is emerging, but to date only accounts for a very small proportion of the whole. The remainder of children are located within the private system. Compulsory education ends at age 16 in the UK, and those electing to continue do so by remaining at their secondary school if it caters for their age group, or they attend sixth form colleges or more vocationally oriented further education colleges often open to adult learners as well.

Major reorganisation of the educational system in England took place in the 1960s and 1970s with the move to the comprehensive system, and the details of this have been documented in the education literature (see, for example, Moon, 1994; Chitty, 2002). We also cover this territory in the education chapter in this volume (Chapter Six), and in an accompanying article (Symonds and Hagell, 2011). Here we are concerned mostly with the use of time at school, and at a later stage we draw these themes together.

There are two questions for us at this point: how much time do secondary-aged children spend at school, and what are they doing with that time? On average, children of lower secondary school age (11-16) will spend around 180-200 days at school, for periods of, on average, 6-7 hours per day (see, for example, the Euronet survey of 11 European countries and the USA – see Flammer and Schaffner, 2003). There are differences, reflecting international variation in the organisation of the school day, and it is surprisingly difficult to pin these down. Most data are compiled from government recommendations and requirements, and in very few cases from surveys of schools. Data from the International Review of Curriculum and Assessment Frameworks Internet Archive (for example, INCA, see O'Donnell et al, 2010) demonstrate the variety. Germany and Hungary, for example, teach in the mornings but manage to achieve around 30 hours per week with 16-year-olds. England teaches 9am to 3.30pm on average, achieving around 25 hours per week. Korea teaches from 8am until 4pm, often over six days a week, achieving up to 1,160 hours per year. Average weeks of school also varied, from around 35 (for example, Japan) to 40 or more (for example, Sweden). The UK tends to sit in the middle or lower half of the distribution of indices such as days and hours of teaching. Interestingly, if one compares aggregate levels of school achievement from PISA studies (Programme for International Student Assessment) (see, for example, PISA, 2006) with INCA data on hours in school, time in school does not necessarily correlate with achievement (at the ecological level).

The amount of time spent at school varies on a number of dimensions including hours in school, average hours on any given day and number of weeks of attendance. In Figure 4.1 (from Symonds and Hagell, 2011), we have plotted the number of hours of teaching against the number of days in the school year, which is a different way of showing the international variation. Some countries, such as Japan, Ireland and France, have both low numbers of hours (relatively speaking) and fewer days at school. Other countries have higher hours and/or days, in varying combinations.

Figure 4.1: Amount of time spent in lessons in the school year: international comparisons

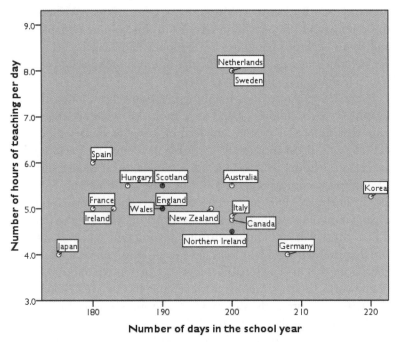

Source: Reproduced with permission from Symonds and Hagell (2011)

Has the amount of time spent at school changed in the last few decades? In some countries, evidence suggests that the number of hours young people actually spend engaging in *formal* school-related learning activities per day – meaning contact hours or classroom hours – has decreased in the past 20-30 years. Zuzanek and Mannell (2003) used data from national time use surveys in Canada and Finland to examine changes in the amount of time adolescents between the ages of 15-19 spend on school-related activities. Time spent attending lessons, doing homework and travelling to and from school had decreased between the 1980s and the early 2000s by as much as 1.5 hours per day in Canada and about 20 minutes in Finland. Similar data from two national time use surveys in France suggested a decrease of nearly 40 minutes per day between the mid-1980s and late 1990s (Chenu, 2003). This was not universal – there have been reports of increases in time spent in school in Germany and Norway. And national USA data (National Center for Educational Statistics, 2005) suggest that between 1981 and 2003 there was also an increase in the USA. So there are reports of both for increases and decreases, and it is hard to tell how much of the variation is due to different ways of coding categories of time use. We could not uncover any comparable published data for the UK.

Apart from the amount of time spent at school, is there any evidence that the organisation of the school day has changed? There is a very limited literature to draw on here, particularly if our focus is the UK, and we recently reviewed some of the key themes elsewhere (Symonds and Hagell, 2011). What we found was that UK school timetables and calendars are remarkably similar to those of 30 years ago, despite schools having considerable freedom to reorganise things if they so desire. There is evidence, however, for subtle shifts brought about by the introduction of the National Curriculum (in 1988) which has possibly reduced 'discretionary' teaching time, evidence for a reduction in the amount of break time across the day (Blatchford and Baines, 2008), and evidence for shorter school days but more 'extended' or optional schooling after school finishes. These issues appear to be driven more by school management priorities than by reform based on consideration of what might work best for adolescent development.

Where we have far fewer data is in relation to the 16-18 year age group in the UK. We do know, as is documented in the education chapter (Chapter Six), that a growing proportion are indeed staying on into some kind of education, rising from just over 40 per cent staying on at 16 in 1985, to approximately 70 per cent in 2007 (Symonds and Hagell, 2011). The majority of those staying on will remain at school (86 per cent; DCSF, 2007b) rather than move to college. These shifts will undoubtedly have implications for their time use both while they are at school and also in relation to the rest of their time, but this has not been a focus of previously published work.

Leisure, socialising and free time

One of the striking features of modern industrial life is the growth of leisure time in general, and young people have not been exempt from the particularly strong trend in this area. But how this is structured and organised may be particularly important, both for understanding the meaning of leisure, and also for relating this to the mental health and well-being of UK young people.

As with economically and culturally similar countries such as the USA, Canada and France, young people in the UK between the ages of 16-24 have been estimated to have an average of around 6.5 hours per day as leisure or 'free time', that is, time not used for sleeping, eating, personal care, domestic work, travel or paid work or study (Gershuny et al, 2006, for the ONS). This statistic is likely to over-estimate the amount of free time available to younger UK adolescents under the age of 16, still in compulsory education, for whom much of this time will not be discretionary but will be dictated by family and others (Larson and Verma, 1999).

However, there are also hints that there may be differences between UK adolescents and those elsewhere. It has been suggested that, when compared with economically similar countries, young people in the UK spend more time with their friends than young people in countries such as the USA, Canada and Spain. Thus the UK ranks among the highest in the proportion of 15-year-olds spending time with friends four or more evenings per week (Margo and Dixon, 2006). That said, there has also been a reported *decline* in the amount of time spent communicating with friends and parents over the last three decades (Margo and Dixon, 2006; DCSF, 2007b), but it is hard to know whether this is not just a methodological artefact from, for example, increases in other kinds of communicating such as on mobile telephones.

Peer group research and time use research do not intersect very well in the literature. The former is more theoretically driven and more attuned to developmental considerations, but tells us very little about time trends. The latter gives us some statistics to compare, but their meaning is obfuscated. What we want to know is whether there is indeed an increase in the time spent in peer group settings, and whether this is distinctive when compared with other similar Western countries, but Feinstein's review revealed little that would help us in this respect.

Sport and active leisure

Given the emphasis in much of the literature not only on the importance of longer-term trends in physical exercise, but also of the importance of sports and other forms of 'constructive group-based activity', this is an area where understanding the time trends could potentially prove to be important. For European countries, estimates for the time spent on sport ranges widely between from 21 minutes per week in Bulgaria to 86 minutes in Norway, and that in East Asian countries less time is spent on such activities, only up to 10 or 20 minutes per day (Larson and Verma, 1999). Participation in the USA is generally higher (National Center for Educational Statistics, 2005), but rates of USA participation in overall physical activity has declined in the past 30 years for both children and adolescents (CDC, 2008). On the other hand, in Canada, involvement of adolescents in physically active leisure reportedly increased from 40 minutes a day in 1981 to 60 minutes a day in 1998 (Zuzanek and Mannell, 2003).

Scottish survey data from 2008, based on 11- to 15-year-olds in 50 secondary schools, painted a fairly positive picture. Only one fifth of children reported doing no sports or recreational activity outside school in the previous year, and on average they stated that they spent 2.5 hours in PE (physical education) at school per week, with an additional 1 hour and 17 minutes on optional sport activities outside school (Scottish Government, 2008). However, systematic comparisons of rates for similar representative samples of children from different countries including the UK, looking at time trends, was not readily available to us from our literature search.

Information technology and electronic media

Similar to their European and North American counterparts, the use of electronic media has increased in prevalence among young people in the UK in recent years. A recent survey reported that four out of five 5- to 15-year-olds in the UK have access to a computer at home and three quarters of European children are connected to the internet, mostly at home (see, for example, Hasebrink et al, 2009). About 85 per cent of 12- to 15-year-olds owned a mobile phone in 2007, and many used it every day, mostly for text messaging (DCSF, 2007b). Recent estimates are likely to be higher.

In a cross-Europe comparative report, Hasebrink et al (2009) identified 12 different kinds of online 'opportunities' such as education, entertainment, information searching and social networking, but found little evidence allowing cross-national comparisons on take-up of the different types of use. However, Northern European countries were classified as both 'high use' in comparison with other countries, and 'high risk' in that more children had engaged in online activities that might be thought as not good for them (giving away personal information, seeing pornography).

In terms of time trends, clearly these types of activities did not even exist as possibilities 30 years ago, so there are obvious shifts, but that is not the key question. The key question is whether the types of things that are being done with new media are (a) using equal or increased amounts of time than that spent previously on the similar but old fashioned versions of media, and (b) whether the meaning and consequences of new media use are different from those of 'old' media. In relation to point (a), there is a debate about the extent to which video gaming and online activities have replaced hours previously spent viewing television, or whether they have eaten into time previously spent doing something else. For example, in the UK in the mid-1990s, young people between the ages of 12-15 averaged 2.8 hours per day viewing television (Larson and Verma, 1999); recent estimates are similar (Mayo and Nairn, 2009), suggesting that new media use may be additional.

In relation to the second point, studies reporting rates of use of electronic media often fail to take account of the sorts of issues that Eccles has raised about what the meaning of the activity is, and how it fits with what the child needs to support development of autonomy and identity (Gross, 2004). Are young people using computers to do homework, or to communicate with friends, or to communicate with strangers? Do they retreat to their own rooms and take part in solitary activities or are they taking part in meaningful social interaction? Is any of this qualitatively different from the way in which 1970s and 1980s teenagers watched a more limited range of broadcast programmes and spoke to each other on land lines? From a detailed study of adolescent internet use in the early 2000s based on a sample of 7-10th graders at California public schools and employing daily diary methods and logs of instant messages, Gross (2004) concluded that, in spite of the explosion of online communication, young people were primarily using the new tools to achieve exactly the same functions as the older ones: to engage in social interactions and to experiment with identity formation.

Family time

The balance and content of time with parents has been the focus of some attention in the literature, and most accounts report that young people are spending more time with their parents than they did in the mid-1970s (for example, 99 minutes per day in the mid-2000s compared with 25 minutes in the 1970s; DCSF, 2007b). The chapter in this volume exploring adolescent relationships with their parents reports similar data (Chapter Five).

What they are doing with this time again needs unpacking. Is this quality time or just a function of the fact that adolescents are likely to be at home more if they are not living independently? Families in the UK are reported to now eat together less often than they did 30 years ago. For example, a MORI study in the UK in 2001 found that only 15 per cent of families sampled ate together in the evening (Mayhew et al, 2005). On the other hand, the ways in which families socialise with each other may have become more fluid and less traditional but no less meaningful. This is an area of research where attention to the various subgroups is important; we might have different questions about how family time is being used for younger versus older adolescents, for example.

In this section we have briefly summarised some of the findings – and the questions they generate – concerning time trends in the structuring of school time and how this may differ in ways that matter to adolescent development, and we have provided a more cursory examination of some other areas. In the next section we draw on two of the UK's time use surveys to try to make a more direct comparison in estimates of adolescent time use across 25 years, addressing particularly the question of the balance of time between different activities.

New analyses of UK data on time trends in young people's time use from 1975-2000

Only two of the seven formal UK time use studies currently available contain information on children: the 1974/75 survey (which was originally the BBC People's Activities and Use of Time Survey), and the 2000 survey (Fisher and Gershuny, 2009). These are available for secondary analysis in the Multinational Time Use Study (MTUS) dataset (MTUS, 2009). Considerable effort at the Centre for Time Use has gone into harmonisation and synchronisation between data sets at different time points.

To make the comparisons more meaningful than many of those in the existing literature, we have chosen to focus on two main age groups. First there are those aged 11-15 years inclusive, who will be within Key Stages 3 and 4 in the UK education system, starting with the transfer to secondary school[1] and ending with the General Certificate of Secondary Education (GCSE) examination year. Our analyses here are based on 993 children in 1974/75, and 717 in 2000. Second, we then look separately at those aged 16-18, who in theory should be post-compulsory education, and eligible, through their age and the rights that come with it, to make more autonomous decisions about how to spend their time. Analyses for this group are based on 611 young people in 1974/75, and 337 in 2000. These splits make sense within the current UK context, but will not necessarily work for cross-cultural comparison.

Data were collected using time use diaries, and we have restricted analysis to typical, term-time weekdays. The samples were weighted to the general population. They were fairly small groups for the purpose of time use analyses, but we felt it was important to look at time use separately for these two age groups. Full information on how the data were collected is available on the website for the Centre for Time Use Research at the University of Oxford (www.timeuse.org/), and also in Fisher and Gershuny (2009). For more details on our analyses, contact Ann Hagell at the Nuffield Foundation.

Traditionally, time use research collapses the array of original variables into groups reflecting related activities (paid work, unpaid work, personal care etc). There is a constant tension between wanting to retain the detail of the data, and needing to group variables for summary purposes. If they are collapsed too far, the groupings become too broad to be very meaningful. On the other hand, retaining all the items separately in their original form becomes unmanageable in analyses and graphs, and in many cases patterns for individual items are not terribly revealing. For the purposes of some of the following analyses, we created eight new domains based on those used in prior time use studies, but with some adjustments for the fact that these were young people, not adults. Our domains included: sleep; domestic activities; travel; education; employment; traditional media use; structured leisure and unstructured leisure (including new media[2]). Box 4.3 shows the different kinds of activities that went under different headings. Cronbach's alphas for these domains are low (mostly 0.3s and 0.4s, with an average of 0.44 in the 1974 data, and 0.34 in the 2000 data), indicating rather heterogeneous groupings. These should not, thus, be regarded as robust subscales. In fact, although we have referred to the original variables as if they were individual items, they too are domains, in that most of them will also include a range of different individual activities.

Box 4.3: Time use activity domains
Sleep

Domestic: housework, odd jobs, childcare, meals and snacks, cooking, washing up, dress/personal care

Travel: free time travel, domestic travel, travel to/from work, walking

Education: school, classes, study, homework

Employment: paid work, paid work at home, paid work second job

Traditional media use: read books, listen to radio, listen to recorded music, read papers, magazines, watch television or video

Structured leisure: active sports, passive sports, cinema or theatre, excursions, civic activities, religious activities

Unstructured leisure: entertain friends at home, visit friends' houses, dances or parties, shopping, restaurants and pubs, other leisure, gardening, knitting, sewing, relaxing, conversations

---

Results

For the purposes of this chapter, we highlight some summary findings and interesting patterns from these two datasets. Figure 4.2 presents comparisons between the two age groups and the two time periods, using eight collapsed domains of activity.

Figure 4.2 shows that the average level of participation in different domains varied by age, and summarises the most noticeable shifts. These were the increases in sleep, travel and overall time in educational activities for both age groups over time; much smaller increases in structured leisure and travel; and decreases in domestic activities and employment for both age groups over time. We should note that the increase in education for the older age group related to an increased *proportion* of the age group who took part in education in 2000 rather

Figure 4.2: Trends in time use: comparing average time spent in different categories of time use (term-time weekday) for two age groups in 1974/75 and 2000

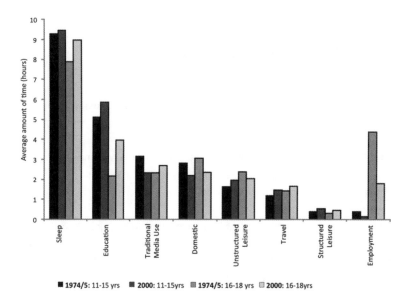

■ **1974/5:** 11-15 yrs   ■ **2000:** 11-15yrs   ▨ **1974/5:** 16-18 yrs   ▢ **2000:** 16-18yrs

Notes: Baseline numbers for 11- to 15-year-olds were: 993 in 1974/75 and 717 in 2000. Baseline numbers for 16- to 18-year-olds were: 611 in 1974/75 and 337 in 2000

than from increased time in education for those who participated, and as discussed earlier this seems a fruitful area for further investigation. A small number of younger children had paid work after school in 1974/75, and almost none did in 2000. But overall there are relatively small changes for the younger age group, and more significant ones for the older group.

Two domains show possible evidence of an age/year interaction, and these are media use and unstructured leisure. It seems likely that part of the explanation here lies with how the two age groups have accommodated different kinds of new media (remembering that this is a part of the 'unstructured leisure' coding), although we need to note that the data from the second survey are not current: there have been many developments in new media since 2000. There were few overall changes in structured leisure, which accounts for a relatively small proportion of time of UK adolescents. It would be interesting to have cross-national comparative data here too.

These results relate to a summary measure across the 24-hour period and, following Gershuny (2004), we went on to construct 'pictures' of the allocation of time use for the four samples (two different age groups, two different periods), showing the pattern of time use on an hourly basis on an average term-time day. These are shown in Figure 4.3. Looking first at the two graphs relating to the 11- to 15-year-olds (Figure 4.3A and B), the general shape of the day is fairly similar in 1974/75 and 2000. The most noticeable change relates to the virtual disappearance of the break in the middle of the day (the peak at around 12.00 in Figure 4.3B), which reflects the reduction in the school dinner hour (see, for example, Pellegrini and Blatchford, 2000, 2002; Symonds and Hagell, 2011). A second shift relates to a little more unstructured leisure in the afternoon hours than previously for this younger age group, and a little less 'media' use. Again, this probably reflects coding comparability issues, as the unstructured leisure code includes some new media use. There has been a slight diminution in paid employment. But overall the picture is one of very similar structuring of young people's lives. Before 16 years, most of secondary school time will be teacher contact hours or clear assignments, highly structured.

In the pictures for time use by 16- to 18-year-olds (Figure 4.3C and D), the time use shifts are most evident. These two graphs from 1974/75 and 2000 look quite different, driven by the reduction in the proportion at work, and the increase in the proportion in education. It is clear that these years witnessed a substantial change in the pattern, for the cohort as a whole, after the end of compulsory education at age 16, with the much discussed 'collapse of the youth labour market'. As the education chapter in this volume also makes clear (Chapter Six), three decades ago a substantial minority of young people went straight from schooling at 16 into paid employment. This is no longer the case, with comparatively small numbers of young people in paid work between 16-18 years. But the point about the time use studies in conjunction with the questions above is that they could, potentially, help us get a clearer picture of what this actually means for young people.

Paid employment is, of course, itself a highly structured activity. Young people in paid work are almost always in contact with older people and doing activities that are supervised and which forms part of work socialisation. Of course, this is not to romanticise: many young people who were in paid employment in the 1970s were likely to be in rather routine, low paid jobs. But in comparison, many of those young people in education now will be in settings where contact hours and supervision accounts for less time than it would have done during the

Figure 4.3: Proportions of adolescents engaged in different activities throughout the average term-time weekday, for 11- to 15-year-olds and 16- to 18-year-olds in 1974 and in 2000

A: Timing for children 11-15, 1974/75, Mon-Fri, term-time (*n*=993)

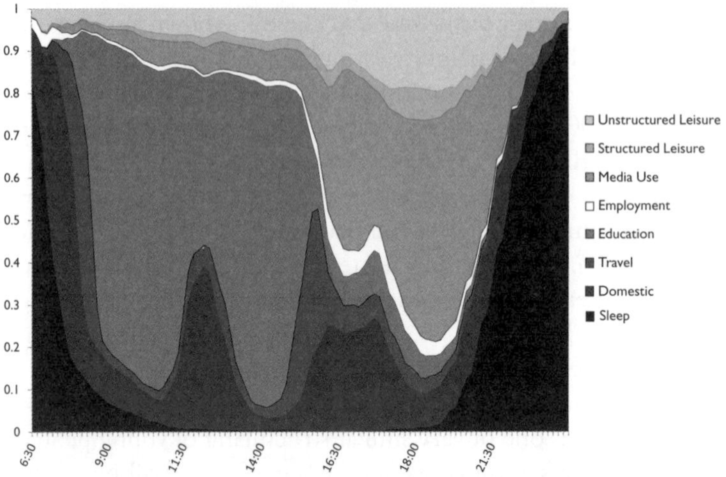

B: Timing for children 11-15, 2000, Mon-Fri, term-time (*n*=717)

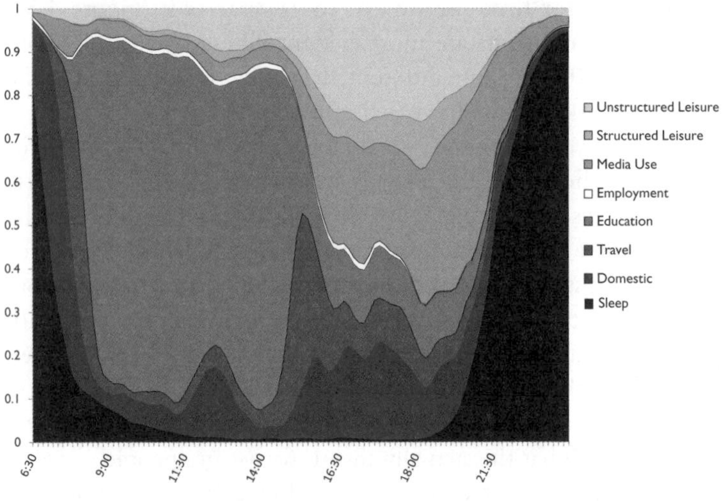

GCSE years up to age 16. There is also now a tail of education that takes place in the early evening.

The visual representation focuses us on the importance of what is happening to the group of young people who might previously have gone to work. For some this may represent enhanced opportunities, but for others it may not. It entirely depends on what they are doing in that educational setting, and how well it is suited to their needs. However, the analysis above suggests that this is indeed a fruitful area

C: Timing for children 16-18, 1974/75, Mon-Fri, term-time (*n*=611)

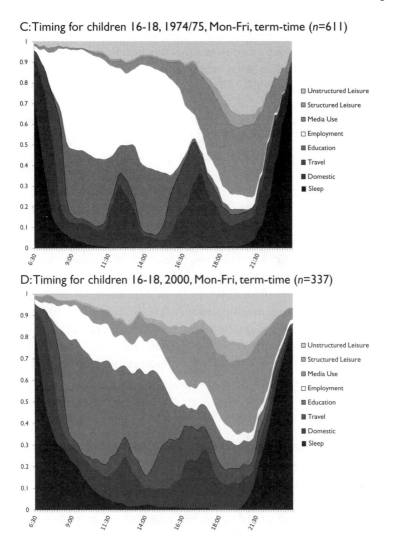

D: Timing for children 16-18, 2000, Mon-Fri, term-time (*n*=337)

for research, as we seek to establish *which* groups of young people have structured days – and how structured these are – and which have less structured ones. Understanding these patterns for different groups of young people seems an important priority.

Of course this final figure (Figure 4.3D, age 16–18 in 2000) offers a pictorial representation of the elongation of adolescence, much discussed in the adolescence literature. The pattern of life from the earlier teens has been extended much further into the upper teens than it was 25 years previously. Of course, the general results only present a gross measure of population shift, rather than anything very revealing about the lives of individuals. They undoubtedly mask variation between groups, and may obscure some trends that go in one direction for some groups, and in another for others, thus cancelling each other out, and some areas where this type of work would be useful has been suggested above. This is where time use analysis needs to focus more attention.

For example, we took a look at how the time use patterns varied by income group (lowest 25 per cent, middle 50 per cent and top 25 per cent), looking just at the 16-18 age group where the most changes had been witnessed. It became clear that the smallest changes were in the highest income groups, where large proportions were in education at both time points. The biggest changes were in the middle income group, where the proportions in education rose the most. The rise in time spent in education fell in between these two, showing a moderate but potentially meaningful shift that might in some cases reflect a loss of job opportunities for young people, and the decline of the apprentice system, rather than a positive desire to be in education. Interestingly the higher income group in 2000 was spending twice as much time in paid work as the other groups, two hours a day on average. This may suggest that those with higher socioeconomic status are more likely to obtain the few part-time employment opportunities on offer in the shrinking youth labour market.

Conclusion

We began by asking what we already know about (a) why time use is important and (b) whether it has changed. A number of different veins of research seemed to have posed relevant questions, in particular the work on out-of-school activities and on finding a good match between young people's developmental needs and engagement in appropriate social structures, including those that provide opportunities for socialisation and constructive achievement. The Feinstein research team particularly stressed the importance of the person–environment fit for successful youth development, and their review of the existing research suggested that there was some evidence that engaging in supervised and structured constructive activities was associated with lower levels of both internalising (for example, depression) and externalising problems (for example, delinquency). It is not, of course, clear that this is entirely a causal relationship (as some of it may be to do with selection issues) and very little of the research directly looked at mental health symptoms of the kind that were described in Chapter Two. In addition, much less attention had been paid to non-discretionary use of time, which for this age group is often set within social institutions such as schools. And although there were some emerging attempts to look at time use in the round – the patterning of the whole day not just a few discretionary hours – research here was less extensive.

Against this background, good trend data on time use by UK adolescents seemed to be missing, and so in the second half of this chapter we looked at some preliminary analyses that begin the process of addressing this gap. One of the main findings was the way in which the lives of 16- to 18-year-olds in 2000 had become more like those of their younger peers with respect at least to the social and structural constraints on how they used their time. The proportions of this age group who were in education rather than employment (unlike their peers 25 years earlier) were clear from the graphs. There were shifts too in other aspects of the day, such as leisure and use of media, but in part they seem likely to be driven by these bigger social changes to do with the demands placed by the big institutional structures of society.

The broad pattern is, of course, familiar from other research (see, for example, Bynner et al, 2002). What is different about these analyses is the focus on time use. This raises questions about the importance of looking at the education and employment trends as they relate to (a) what is going on in those settings and how that might have changed, and (b) what the knock-on implications are for the rest of the day. We talk about social *categories* that describe how young people spend their time (in education, in work) but have little sense of how the way that education or employment may be structured – in terms of 'contact hours', 'adult supervision', 'constructive structure' and so on – and these will have changed dramatically for some groups of young people.

For example, those in the 16-18 age groups who are on traditional A-level courses in schools will experience school as having a considerable amount of structured time, and where it is unstructured ('study time'), their goals will be clear and there will be an emphasis on ways that their use of it can be monitored in the long term (exam results). But for young people, those in sixth form colleges or in further education doing different kinds of qualifications, the educational settings may be rather less structured, with fewer contact hours each day, and far fewer each week. This means that young people on those pathways may in fact be more reliant on autonomous self-direction than their counterparts doing A-levels, and they are certainly more so than they would have been in the traditional workplace in which young people had their first jobs 35 or so years ago.

The important thing is that these patterns may have social and emotional consequences, as well as different educational outcomes. This should all be a legitimate part of how we think about time use for these age groups. As we have seen, there is a growing literature on the importance of the components of out-of-school activities for young people's positive development, including discussion concerning the implications of very structured versus unstructured activities, the role of adult leaders and mentors and the type of skills being shared and learned in these settings. This is very important but there is much less on the settings of school and education for the older age group, especially if we want to know about these in comparison to other settings.

For example, one implication of the time shifts we noted might be an increased element of age segregation for this post-compulsory school age group. In a work place, a teenager is likely to be in the minority among adults of a fairly wide age range. In a life dominated by college, there may be fewer adults, presenting a restricted range of occupational roles, that is, teaching, to model from. We do not know whether this is so, much less whether it has consequences. But it may prove to be a fruitful way to structure comparisons of young people on different educational tracks, either in the UK or in comparison with other countries.

One issue that has been relatively neglected in the time use research and in this chapter is the issue of heterogeneity. We have taken only a brief look at how things might have changed differently for young people in different socioeconomic groupings, and this undoubtedly deserves more attention. In addition, time use data have a number of important limitations, and as with most population-based data sources, they are best thought of as measures that benefit from validation and triangulation from other sources. It is critical to emphasise again that all these data are self-reported, and there is no observational information. We have bolstered some of the evidence from empirical time use studies with information about the typical structure of schooling and how this varies. But we have been able to do so only in the most cursory way; this is an area that would benefit from more analysis.

There are, of course, many areas of everyday life and time use that we have not been able to cover. We have not studied the interaction of income and spending money with these trends, and, given the fall in working, the rise in educational involvement and the reduction of state benefits for the 16-18 age group across this period, it seems likely that disposable income patterns have changed and that they might play an important part in how people use their time. We have not looked at how the introduction of new media has changed the way people organise their time; one of the biggest differences in daily living for teenagers between 1974/75 and 2000 must be the assumption of being constantly accessible to friends and relatives, being contactable by telephone at all times of the day and night and by being online in various forms of internet communication. But this is a topic for a rather different type of research.

What this chapter does do is raise interesting questions that encourage us to go below the surface of the patterns of participation in broad categories of activity. Time use data can be seen as an indicator of how social institutions and interaction 'work' in different countries, over time and for different groups, given that socialisation, task-based achievement and the development of competencies and skills are all acquired from interactions with social structures such as school, families and peer groups. This could open up a seam of richer and more detailed inquiry about how this matters and what it matters for. These issues give some sense of the complexity involved in interpreting findings from what, at face value, can seem very straightforward data about time use and its association with mental health.

Notes

[1] It is possible that some of the sample was in a middle school system, but they would be in a minority.

[2] The MTUS coding scheme designates using computers in leisure time (for gaming and for electronic communication) as 'other leisure'. This variable is included in the 'Unstructured leisure' domain as it also incorporates leisure activities such as artistic pursuits and is therefore not strictly able to be categorised as 'media'.

Acknowledgements

This document presents results drawn from the MTUS, but the interpretation of these data and other views expressed in this text are those of the authors. This text does not necessarily represent the views of the MTUS team or any agency which has contributed data to the MTUS archive. The authors bear full responsibility for all errors and omissions in the interpretation of the MTUS data. We are very grateful to two referees who provided helpful comments on an earlier version, and to Dr Kimberly Fisher for advice on using the MTUS data.

FIVE

Trends in parenting: can they help explain time trends in problem behaviour?[1]

Frances Gardner, Stephan Collishaw, Barbara Maughan,
Jacqueline Scott, Karen Schepman and Ann Hagell

Introduction

Has parenting changed over recent decades? Do parents supervise and control their offspring more or less closely than they used to? Do they show more or less parental involvement? Spend more or less time in caring for young people, in conversation and joint activities? The period from 1970 to the end of the 1990s saw a rise in behaviour problems by young people. Over the same period there were dramatic changes in family size and structure, and in the working lives of parents. Understandably, people have questioned whether there is a link between these trends. Debates have raged over a possible decline in family values and structures, the implications of working parents, the role of fathers, or the length of time children spend in daycare. But are these concerns well-founded? What evidence do we have for thinking that parenting is changing? And what do any changes actually mean for young people, especially those aged between 10 and 20 years old?

As part of the Nuffield Foundation's Changing Adolescence Programme, Professor Frances Gardner, Dr Stephan Collishaw, Professor Barbara Maughan and Professor Jacqueline Scott, from the Universities of Oxford, Cardiff, King's College London and Cambridge respectively, undertook a study of time trends in parenting. The project focused particularly on the relationship between parenting and behaviour problems in teenagers. As Stephan Collishaw demonstrated in Chapter Two, UK adolescents' 'externalising' behaviours such as lying, stealing or disobedience, as rated by parents when their children were aged 15/16 years, rose through the 1970s, 1980s and 1990s, levelling out and falling slightly in the 2000s. We know that parenting styles influence the development of youth anti-social behaviour at an individual level (see, for example, Loeber, 1990). However this study by the Gardner team for the Nuffield Foundation is the first study to examine whether there is evidence for change over time in parenting practices and relationships, and to explore whether these might explain generational changes in rates of adolescent problem behaviour.

The questions were addressed by the research team through a review of published evidence, and analyses of two sets of UK nationally representative data. The first of these data sets was the British Household Panel Survey (BHPS) with annual data on parenting reported by teenagers and their parents from 1994 onwards. The second data source came from a related Nuffield Foundation-funded project – Youth Trends – a study specifically designed to explore causes of trends in youth mental health. Youth Trends compared a large representative sample of 16-year-olds (members of the 1970 British Birth Cohort Study, BCS70) studied in 1986 with a new representative sample of 700+ 16-year-olds studied 20 years later, in 2006. Identical questions were used to assess parent-rated behaviour problems and youth ratings of parenting behaviours in both studies (see Collishaw et al, 2011). In this chapter, the main results of the review and new analyses are summarised, and selected findings are highlighted. A fuller account can be found in various publications from the Gardner team (Collishaw et al, 2007, 2011; Schepman et al, 2011).

What do we mean by 'parenting of adolescents'?

When we think of parenting, we often think of small children. But families are still a very important part of the lives of teenagers and young people. From the point when children can walk down a street on their own, catch a bus and find their own way home, there is a change in the skills required from parents (Steinberg and Silk, 2002). Parenting moves to being about aiding independence and helping young people to exercise that independence sensibly. Parents need to balance their children's needs for autonomy with a need to provide structure, protection and boundaries.

Teenagers can, and should, escape from the family home; they spend much of their time elsewhere, and they are open to peer group and community influences in a way their younger siblings are not. They are active agents and their perspectives and choices play an important part in what happens. Parenting adolescents is often seen as particularly challenging, with the new demands of puberty, peer influence and risky behaviour (Smetana et al, 2006). In some ways today's adolescents are introduced to elements of growing up at an earlier age than previous generations; in other ways, the period of semi-dependence on their own families lasts for longer than it has done at times in the past (Mortimer and Larson, 2002b; Furstenberg Jr et al, 2005; Coleman, 2011). With extended transitions from childhood to adulthood, one implication for parenting might be that the supervisory and supportive elements continue for longer into the late teens and early 20s.

Gardner et al's review for the Foundation focused particularly on two aspects of parenting that have been shown to be related to behaviour outcomes for children. These are measures related to parental involvement and warmth, including parental interest, time spent in joint activities, meals and quality time, and measures related to parental control, including monitoring, supervision, expectations, discipline and conflict. Research evidence from both longitudinal studies and from randomised intervention studies have indicated a causal role for these factors in the start and continuation of behaviour problems (see, for example, Loeber and Stouthamer-Loeber, 1986; Baumrind, 1991; Gardner et al, 2006). Although parenting is not the whole picture by any means, some researchers have estimated that it may account for around 30 per cent of the variance in behavioural outcomes for young people (Patterson, 2002).

In this chapter we look at how parenting has changed, both in terms of the shifts in family formation and structure, and the time trends in supervising, monitoring, parental involvement and responsiveness. We then look at the question of whether the trends could be related to trends in adolescent problem behaviour.

How has parenting changed?

Shifts in family formation and structure

There is no doubt that there have been dramatic changes in family size and structures, and in the working lives of parents (Scott et al, 2004). Detailed accounts are given in reports from the BCS (see, for example, Ferri et al, 2003) and in official statistics from the Office for National Statistics (ONS). Box 5.1 presents a brief outline of some of the main changes that have been seen in the circumstances of families over recent decades.

Box 5.1: Key changes in families in the UK, 1970s-2000s

- *Family formation: later and smaller.* There has been an overall trend to later childbearing, and to smaller families, with 84 births per 1,000 women aged 15-44 in 1971, decreasing to 56 by 2003. As a result, families have become smaller.

- *Family type: less marriage, more variation.* More parents cohabit, and fewer marry. The number of marriages dropped from 480,000 in 1972 to 266,000 by 2009, while divorce rose by about a third over the period to 167,000 in 2003, falling back to 114,000 by 2009. The average age at first marriage increased from early 20s to 31 for men and 30 for women in 2007. Over the same period, cohabitation for women tripled to around a third of 18- to 49-year-olds. Although very few births happened outside marriage in the 1960s, by 2008 45 per cent of children were born to unmarried parents, mostly to cohabiting couples.

- *Family restructuring: a more common experience.* The number of children under 16 experiencing divorce had risen to just over a fifth of all children by the early 2000s, although it had peaked in the mid-1990s. Children increasingly experience a variety of different family structures, including step-parents and siblings, and lone parents. The proportion of children living in lone-parent families tripled between 1972 and 2006, to 25 per cent.

- *Maternal employment: increasing.* Many more mothers now return to work outside the home early in their child's life. In 2009, over 80 per cent of mothers of children aged 11 or over were working at least part time, a slightly higher rate than that for women with no dependent children.

- *Family economic circumstances: more inequality?* Rates of child poverty rose markedly between the mid-1970s and the late 1990s, and then started to fall through the early 2000s until 2004-05. However, the pattern is less clear after this point and recent estimates suggest that the trend might be levelling out. Household income inequality grew in the 1980s and stabilised in the late 1990s, although again the direction of more recent trends is unclear.

Sources: Statistics collated from the ONS (www.ons.gov.uk), UK National Statistics Publication Hub (www.statistics.gov.uk), Brewer et al (2011), Cabinet Office (2008); and a summary of ONS historical data (www.2as1.net/marriage_ research_3.html)

So there is indeed evidence for longer-term dramatic changes in the ways in which families are organised, relating in particular to the size of families, the extent of family breakdown and reconstitution, and in the proportion of women working. A key question is what impact, if any, these changes have had on parenting and young people.

Time trends in supervising and monitoring

For all the debate and discussion, there is a surprising lack of robust data on trends in parenting behaviour, particularly for adolescents. Gardner's review team explored the published data but found that there were *no* studies across time based in the UK and dedicated to answering these questions. We looked at this issue in Chapter Four where the whole issue of what we know about how different groups of adolescents spend their time, and how it may have changed, was considered. But looking particularly at parenting, the review team found that there was information that could be drawn on from some rather varied sources to begin to piece together a story, or at least the outlines of one. Published research indicates that parents today exert more control than in the past, restricting the range of out-of-home activities that children are able to engage in. There has, for example, been a decline in unsupervised walking to school (Hillman, 2006; Sonkin et al, 2006), and in the proportions of children allowed to play locally without an adult present (Gill, 2007; Gleave, 2008). But this information relates to younger children.

With older children we refer more to monitoring and supervision – do parents know where their teenagers are, what they are doing and with whom? Can they stop them or influence them if they want to? More recently the notion of monitoring has been challenged – Swedish researchers have suggested that it may not be so much an index of how active parents are in supervising their children, but may reflect instead the quality of their relationship with their child – does the child feel confident and close enough to tell them what they are up to (Stattin and Kerr, 2000)? The fact is, however, that Gardner et al were unable to find any published evidence on how or why parents' monitoring had changed over time.

What the research team did do was to present new data from Collishaw's Youth Trends survey, looking at adolescent and parent reports of monitoring and supervision (of 16-year-olds) in 1986 and 2006 (Collishaw et al, 2011). A selection of the findings from this exercise are presented in Table 5.1, which presents the adolescent reports of parents' monitoring and expectations.

These data showed that young people in 2006 reported that their parents more closely monitored their out-of-home activities than youth in 1986. The proportion of parents who routinely asked their teenagers who they were with increased, for example, from 67 to 77 per cent over this time; and the proportion of youth who said they actually told their parents who they were with also increased from 78

Table 5.1: Youth reports of parental monitoring and expectations, 1986 and 2006 (%)

	1986 (%)	2006 (%)
Parent asks young person who with	67.0	78.0***
Parent asks young person where going	78.2	87.1***
Parent asks what young person will do	47.4	65.7***
Parents expect me to ...		
Go to school	93.1	96.9*
Do homework	89.8	94.9**
Help in the house	94.8	95.6
Be polite to them	74.9	86.3***
Tell them time coming home	82.7	88.2**
Tell them where going	85.6	93.2***
Tell them who with	74.3	88.2***
Tell them if in trouble	88.1	97.5***

Notes: *$p<0.05$; **$p<0.01$; ***$p<0.001$.
Based on sample $n=4,524$ in 1986 and $n=716$ in 2006.
Source: Data selected from Collishaw et al (2011)

to 86 per cent. Parents' expectations of good behaviour also appeared to have risen over this period. For example, between 1986 and 2006, the proportion of young people reporting that their parents expected them to do their homework increased from 90 to 95 per cent, and that their parents expected them to be polite from 75 to 87 per cent. In total, on seven out of eight measures of parental expectations, significant increases were seen. An important question is whether these changes have occurred for different subgroups of young people – boys and girls, poorer and better-off families. Girls reported greater parental monitoring and parental expectations than boys in both surveys, but increases over time were observed for both genders. Interestingly, single parents and poorer parents showed the greatest increases in parental monitoring between 1986 and 2006.

Looking at a different aspect of control and supervision, Youth Trends also showed that the proportion of young people being told off by parents was higher in 2006 than 1986, and that young people with problem behaviour in 2006 were subject to greater control than children with the same levels of problems in 1986. An important issue is whether changes in parental control are a reflection of changes in youth behaviour. For example, increased youth anti-social behaviour may prompt increased parental vigilance and behavioural control. However, additional analyses suggest that this is unlikely to be the whole story. For example, when looking at a different aspect of parental control –

'child being told off when they did something wrong' – young people in 2006 were subject to greater control even when compared with children with the same levels of problem behaviour in 1986.

Figure 5.1 shows how parental monitoring varied by social disadvantage and by cohort, but interestingly, also shows that differences by family type and income reduced over time. Social disadvantage was strongly related to parental monitoring in 1986, but not in 2006. Importantly too, technological change (mobile phones, for example) has increased the resources available for monitoring and the focus has changed, to include what young people are doing online as well as out of the house.

Figure 5.1. Mean parental monitoring score by social disadvantage and cohort (Youth Trends, 16-17 year olds).

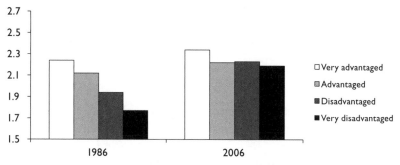

Note: Composite score made up of three youth-rated parent monitoring questions in Youth Trends.

Source: Nuffield Foundation (2009b)

An important feature of the review was the ability to replicate key findings in an independent set of nationally representative data (BHPS). A strikingly similar pattern was shown in more detail throughout the 1990s, from the BHPS data, as illustrated in Figure 5.2. These suggest that there were fewer young people out late without parents knowing where they were by 2005, and there has been greater convergence between social groups in parental monitoring in more recent years.

In summary, while we do now know much about why monitoring has grown, it is striking that the different sources suggest that it has, and that is has grown most in the more disadvantaged families. We will return to the issue of links with adolescent problem behaviour, but it seems clear that parental control has not declined as many have suggested and thus cannot provide an answer. Instead, the increased levels of parental

Figure 5.2: Youth out later than 9pm without parents knowing where: associations with lone-parent status and poverty (BHPS, 14- to 15-year-olds)

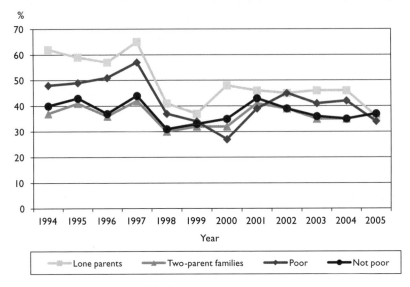

Source: Nuffield Foundation (2009b)

control may be a response to changes in youth behaviour and may even have mitigated against even greater increases in problems.

Time trends in parental involvement and responsiveness

Gardner et al's literature review concluded that there were no existing studies of time trends in parental responsiveness, warmth or perceived support towards adolescents. Without direct measurement of the key constructs, this is a very difficult topic to investigate. However, two indirect measures of parental involvement that have been the subject of considerable public debate are those of the amount of parents' time spent with children, and the frequency of shared family meals. In both cases they offer opportunities for fostering family cohesion and better quality parent–child relationships.

Studies based on UK nationally representative time use surveys have found steady increases in parents' time spent caring for children (as a main activity), from about 20 minutes per day in the 1960s to about 70 minutes in the 1990s (Gauthier et al, 2004; Sullivan, 2010). This is echoed in a number of studies from many other countries. In contrast, the literature review identified some tentative evidence of an overall decline in family meals since 1970s (see, for example, Cheng et al, 2007). New analyses of family meals from Youth Trends and the

BHPS concur, also showing evidence of a decline in the proportion of teenagers reporting eating a family meal with their parents more than once a week, from 83 per cent in 1986 to 72 per cent in 2006. Interestingly, again, there were only small differences in the frequency of family meals in different income/socioeconomic groupings, and in different family types.

A crucial point is that time use diaries and data on family meals reveal little about the quality of parent–child interactions, or about young people's perceptions of levels of parental support. The Youth Trends study enabled the team to also examine changes in youth-perceived parental responsiveness.

Young people's ratings of how much parental interest they received was very similar in 1986 and 2006 – in both cohorts a majority of the adolescents (66 and 67 per cent) felt that their parents wanted to hear their ideas. Their own reports of the amount of 'quality time' spent with their parents, that is, free time that they opted to spend together, increased between 1986 and 2000 ('most days' increasing from 23 to 30 per cent for mothers, and from 10 to 13 per cent for fathers). As we found in the chapter on time use (Chapter Four), a missing bit of the puzzle is how much young people's time (and variably for the younger adolescents and older ones) is actually spent in parents' company, or in other adult company, and the extent to which this has changed.

Taken together, these data are suggestive that there has been no major detrimental change in parental involvement and responsiveness. However, in the absence of high-quality comparable cross-time data on parental warmth and family cohesion, they should perhaps be viewed as preliminary.

Could the results be due to methodological artefact? Playing devil's advocate, we can expect that people will question results such as those relating to monitoring and parental expectations, and suggest that young people are more sensitised to their rights and so thus report more surveillance. Perhaps young people notice their parents parenting more now than they did previously, because of the increased media attention to it. However, there are two reasons why we think these artefacts cannot explain the findings from these Nuffield-funded studies. The first is that in many cases the sources of the information are both the young people *and* their parents. In addition, virtually all of the trends were going in the same direction, even if measurement was very different. These facts increase our confidence that the results reported here reflect real phenomena, although that is not to deny that more research is needed to replicate and extend the findings.

Could trends in family structure account for trends in adolescent problem behaviour?

The Gardner review reported on well-known trends for shifts in family structure over the time period, and the implications of this has been extensively discussed elsewhere in the literature. In order to look more closely at the implications of the shifts, Stephan Collishaw and his colleagues undertook a series of additional analyses directly asking whether the historical trends between family structure and adolescent conduct and emotional problems were connected (Collishaw et al, 2004, 2007, 2010). Using data from repeat national cohorts, these analyses demonstrated that increase over time in conduct and emotional problems remained significant when statistically controlling for change in family composition. While changes in family structure accounted for some of the observable change in time trends in adolescent well-being, on the other hand, they were only a small part of the explanation. We return to this issue in more detail later.

This is consistent with results from a number of large-scale longitudinal studies generally that also support the conclusion that family structure on its own does not explain children's outcomes; it is what divorce and breakdown mean to the family atmosphere and family relations that matters (see, for example, Amato, 1993; Simons et al, 1994). In addition, there are issues of 'selection', in that families with pre-existing problems will be more likely to separate, and so may have higher rates of risk factors that predict to child outcomes that are nothing to do with the fact of separation itself. In fact, Collishaw et al showed youth behaviour problems rose within each of the different family types, not just in divorced families (Collishaw et al, 2007), as demonstrated in Figure 5.3.

However, understanding the relevance of the trends in family structure remains somewhat incomplete. Although there were increases over time in conduct and emotional problems among all family types, the rates among adolescents in non-intact families were expected to be higher than in intact families (as found in other studies). Thus, despite an equivalent increase in adolescent conduct problems for intact families, the prevalence of non-intact families has increased dramatically, potentially increasing the absolute number of children with the kinds of behaviour problems that can arise from family conflict. It is possible this has had subtle effects on the cohort as a whole.

One way of thinking about this leads us to think about dynamic causes, but this is not well captured by repeated surveys. If, for instance, young people in lone-parent families or stepfamilies are more likely to

Figure 5.3: Parent-rated behaviour problems (% high scores) by family type and cohort: evidence from three UK cohorts

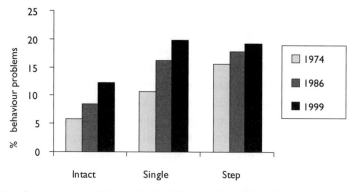

Note: Baseline sample 1974 n=10,343; 1986 n=7,234; 1999 n=860.

Source: Collishaw et al (2007)

act out in various ways, this could set 'norms' for young people in other families: both in terms of what is seen as 'normal' and in the sense that it may create youth peer groups where acting a certain way is seen as more desirable by young people themselves. When this is measured again at the next survey, it may appear that young people in all family types are showing increased conduct or emotional problems. But if the driver is partly the norms set by young people in non-intact families, a common-sense view might be that family change has been a cause of this trend. However commonsensical this may seem, the data we have are not well designed to understand that kind of dynamic causation. We simply do not know if the fact that trends for young people in all family types are a result of changes driven partly by family composition or other non-familial social change. This is an issue we return to in the Conclusion.

However, in order to look a little more at the contribution of shifts in family structure, and to begin to estimate what the size of the effect might be, Collishaw and colleagues undertook some 'counterfactual' analyses specifically for this chapter. For these analyses, the question was 'How much lower would the population rate of conduct and emotional problems be if there had been no change in family composition in the years from 1986 to 2006?' By using problem rates within each family type in the earliest study, and modelling what problem rates would look like by 2006 if the composition of family types had not changed, Collishaw demonstrated that approximately 15 to 30 per cent of the actual observed change in emotional and behaviour problems could be estimated to be attributable to the change in family structure; approximately 70 to 80 per cent could not. These findings confirm those of others that changes in family composition are likely to be part of a complex web, working with other social factors in leading to youth outcomes (West and Sweeting, 2003; Eckersley, 2007; Collishaw et al, 2010, Sweeting et al, 2010; Schepman et al, 2011). For instance, they may interact with factors such as the rises in substance misuse noted in other chapters, or have greater or lesser effects depending on whether intermediate pathways hold.

Aside from these rather complex changes arising from changes in family structure, however, the evidence from the other trends suggested that, rather than an overall decline in parenting, there were encouraging signs of improvements in, for example, monitoring and supervision, and quality time spent together for this older age group. The only variable that showed the opposite tendency was family mealtimes. On balance, it thus seems unlikely that the time trends in rates of youth problem behaviour described at the outset could be accounted for primarily by a decline in the general *quality* of parenting. At a time of heightened anxiety over parenting, this is heartening.

That said, the Gardner et al review did draw attention to some interesting results that linked parents' own mental health to that of their teenagers. As Figure 5.4 demonstrates, secondary data analysis showed that there has been a general increase over the past 20 years in self-reported distress among parents (the Malaise Inventory in Youth Trends and the General Health Questionnaire, GHQ, in BHPS), and these increases in distress have affected single parents and parents on low incomes to a greater extent than they have other families (see Figure 5.4).

This is a crucial finding, and one that requires more thought. Is parenting becoming more stressful, particularly for socially disadvantaged families? Parent emotional problems are critical for understanding links between social context, parenting and children's outcomes. Parents may be finding the task more difficult, both because of the demands on parents of social change and elongated adolescence, but also because of rising levels of youth problem behaviour generally. Social disadvantage may, itself, cause more distress now than it has done at different periods in the past (perhaps because there is less absolute disadvantage?), and this might have an impact on parenting practices. As a result, some parents seem to be showing more distress, and this may be negatively affecting some young people. Parent depression is perhaps the best established risk factor for development of emotional problems in offspring, and so increases in parent depression would be expected to lead to increased problems in offspring over time. This is one avenue of further research currently being addressed by the research team. Further analyses of the Youth Trends data by Karen Schepman and colleagues (2011) have already demonstrated both cross-sectional and prospective correlations between maternal emotional problems and adolescent mental health symptoms.

Figure 5.4: Mean parental Malaise Inventory score by degree of social disadvantage and cohort (Youth Trends, 16- to 17-year-olds)

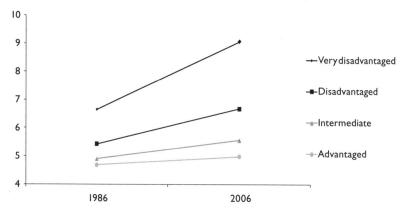

Source: Nuffield Foundation (2009b)

Implications of trends in parenting

The first point that needs facing head on is the paradox that, according to the measures that were available in the Nuffield-funded analyses, *average* ratings of 'good' parenting appear to have improved over a period when average youth problem behaviour has worsened. What does this mean?

The most important thing to stress is that it does *not* mean that parenting does not matter. Decades of longitudinal research have shown us that, at the individual level, parenting is one of the most important predictors of children's outcomes. In the Youth Trends study undertaken by Collishaw there was a strong correlation at the individual level between a family's parenting and their child's behaviour problems in both cohorts (1986 and 2006). We are making an important distinction here between the relationship between parents and their own child versus correlations at the level of the whole cohorts of young people aged 16 at different points in time. If we look at the population level, improvements in parenting do not seem to have been accompanied by improvements in the overall levels of behaviour problems – except perhaps until recently. But investing in parenting interventions remains a very effective way of improving outcomes for individual children (Gardner et al, 2006; Piquero et al, 2008). Another way of looking at this is that if, on average, parenting improvements had *not* taken place, the average outcomes for young people might indeed have been worse.

An analogy might help explain the difference between predicting cohort differences, and predicting individual outcomes. The one that we have used in other contexts is that of height. The best predictor of a child's height is his or her parents' height. About 80 per cent of the variations in the population in height are due to genetic influences. However, in the first half of the 20th century, the height of the whole population of children rose by around 12cm over a period of just a few decades (Rutter et al, 1998). This was obviously not driven by genetics; it related primarily to improvements in nutrition. So at the individual level genetics was the best predictor of individual height (Joe still grew to look like his parents), but at the population level the most powerful cause operating on height during that period was what children were eating (Joe's whole class was taller than their parents' classes had been at their age because of better diets).

So while parenting is very important at the individual level, something else seems to be operating on youth behaviour at the cohort level. Some changes in family structure may have increased the challenges for some parents, and there was evidence to suggest that a small proportion of the overall increase in conduct disorder may have been attributable to changes to family structures; there may also be a dynamic element to this that is in fact not well captured by our evidence and the analyses we can carry out. However, trends in parenting behaviour had, if anything, improved overall, and so deteriorating standards of parenting seem unlikely to be the explanation for the cohort's increases in behaviour problems over and above the rather modest effects due to family breakdown or shifts in family form. One could argue that improved parenting could well have been a *response* both to a world that is perceived as presenting more challenges and dangers to young people, and to a cohort of teenagers, some of whom were proving to be more difficult to manage at times. Indeed, the team's analyses of the Youth Trends data suggested that trends in problem behaviour would likely have been more marked had there not been the improvement in parenting observed in that study.

Various other possibilities could be hypothesised, and indeed much of this volume tries to consider them in turn. Parenting may have been improving but perhaps this was in the context of other influences that might have made this period more challenging, such as the collapse of the youth labour market. One challenge this presented may have been the loss of adult structured activities and opportunities to learn and achieve that work brought to many young people who did not stay on in school. We also examine changes in the neighbourhood and peer groups in other chapter in this volume (Chapter Eight). Yet overall, the main findings about parenting are good news, and provide material for a more nuanced debate about how parenting has changed. They raise interesting questions that we need to answer about what *is* going on in families, and about how we need to provide positive and constructive support for parents who may have an increased need for it during changing times. We begin here to identify some discussion points for further debate, and potentially, further research:

- *The importance of different contexts for parenting* One of the first discussion points to arise from this study concerned the possible role of the local neighbourhood in setting a context for parenting parenting (see, for example, Kotchick and Forehand, 2002). If you are living in a safe, wealthy area, with low crime rates and strict schools, your parenting may take a different form compared to someone living in an under-resourced area with high crime rates, where you are concerned for the safety of your children. In the latter case you might try to be stricter and more controlling, to compensate; the meaning of your monitoring and supervising behaviours, for example, might be different in different situations.

- *The role of social norms and expectations* One issue that our data do not make it easy to consider is the importance of the reinforcing effects when parenting norms are shared and applied consistently not just by parents but also by neighbours, schools, other adults and employers. There is indeed some evidence that being a good parent of an adolescent is more effective if it fits in with the general neighbourhood ethos, where everyone locally shares some values and styles (Smith, 2004). This may be related to some of the questions we pose elsewhere about the implications of extended periods of adolescence for the sort of informal socialisation that perhaps used to come more from being part of the world of work. It could be hypothesised that this is a particularly adolescent issue, as adolescents are 'out there' in the local neighbourhood or outside the home in a much more active way than primary school age children. How can we learn more about the role that the context for parenting plays in the story?

- *The strains placed on many parents by extended adolescence* We mentioned at the outset the elongation of the period of adolescence, brought about partly by the collapse of the youth labour market, leading to the increase in educational participation through the late teens, changing patterns of independent living, delays in family formation and non-linear progression away from home, back again, and then away again. While this has been considered with respect to the effects on young people, less is known about implications for parents. These are clearly financial, but also emotional, in that a young person in your house potentially requires more support, and provokes more worry, than one living several miles away. Almost a third of young men in the UK aged 20-34 still live with their parents (ONS, 2009). Is this increasingly stressful for parents? Again, this is an issue we turn to in our conclusions.

- *The paradox of improvements in parenting combined with a decline in parental mental health* In some cases parental mental health seemed to have declined over this period, despite overall improvements in aspects of parenting. Where parents had poorer mental health, this was associated with more behaviour problems in the young people. Is there a particular subgroup of parents who are more prone to stress and then are less able to help their children? Who are they, and what can be done to help? As well as extended adolescence as a source of stress, parents are suffering a 'time squeeze' – while spending more time with children, they are also spending more time working (see, for example, Craig, 2006). The cost of trying to do too much could have greater effects on the mental health of mothers in more disadvantaged families.

- *How much variation is there in parents' behaviour and adolescents' experiences?* Socioeconomic groupings seem to be less important than we might have anticipated, at least with respect to these particular variables, but this does not rule out the possibility that significant diverging pathways are being taken by families, with differing implications for their young people. There is also the evidence that parental mental health has declined more in the more disadvantaged groups. Not all families will have experienced social change in the same way, and some young people will remain very disadvantaged by changing circumstances, or even become more so. Elongated adolescence will mean very different things depending on how it is spent (at university, for example, versus unemployment). Some of these themes will be picked up in other essays in this volume, but it is crucial that further research attention is given to the range of experiences that adolescents and their families go through.

Conclusion

Descriptive data would suggest that the tasks and skills required by parents of teenagers have changed. Adolescence has elongated; children are around in the parental home for longer; and the development of new technology creates whole new monitoring challenges. Not only that, but the last three decades have witnessed some quite striking changes in family circumstances and structures.

However, parents seem to be adapting and responding. Despite public concern about declining family life, the work funded by the Nuffield Foundation has found no evidence of decline in parenting over recent decades, based on available youth and parent self-reported data. There was no evidence of parents being more selfish about their own time use, or neglecting supervision and control. The only trend in the opposite direction related to a slight decline in the frequency of family meals. In many more ways, the data suggest evidence of improvement in parenting.

Furthermore, despite widening income inequality and declining social mobility over this time period, there was no evidence that parenting quality has declined in the most disadvantaged subgroups in society. If anything, the opposite appears to be true. It seems unlikely then that change in parenting behaviour is the main explanation for trends in youth problem behaviour. This is not to say that parenting is unimportant; on the contrary, it is one of the strongest predictors, within cohorts, of youth problem behaviour. It is just that its role in causing time trends is less clear.

However, the results did highlight a potential role for parental mental health, and we have hypothesised that parenting may be becoming more stressful in some ways. We draw particular attention to the need for more discussion about the broader, social environment in which we parent. This, we suggest, would complement and extend the current focus on individual parenting classes and family support services. In addition, there have been small but non-trivial contributions to the trends in youth conduct and emotional problems arising from the changes in family structure seen over this period. More dedicated studies of time trends in parenting, and of the changing context and expectations laid on parents of adolescents, may help us to understand more.

Notes

[1] This chapter is based in part on an earlier Briefing Paper published by the Nuffield Foundation (2009b).

SIX

Educational changes and possible links with adolescent well-being: 1970s to 2000s

Ann Hagell, John Gray, Maurice Galton and Colleen McLaughlin

Introduction

Among the various things that may have changed in adolescent lives over the last 30 years are secondary school experiences. Education constitutes a vast and significant social institution with which young people are directly engaged for a great deal of time (indeed, approximately 15,000 hours; see Rutter et al, 1979). We have to start with an assumption that it matters, and if so, that *changes* in educational experiences may matter for changes in social and emotional well-being.

But what do we know about whether school experiences are significant for the kinds of outcomes we are interested in? *Does* schooling matter for mental health? There are two major issues here that we could be interested in. First, there is the question about school 'in general', including the types of schools available, how children are allocated to them, the way in which the day is organised, the type of teaching, the ethos of encouragement and discipline, testing requirements, the social mix and academic streaming options. All these might have changed.

Second, there are the major indices of movement around the education system, the system of transitions and transfers, both between and within schools. By this we mean the transition into secondary school (called 'transfer' in the USA), the transition within school into, for example, the GCSE teaching years, and the transition at age 16 at the point when compulsory education ends in the UK. At this point the transition may be out of the system, or it may be into more education. Educational transitions can be regarded as 'flash points', highlighting particular issues and challenges in getting education right for all young people. Both transition into secondary school and transition at age 16 represent times when cracks in the system might be particularly obvious, and when vulnerabilities can become amplified. On the other hand, they offer opportunities and chances to change track, and they represent the closest thing we have in the UK today to formal adolescent 'rites of passage'. They may offer a prism through which to assess school effects, and they may also have impacts that are rather separate from those of other educational experiences. They offer an interesting chance to explore what has been going on in adolescent education.

We therefore begin this chapter by asking what we know already about whether school matters for adolescent mental health outcomes, including any evidence for the impact of transitions on children's adjustment. We then look for evidence on any shifts and changes that have happened in educational experiences in general, and transitions in particular, that might shed light on time trends in adolescent well-being. In answering these questions, we have drawn in part on a literature review on school experiences and adolescent mental health outcomes undertaken for the Foundation as part of the Changing Adolescence Programme by a team led by John Gray, Maurice Galton and Colleen McLaughlin at the University of Cambridge, together with Barbie Clarke and Jennifer Symonds. The full version of their review is available from the authors (see the end of the chapter for details). In this chapter, we highlight some of the main findings and supplement the review with findings and data from other sources as well, including the Foundation's review on the future of education and training for 14- to 19-year-olds in the UK (Pring et al, 2009).

The Gray et al review concluded that the literature directly addressing our specific questions about changes in the levels of well-being and mental health is not huge. There are various different research traditions that come at the problem from different angles. They often share similar targets (outcomes for children) but start with different questions (do transitions cause dips in attainment? are some schools better than others? does low achievement at school predict behaviour problems?). Some of these questions are indirectly relevant for our purposes, but others are not. In order to create some boundaries around our work in this area, we have thus excluded research on the relationship between school-based achievement and poor mental health (looking at individual results in Intelligent Quotient [IQ] and examination test results etc), where there is already a vast literature indicating a clear, inverse and bidirectional relationship (reviewed in Gustafsson et al, 2010), as this research tends to be about individual academic achievement rather than about schools as systems. However, we have included some questions about increased exam testing and mental health where there has been much less effort to interrogate the literature, and where the school system is likely to be critical to the experience. As in other reviews in this collection, we have focused on the relevance of adolescent experiences for fairly common symptoms of emotional and behavioural difficulties, such as anxiety, low mood and conduct disorder, but if there was evidence that some kinds of school structures are more likely to leave children feeling like failures, or detached from the wider social norms, or likely to truant, then we have included this too. These factors may fall short of being positively correlated with clinical syndromes like depression, but are part of our general concern about social change and adolescent well-being.

Does school matter for mental health?

There are a number of aspects of school and education that might be important for children's outcomes. For example, in a recent systematic review of empirical findings on schooling and mental health outcomes, Gustafsson et al (2010) identified the following categories of indicators worth considering:

- assessment of achievement and teaching: results, learning, assessment, achievement, teaching;
- importance of individual failure issues: truancy, drop-out, school failure;
- role of different ways of grouping students through streaming and selection processes;
- access to special education provision, and inclusive education structures;
- support for relationships: with teachers, peers, bullying, climate, connectedness;
- importance of organisational structures: leadership, management, administration, ethos;
- context of the wider educational system: rewards model, transition system, grade transition, educational reforms and directives.

We have grouped these into four broad areas – school effectiveness (including issues such as how well schools are run), school connectedness (including items relating to schools as communities), the school's role in individual psychosocial development (including issues such as bullying and exam stress), and the contribution of school transitions – and we look briefly at each in turn.

School effectiveness

The question about the role of school experiences is often seen through the lens of the school differences/school effects literature; do consistent variations in the way schools are run have differential effects on the children in their care? In 2002, Michael Rutter and Barbara Maughan provided an overview of research published on this topic since their own seminal work in the 1970s (Rutter et al, 1979). The latter had started a lively debate and stimulated a considerable amount of further research. In their reassessment of the literature, they drew the following conclusions:

• That there is now good evidence that the overall characteristics of the school environment can play a role in shaping pupil achievements. The key features of schools that seem to carry the benefits include the ways both in which they are organised and run (leadership, sensible organisation of class structure), and a clear focus on the purpose of the school to teach and support learning. These things need to be set in a calm and orderly atmosphere, which in turn will support the development of positive teacher–student relationships, and provide opportunities for student involvement at school.
• However, that does not tell us how to bring about change to schools. The authors stated that '… knowing the end result you wanted and knowing how to support schools to bring that about were two entirely different issues' (Rutter et al, 1979, p 454).
• There was some evidence that features of the classroom were as important as, and could be different from, features of the school as a whole.
• Advances in genetic research had not ruled out the importance of school differences but had alerted researchers to the importance of gene–environment interactions, partly through selection effects. Thus individual characteristics can mean that some children bring particular vulnerability or particular resilience to their experiences at school, but on the other hand, individual characteristics can also influence and shape those experiences and aspects of the school environment. This is a much more dynamic model of how nature and nurture interact and affect each other than was in vogue a few decades ago.

The school effectiveness research also suggests that different factors may be important for achievement on the one hand, and behavioural outcomes on the other (Gray, 2004), but it has been suggested that the effect sizes are larger for cognitive outcomes than for behaviour problems (Gray, 2004; Maughan, 2004). There is much less information on the relevance for emotional outcomes.

School connectedness

What emerged as a result of the school effects literature was a new interest in schools as communities that can promote well-being as well as attainment, and the research on 'school connectedness' is an example of this (Battistich et al, 1995; Whitlock, 2003; Blum and Libbey, 2004). School connectedness is the belief of individual pupils that the people who make up the school community (adults and other pupils) care about them, and the feeling that they are a valued part of the community. The Gray et al review conducted for the Foundation as part of the Changing Adolescence Programme provided a detailed account of this area of interest. The review showed that the measures for school connectedness focus on belongingness and support. The characteristics of schools that have high levels of pupil connectedness are positive classroom management, including teacher–student relationships and classrooms with a positive emotional climate (Maughan, 2004), engagement in extra-curricular activities and effective and humane discipline strategies (see, for example, McNeely et al, 2002). Altogether these tend to be referred to as 'school climate' (Whitlock, 2003, p 2), or what Gray et al call the 'supportive school' (Gray et al, 2011). School connectedness has been shown to be related to later reduced violence, less risky sexual behaviour, less drug use and less dropping out (Whitlock, 2003).

However, as, Maughan (2004) suggests, we need to move beyond thinking about effects as they impact on everyone, and consider more (given the genetic variation too) how certain subgroups or 'clusters of individuals' are differentially affected. Studies on subgroups are few and far between. Roeser et al (2000) provide one exception; they identified some 30 per cent of children who were not doing well academically and scored highly on emotional distress, and where the problems become a downward spiral in interaction with features of the school environment, in contrast to the experiences of other groups.

School's role in individual psychosocial development

The problem with most of the research on the impact of school systems on children is that while there are some measures of behaviour in some studies, there is very little on anxiety and depression. The literature on schools as part of the context for individual development gives us a little more to go on in this regard, although the focus on adolescence is less developed. In this kind of research sampling tends to start with children rather than schools, and data are collected from individual children about their school experiences. Schools are not compared – indeed, the children in the sample are likely to have gone to a wide range of different establishments – but differences in children's school experiences are measured, in relation to other outcomes. For example, larger school size has been associated with bullying (Bowes et al, 2009), and reported quality of schooling has been associated with later maths achievement (Lefebvre et al, 2008). Gustafsson et al (2010) concluded, in their review, that there was evidence that an individual child's investment in school followed by experiences of school failure can lead to depression, particularly for young women, but this does not really tell us anything about school effects. They acknowledge that the challenge is to look at relations at a higher level of aggregation, such as at the classroom and school level, in order to untangle the relationships. There is thus a sense in which the school effectiveness is 'top down', but stops a little short of looking at the interaction between the child and the classroom climate, and the individual development work is 'bottom up', but also stops short of this critical middle intersection between the child and their social environment at school.

One area where we might have thought that research on individual psychosocial development could provide a steer relates to the question concerning whether the experiences of examinations and testing are stressful, yet, as we saw in the chapter in this volume on 'stress' (Chaptyer Three), there is surprisingly little evidence on this. Key questions remain unanswered, such as whether taking a few examinations is more stressful than taking lots (or vice versa), whether it is better to have them spread throughout the school years or concentrated in a block at the end, and whether it makes a difference if the stress is induced by an experience that everyone in the class is having at the same time and regards as part of normal school life. However, there is some recent, limited work on what has been called 'school burnout', so that, for example, a recent Finnish study reported that school burnout more strongly predicted depression across time than vice versa, and that young women reported higher levels of both burnout and depression (Salmela-Aro et al, 2009). School burnout is defined as a school-related stress syndrome involving fatigue, cynicism about the purpose of education and feelings of inadequacy. However, there is an immediate problem in that this definition would seem to overlap with some of the key features of depression, so it is hard to sort out cause from effect. Interestingly, a separate study by the same team demonstrated higher levels of burnout for those on academic tracks in comparison with those on vocational tracks (Salmela-Aro et al, 2008).

So, although the work that begins with a focus on individual outcomes provides hints about aspects of schooling that might be important for social and emotional adjustment, such as bullying, quality of teaching and feelings of 'burnout', the work tends not to tell us much about schools as systems, or experiences for groups of children going through the same systems.

What do we know about the impact of school-based transitions?

As we have noted, one particular feature of secondary schools that might be relevant for mental health outcomes are the transitions they imply; into the school in the first place, within the school at different educational break-points and into post-16 (post-compulsory) education. The research questions here tend to have focused on how well the particular developmental needs of individual adolescents (such as need for structure, need for intellectual stimulation, need for adult role models) are met by the school system at the time of transfer – what Jacqueline Eccles has referred to as the 'stage–environment fit' (Eccles et al, 1993).

The *transition into secondary school* has received probably the most attention although, again, much of this work has focused either on achievement, such as scores in maths, science or grade point averages, behaviour, or on positive adaptation to school such as attitudes (see, for example, Roeser et al, 1999; Galton et al, 1999a; Tymms et al, 2008; Galton, 2009). Motivation tends to go up with transfer but then suffers a set-back as the reality of secondary school life sets in. Attitudes to school similarly show a dip.

Much less research uses the kinds of outcomes we are interested in: symptoms of anxiety and depression, for example. There is some evidence for small increases in transition-related anxiety (how worried the children are about the move), which is usually shown to rise before the transition and then comes back down quickly afterwards (Youngman, 1978; Jennings and Hargreaves, 1981; Wigfield et al, 1991; Galton et al, 1999a; Lohaus et al, 2004; Mullins and Irvin, 2005), and general anxiety has shown a similar pattern (Hirsch and Rapkin, 1987). Transition anxiety appears to be offset by parental support (Duchesne et al, 2009). Studies of depression across transition into secondary school and other transitions within school are rarer and the results can be difficult to interpret, as longitudinal studies have shown that rates of depression and social phobia normally rise in girls across adolescence (Costello et al, 2003). Increases in depression have been reported for most transition or transfer points (Rudolph et al, 2001; Little and Garber, 2004). Barber and Olsen (2004) measured symptoms of depression across a series of grade and school transitions using the Children's Depression Inventory, and reported significant increases for most shifts between grades (years), regardless of whether they also implied a shift between schools. In the West of Scotland longitudinal study, West et al (2008) followed a cohort of over 2,000 young people as they moved through and out of the educational system and, unusually, looked at the longer-term implications of what they term 'poorer school transitions', which predicted higher levels of depression at age 15 (measured using a six-item version of Kandel and Davies' depression scale; see Kandel and Davies, 1982). However, depression was not measured at transition so was not controlled for at Time 1 when looking at Time 2 outcomes. This is not to negate the finding, but it introduces the possibility that this may reflect a complicated picture of depression-prone children feeling more anxious at transfer and then subsequently having a worse time and becoming more depressed.

One interpretation of the West et al (2008) findings could thus be that a small group of children were particularly vulnerable at transition, and then remained so. This chimes with a number of studies that suggest that, while the majority of children only have transitory adjustment problems, there is a significant subgroup of young people who find it particularly difficult to adjust and may have longer-lasting problems (Evangelou et al, 2008). Estimates of the size of this group usually hover around the 10 to 12 per cent mark (Galton, 2009).

Transitions may be stressful or upsetting because of a mismatch between what the young person needs and what the school can offer. Post-transition schools are usually larger, more bureaucratic, organised around subject teaching rather than pastoral groupings, and involve more structured, academic contacts with a wide range of adults rather than supportive, personal contact. Middle schools may shed some light on this; middle schools (which are far more common in the USA than in the UK) tend to be more like primary schools, and some research suggests that the transition between the two seems less stressful for children (Lipps, 2005). However, by the nature of the system pupils then have to make another transition at age 14 into high schools, and there is some evidence that this can be problematic, so it may be that the problem is only delayed rather than solved (Benner and Graham, 2007, 2009). It is not known whether this is because of the difference between middle schools and high schools, or whether it is a cumulative effect of having to make two transitions rather than just one, although there is some limited evidence that the effect of frequent transfers on achievement may indeed be cumulative (Alspaugh, 1998; Juvonen, 2004). In addition, we have to be a little careful about generalising from USA middle school research as their middle schools do not bear a great deal of resemblance to the few remaining UK middle schools, which are smaller and tend to be organised differently. There is little published research on the latter, and over recent years most local authorities in England have dismantled any remaining three-tier systems in favour of a single transfer at age 11.

Alternatively, the issue might be something to do with peer group disruption, rather than about school organisation or relationships with adults. Trajectories of peer group affiliations within the classroom have not been subject to much attention. Or is it something to do with the changes to class sizes or models of teaching or pastoral care? Or is it part of the shift to a larger, more hierarchical, environment full of other adolescents engaged in social comparisons with each other? Are these real differences caused by the transition, or are they part of ongoing developmental changes that would have happened anyway, such as those associated with puberty? A number of questions remain unanswered. This is partly because it has not proved possible to randomly assign children to educational settings with anything approaching a true experimental design, but there is a handful of natural experiments that try to untangle some of these issues. Primarily these studies investigate developmental outcomes for two samples of same-aged adolescents who either experience a school transfer or remain in the same school. The results have tended to suggest that many of the changes in social and emotional functioning are a feature of the age group, rather than pegged to school change (see, for example, Barber and Olsen, 2004; Lipps, 2005). Where there are changes, they seem to be related to particular shifts from smaller social and teaching groups to larger classes or schools rather than any other aspects of transitions, but many of the aspects we have raised such as peer group factors have not been a particular focus of much of this work.

Another way of looking at this is to ask about international comparisons. Certainly different transition models are in place across the USA and Europe. And, as we have already noted, North America has a tri-partite middle school system virtually unknown in Europe apart from a few counties in the UK. The Information on Education Systems and Policies in Europe (EURYDICE) Unit at the National Foundation for Educational Research (NFER) collects information on European education policies and on the organisation and structure of the education systems, and in a bulletin published in 2002 they noted four main models of transition in European countries, including:

- a single compulsory education structure without transition (Czech Republic, Denmark, Finland, Norway, Sweden and some other northern European countries);
- automatic transition after completion of primary education (France, Romania, Spain, UK);
- a more flexible system where children have options to transfer into different systems (academic or general) on the basis of teacher/parent consultations and examinations (Germany, Lithuania, Luxembourg, the Netherlands);
- transitions only allowed after acquisition of a primary school certificate which then allows transfer (Belgium, Greece, Italy) (EURYDICE, 2002).

However, as far as we are aware, there are no evaluations of the success or otherwise of the different European models described by EURYDICE, nor any evidence about differential outcomes for either cognitive or social and emotional factors, but it would be useful to widen research to include these models in discussions about the role of transitions in the UK context.

We now turn briefly to evidence of the effects of the *transition out of compulsory education at age 16*. The UK is unusual in having such a low school leaving age, and we have long had many more young people leaving education at this point than, for example, the USA, where rates of high school completion diplomas (usually awarded in the year that the student turns 18) stood at 90 per cent in 2008 (Chapman et al, 2010). Although compulsory full-time education ends at age 15 or 16 in Germany, students must continue in at least part-time education for another three years (O'Donnell et al, 2010). In comparison, the most recent available statistics for the UK at the time of writing show that 72 per cent of 17-year-olds were in full-time education in 2009, falling to 46 per cent of 18-year-olds. Only 33 per cent of 16-year-olds remained in state-maintained secondary schools in this year, and only around 5 per cent were in part-time education at these ages (DfE, 2011). Table 6.1 demonstrates the range of different 'staying on' options for young people in England and Wales, and also summarises the kinds of qualifications they may be doing at these various institutions.

There is a wealth of research on this age 16 transition (into more education, training, employment or none of the above) from educational and economic perspectives (see, for example, Pring et al, 2009). There is plenty of evidence, accumulated over a number of years, that pathways are determined during this transition that will have long-term effects on various psychosocial outcomes (see, for example, Hagell and Shaw, 1996; Wright, 2005). But whether there are short-term implications for the kinds of common mental health symptoms that we have focused on seems largely unknown.

Table 6.1: Age 16 educational options in England and Wales

Locations
Maintained schools
Academies and city technology colleges
Independent schools
Sixth form colleges
General further education (including tertiary and specialist colleges)
Higher education institutions (such as universities)
Work-based learning (apprenticeships)
Courses
Level 3 (GCE/VCE A/AS levels; NVQ 3 and equivalents)
Level 2 (GCSE/Intermediate GNVQ; NVQ2 and equivalents)
Level 1 (Foundation GNVQ; NVQ 1 and equivalents)

Sources: Pring et al (2009); DfE (2011)

So overall, in response to the initial question about whether school matters for mental health, there is both observational and intervention evidence that the answer to this question is a limited 'yes', but many questions remain to be answered. There have been few systematic efforts to look at the range of ways in which structural and institutional aspects of school might affect adolescent well-being, over and above academic and behavioural outcomes. The Gray et al review undertaken for the Foundation highlighted potentially important features of secondary schools such as whether they are well run, calm and orderly, with clear expectations and recognition of the range of individual needs of the young people going through the system. The connectedness of these children and their schools may be important. Overall, however, the results on school transitions are surprisingly equivocal with respect to whether there is an impact and of what nature, and again the focus is normally on academic outcomes. One hypothesis that is emerging is that it is change in classroom organisation and school climate that may be important for emotional well-being, rather than change in school per se. This may have particular importance for UK adolescents at age 16, when many more of them than in other countries lose that structure. Studies do not reveal what actually might be going on causally, nor have they managed to untangle whether a large part of the pattern is attributable to other developmental changes going on at the same time, and it should also be emphasised that most of the existing research suggests that, at least for the youngest age groups, the effects are fairly short-lived if children are well supported by both schools and families, and if they do not have additional educational needs. Key questions surrounding the different experiences and trajectories of young people who are less well supported and less academic remain, particularly in relation to our central question about well-being.

What has changed? Time trends in the structures of secondary education in the UK

So if school matters (albeit as part of a larger picture), has the schooling system changed in ways that would increase any negative impact? Three sets of changes can be identified that might be important, and here our focus is firmly on the UK. First, in the 1970s, there was the move to the comprehensive system for a larger proportion of the school-aged population. Second, there are the constraints of the National Curriculum and the significance of a more widely shared exam experience. Third, there have been changes to what happens to young people at age 16; despite the lower staying-on rate in the UK, the current figures cited above are the highest they have been for the last 30 years, and the implications might be both positive and negative.

The move to a comprehensive secondary education system

During the 1960s, Labour government policy was to move from a tripartite education system (of grammar, secondary modern and technical schools, although very few of the latter were ever built) to a system of comprehensive education (non-selective secondary schools for all). Despite Conservative opposition, the policy unfolded as planned throughout the 1970s and 1980s. Many grammar schools became comprehensives or went independent. The proportion of young people attending comprehensives went from 9 per cent in 1965, to 79 per cent in 1977, and to 87 per cent in 1994 (Benn and Chitty, 1996).

Despite the broader changes to the educational system, evidence that there have been changes to the classroom climate itself is weak. Indeed, superficially things in the 1990s and early 2000s look fairly similar to the 1970s and 1980s; the system of a relatively unchanging form group for pastoral care, and the gradual introduction of ability grouping for most teaching reaching a peak at GCSE entry (or equivalent), has not changed greatly. It also occurs across school type; there is likely to be as much grouping in most grammars as there is in comprehensives – there are top and bottom groups in both. The difference lies in the absolute ability level of the groups. There were experiments, particularly in the 1970s, with systems that abandoned grouping and taught across ability ranges in single classes, but the pendulum has swung back to a more traditional model. In the UK this has tended to mean subject-specific grouping, rather than USA and Canadian systems of whole-school tracking, where children are in the 'advanced' track for all subjects, for example. Evidence on the effects of ability grouping is equivocal; some studies have suggested impacts on academic achievement and self-esteem, others less so, with the balance suggesting small effects that are subject-specific (Ireson et al, 1999). There has also been little change in class sizes; the Department for Children, Schools and Families, for example, regularly undertakes a census of the number of children in class in all maintained secondary schools in England and Wales on one day in January (approximately three million children), and this has ranged from 22.1 in 1978, through 20.7 in 1988, 21.9 in 1998 and 21.3 in 2007 (O'Donnell et al, 2010).

However, with respect to the things where we have evidence that schools make a difference, such as the internal organisation of classrooms, purposeful leadership, positive teacher–student relationships and 'supportive school' environments, there is no evidence available on time trends. It seems plausible to assume that many things have in fact progressed following the debates that 15,000 hours (Rutter et al, 1979) and the school effects world provoked in the 1970s. Regardless of school type, there is a great deal more awareness about the importance of children's everyday environments for their well-being, and every year more schools are rated as 'good' on the government's 'objective' ratings, but of course these ratings only go back a few years.

Introduction of the National Curriculum and extension of GCSE examination

In 1988, the National Curriculum was introduced in England and Wales, introducing standardised taught content across all state-funded schools, and allowing national assessments that could help identify failing schools. As well as a change in what was taught, one of the significances of the introduction of the Curriculum, as Gray et al's preparatory review of this topic pointed out, was that pastoral care provision by teachers in secondary school came under considerable pressure; it is now usually provided by other personnel in designated timetable slots, rather than being woven into the fabric of overall provision.

But perhaps more significantly, it is the introduction of widespread examinations that may indicate most change. For children of higher ability (more of whom will have been in grammar schools in the past), experiences were probably not dissimilar between the 1970s and the 1990s regardless of the type of school they were in. But for children in the middle/bottom ability groupings, who may well have not sat many exams at all in the 1960s and 1970s, or may have taken the less challenging CSEs, there have been a number of implications. These include (a) the introduction of a widespread modular GCSE/AS/A-level system meaning continued public examination testing for several years in the mid-teens, (b) more children on what we might call the 'academic' track (as opposed to 'vocational'), and (c) an increase in the overall number of years of education.

As a result of these changes, more children have 'success' at school. In their review of education policy in the UK since the Second World War, Machin and Vignoles (2006) note that the proportions reaching the equivalent of five or more grades A★ to C at GCSE stagnated from around 1970 to the mid-1980s, when around half were leaving full-time education at age 16 with no qualifications at all. From the mid-1980s onwards, the proportions staying on and exam achievement both began to rise rapidly. Figure 6.1 illustrates these trends.

Trends in the proportions staying on past age 16

Figure 6.1 demonstrates the rise in young people staying on, but 'staying on' can mean a number of different things. Table 6.2 presents more detail on participation in education and training by 16- to 18-year-olds in England and Wales from 1985 to 2003. This demonstrates that only a relatively small proportion are actually staying on at school; the majority go to a combination of different kinds of colleges and will be taking a wide variety of courses (see Table 6.1). In fact, the proportion staying on at school has not increased by very much; more of the increase comes from college participation. As Pring et al (2009) pointed out in their review of the future of education and training for this age group, learners at this level are funded at a higher level if they are in schools in England than if they are equivalent learners in further education colleges. As the latter tend to have lower levels of prior qualifications

Figure 6.1: Staying on at school and exam achievement in the UK, 1950–2000

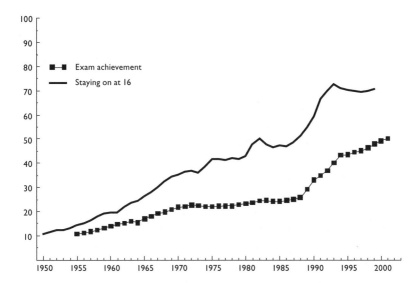

Note: Staying on is defined as the percentage of pupils staying on after the compulsory school leaving age. The exam achievement series measures the percentage of school leavers achieving five or more higher grade GCSE (or O-level) passes. Data for 1994-2000 comes from DfES (Department for Education and Science) Statistical Bulletins. Before 1994, data are taken back using a series provided to Machin and Vignoles by Duncan McVicar (see McVicar and Rice, 2001, for details).

Source: Reproduced with permission from Machin and Vignoles (2006)

Table 6.2: Participation in education of 16- to18-year-olds by institution type, England, 1985-2003

	1985	1990	1995	2000	2003
Full-time education					
Maintained schools	11	13	17	18	18
Independent schools	3	4	5	4	4
Sixth form colleges	3	4	7	6	7
Further education colleges	13	17	23	20	20
Higher education institutions	2	4	7	7	7
Part-time education					
Further education colleges	15	14	9	6	6
Total (full-time and part-time)	48	56	66	63	62

Note: Rounding means some columns do not equal 'total'.
Sources: DfE (2011) and www.education.gov.uk/rsgateway/DB/SFR/s000938/index.shtml

and to come from less privileged backgrounds, Pring et al (2009) suggested that this was potentially inequitable.

The concern is that a proportion of this higher rate of 'staying on' derives from a lack of alternatives given the collapse of the youth labour market, and in particular of the market for unqualified young people, and the fading away of the old apprentice schemes, rather than from an 'opt in' to more education. With respect to our main focus on well-being and mental health this raises some particular questions. Certainly there are negative implications for young people who fall out of all the categories at this point ('not in education, employment or training', NEET; cf Bynner and Parsons, 2002; Pring et al, 2009), but there is less discussion about stage–environment fits for this age group in these different educational environments. No doubt for many – possibly for most – these environments provide useful and positive experiences, but it may be that for a minority who would otherwise not have stayed on had there been jobs available, that this becomes a less positive experience.

Have these 'staying on' trends affected everyone equally? Machin and Vignoles (2006) emphasise the introduction of innovative market-oriented reforms, including more parental choice and school accountability, and note that, despite increases in examination success, some of these policy initiatives may raise inequality because richer parents take more advantage of a more market-oriented system. The UK still has a particularly distinctive 'tail of poor achievers', according to their analysis (Machin and Vignoles, 2006, p 4). Yet their own analyses of staying on rates by parental income groups using the big British birth cohorts suggest *less* educational inequality during the more recent years. On the other hand, Goldstein and Noden (2003) have used multilevel modelling approaches to look at social segregation in local education authorities, demonstrating an increase in variation between schools in the 1990s, towards the end of our period of interest. They suggest that this is partly because of an increase in the proportion of schools with control over at least some of their intake (some comprehensives retain selective components, albeit informally). The evidence on the contribution of educational reforms to increased social inequality is thus equivocal.

In conclusion, we have looked at three areas where there is evidence for change in adolescents' experiences of education over our period of interest, including changes to the examination and assessment regimes, and changes in the proportions staying on after the end of compulsory education at age 16. Finally, returning to the transition from primary school and between grades, it is worth noting that there have been few noticeable changes in this area apart from perhaps an investment in transition programmes where primary children visit secondary schools prior to transfer, and attend 'induction days', or have a few weeks of protected transition time at the start of the new year in the new school. Evaluations of these schemes suggest they help – a little (Shepherd and Roker, 2005) – although they tend to be rather limited in their reach. There is no evidence that we have unearthed that suggests that transitions are becoming more challenging. The only example we have found of a repeated study of school transitions in the UK across our time period of interest was undertaken by Maurice Galton and colleagues. Having undertaken a study of school transfer from primary school to secondary in the 1970s (Galton and Willcocks, 1983), they repeated the study in the late 1990s after the introduction of the National Curriculum (Galton and Hargreaves, 2002; Galton et al, 2003). The introduction of this Curriculum had caused some primary/secondary coordination difficulties, because the links between Key Stages 3 and 4 were not as smooth as they were intended to be, but the authors do not indicate that it has played any special part in changing children's experiences of the transfer. In fact, the problems of different teaching modes and styles seemed to persist between primary and secondary, regardless of what was being taught. The observational comments from secondary school classroom teaching were very similar to those of 20 years earlier. They concluded that many of the features of transition had not changed in 20 years, and indeed that there was evidence that transfer was a less stressful experience at the end of the 1990s compared to the 1970s (Galton et al, 1999b).

Many of the changes we have noted are undoubtedly positive, but we have used this brief review of some of the significant shifts to illustrate that there may be questions about whether the impacts might be more mixed for certain subgroups.

What do young people say?

Have young people's reports of their educational experiences changed over recent decades? In their review for the Foundation, Gray et al assessed the evidence particularly from repeated surveys of the Health Behaviour of School-aged Children surveys (see for example, Currie et al, 2008), which have data for the last 10 years on self-reported feelings of being pressurised by schoolwork. These data reveal that quite high proportions of English young people felt they were under some, or a lot of, pressure in recent years (60 per cent of 15-year-old boys and 70 per cent of 15-year-old girls in 2005/06, for example), in comparison with those from other countries. Gustafsson et al (2010) also gave self-reported anxieties and worries serious consideration. They noted that children tended to be rather circumspect about the effect of school when they were actually embedded in the system, but spoke more freely of their negative experiences after the event, when they were older. For children encountering academic difficulties, they comment on a tendency for more aggressive reactions from boys, and more evidence of tendencies towards early depression among girls. A large number of qualitative studies report on the importance of relationships with teachers, other school personnel and peers, and comment on the stress of the experience of streaming, ability grouping and selection through increased competition and comparison. Children certainly worry about school; it features highly on self-generated lists of things that concern them (Gullone and King, 1992). However, we do not have reliable comparative data from before the start of the 1990s in order to assess longer-term trends on these self-reported variables.

Studies have also widely reported children's self-perceived worries (and excitement) before transfer, and disappointment and adjustment afterwards (reviewed, for example, in West et al, 2008). With respect to time trends across our period of interest in the UK, however, once again we are left with a paucity of evidence, apart from Galton et al's (2003) results. One final study worth mentioning, however, is a USA-based analysis of the worries and stressors of 7- to 12-year-old children in the mid-2000s, compared with items and results from previous instruments over the preceding 30 years. The results suggested new stressors emerging that reflected the changing experiences and expectations of school-aged children, beginning in the 1980s with more evidence of feeling pressurised by parents and other adults in the context of good grades (Ryan-Wenger et al, 2005). In addition, it may be important to remember the results of the Finnish study showing higher levels of school stress in academic tracks when compared with vocational education (Salmela-Aro et al, 2008).

With respect to self-reported variables from the post-16 period, there is little to go on. There is an interesting qualitative literature on the experience of low paid insecure work patterns among young working-class men at a time when there are few other options for them (MacDonald, 2009), but much less on the experiences of those left in education at this time. Others have noted that while educational aspirations have risen in recent years, and that young people accept they need to invest more in education, matching aspirations to realistic expectations and maintaining a sense of direction and purpose may be more challenging (Schoon, 2006; Biggart, 2009). But repeated survey information on these kinds of variables for this age group across our time span is not available.

Are there trends in other 'school-related' problems?

We have found little in the way of direct evidence for changes in educational experiences being correlated with changes in adolescent mental health outcomes, although some hypotheses are emerging. Before concluding, however, there is one last question we can ask that might shed some indirect light on the issue. Although we uncovered little in the way of specific information about trends in symptoms of depression and anxiety in the educational setting over the last three decades, are there trends in other 'school-related' problems that would suggest something negative was going on in the school domain? Are there alternative indices that might indicate some changes were having a detrimental effect? The three that immediately spring to mind are school exclusion rate data, truancy data and bullying data. If school as a social context has become a more challenging or threatening environment for adolescents, we might expect to see significant time trends in these over our period of interest.

Interestingly, school exclusion data (school 'expulsion' as it was known earlier) was not routinely recorded in the UK until around 1990. The two current official definitions of exclusion (fixed-term exclusion and permanent exclusion) have been reflected in official statistics since 1994-95 (Gordon, 2001). We have not been able to track down any publications on historical trends in school exclusions or expulsions in the UK between the 1970s and the late 1980s. In their review for the Foundation, Gray et al constructed a timeline from 1990 to 2006 by using different sources, and this showed a considerable rise in the 1990s, falling back in 2000. Levels are still at least three times those of 1990 (at just under 8,000 per annum in secondary schools). We do not know, however, what was happening before 1990. Of course rates of school exclusion will be very much affected by policy, but they may also reflect underlying levels of conduct disorder (which we have seen went up at times during this period). It would also be possible to speculate about the relevance perhaps of changes in tolerance of certain behaviours – is bad behaviour in the classroom less tolerated? Is it more likely to be dealt with by the school than by individual teachers? Schools may be concerned about disruption to other pupils (in an era of concentration on exam results and school league tables), and there may be interactions with the trends outlined above where some children who would previously have left school may now be retained for longer.

Truancy data are similarly restricted. Department for Children, Schools and Families (as it was then) statistics track trends from the mid-1990s (www.education.gov.uk), and these demonstrate that the percentage of half-days missed due to unauthorised absence in secondary schools ranged from around 1 per cent in 1996 to 1.5 per cent in 2006. Ofsted have made the link between good quality educational provision and school attendance (see, for example, Ofsted, 2007), and by provision they mean the school's rating of being, for example, 'outstanding', and factors such as leadership and management, teaching skills and examination achievement. Ofsted also noted that authorised absence had improved over time, contrary to the data for unauthorised absence (what we would indeed regard as truancy), and that schools vary enormously (Ofsted, 2007). As an indicator of how hard it is to know exactly what these kinds of trends are really reflecting, they noted that schools had moved away from authorising holidays in term time; these were now more likely to be recorded as unauthorised absence.

Bullying is interesting because it has been subject to enormous interest and intervention over the years since the 1980s. There is also clear evidence that it is associated with psychiatric symptoms for the victim and also the perpetrator (Kumpulainen, 2008; Arseneault et al, 2009). A meta-analysis of the victimisation-adjustment literature concluded that the largest effect sizes were for depression – around 0.29 when multiple informants were used, rising to 0.45 when the child was the source of all the data (Hawker and Boulton, 2000). Significant effects were also found for loneliness, self-esteem and anxiety but estimates of prevalence vary quite substantially; a recent estimate suggested they ranged from 9 to 32 per cent for experience of victimisation (James, 2010).

There is a public perception that bullying has been on the increase, and as we know, conduct disorder has risen over this period and is likely to be correlated with bullying (Wolke et al, 2000). A rise in sensitivity to bullying and programmes could be hypothesised to either contribute to perceptions of a rise in the underlying behaviour, or, alternatively, could have helped to bring levels down. What we really need, of course, is good repeat epidemiological data. In searching for relevant data, the Gray et al review for the Foundation identified the Health Behaviour of School-aged Children as providing some data on the topic, but only for the 2000s. These have in fact shown a recent small fall in bullying across the last decade, and have also suggested that

English adolescents were somewhat less likely to report being bullied than their counterparts across the other countries in the study. However, we have not uncovered any reviews of English data on bullying trends that cover our longer period of interest back to the 1970s, and it seems likely that comparable, repeated surveys do not exist to establish a meaningful baseline.

In the last 10 years schools have become places where it seems fair to assume the majority of young people are safer than they used to be; there are clear procedures in place for dealing with bullying; truancy is more rigorously policed and government initiatives to deal with both have been widely implemented (DfE, 1994, 1999). The rise in exclusions since the early 1990s could reflect these initiatives (which may have led to increasing intolerance of the behaviour) or this could be the result of rising levels of conduct disorder (see Chapter Two). As indices of school-related problems, these three are not as revealing as we might have hoped and, more problematically, the data available to us do not go far enough back into our time period for us to be sure about the trends.

Conclusion

The literature search undertaken by Gray et al as part of the Changing Adolescence Programme, and other sources such as the Nuffield Foundation's 14-19 review (Wright, 2005; Pring et al, 2009), have revealed that there have been some major changes in the basic structure of school experiences for adolescents over the last 30 years. These have included:

- much more attention to attainment and examinations, applying more widely across the ability and socioeconomic range;
- a significant increase in examination participation and 'success';
- a major shift to comprehensive education in the 1970s;
- a significant increase in the number of children staying on at 16 years and thus having longer 'school experiences' than previously;
- more participation in a variety of non-school post-16 educational routes than in previous decades.

Research evidence to suggest that any of these are associated with aspects of adolescent well-being and emotional adjustment is distinctly lacking. The evidence available to us suggested that aspects of school and classroom organisation, and social relationships in the educational arena, are key correlates of mental health symptoms, but it has proved very difficult to assess whether these specific aspects of the educational system have changed particularly over time.

It is easier to establish that more children are involved in education for longer than previously, so exposure to educational environments is more intense (with the stress on examinations) and more extended than previously. These trends do raise some important questions. First, what is the impact of the increased educational participation of the lower achieving, lower socioeconomic groups? More young people may be in education, but this may mean very different things for different groups of young people on different educational 'tracks' in different kinds of educational provision. Some of the research we have cited has touched on this topic; to date, evidence on whether social inequality has shrunk or been expanded by increased educational participation is equivocal. But the issue of subgroups with different experiences of schooling is one that deserves more attention. We need to consider who may be more vulnerable to these social changes, rather than assuming that the effects will be similar for all (Rutter and Maughan, 2002). In particular, a big question mark hangs over the effect of increased examination participation and associated school pressure on groups of children who may in the past have been destined for non-academic pathways. At the end of our time period, more adolescents expected to remain in education even if they were not achievers, and even if they disliked school (Schoon, 2010). Current educational literature is very focused on academic outcomes particularly for the older age group, rather ignoring the social and emotional aspects of life in education.

Second, we do not know enough about peer group effects in the educational setting. These have been left out of the equation in education research, although hints at social comparison effects have arisen in the work that we have reviewed here. But put together with our findings in the chapter in this volume on activity patterns and time use (Chapter Four), which highlighted the possibility that adolescents were living more age-segregated lives, with longer periods in education and pseudo-education, and findings on the importance of peer group behaviour in the picture of time trends in drug and alcohol use, there is obviously a need to look at peer group relations and influences in the context of social change across a number of different domains including education. Also, as the schools research points out, it is as much classrooms as 'schools' that are salient for outcomes, and the people filling those classrooms are peers. Selection effects are likely to be a complicating factor here; schools vary massively in their intakes and having a heavy concentration of other people with difficulties in a school/classroom may be problematic in itself ('contextual effects').

Contagion, or 'deviancy amplification' effects may also be important; if a significant proportion of the classroom shows symptoms of conduct problems or depression and anxiety, what is the effect on the whole class? This has been demonstrated at the primary school level (Kellam et al, 1998) but could be extended to the secondary level. Our school settings may not adequately tackle the increased intensity of same-age peer group relations that seems likely to be a key part of social change for this age group over the last three decades.

It is clearly important to draw together all aspects of adolescent lives and experiences in the school setting, and to relate these to each other, in order to get an accurate picture of social change in this context. It may well be the case that a number of interesting divergent trends are emerging, with some factors being important for social adjustment and psychological health, and others being important for academic success. The work of the Changing Adolescence Programme began the process of drawing questions – if not evidence – from a range of different disciplines and perspectives, and it is likely to be helpful to continue this exercise if we are to understand the complex and significant role of secondary school experiences for young people today and in the next few decades.

SEVEN

Trends in adolescent substance use and their implications for understanding trends in mental health

Ann Hagell, Judith Aldridge, Petra Meier, Tim Millar,
Jennifer Symonds and Michael Donmall

Introduction

A clear social change over the second half of the 20th century was the increase in the proportion of young people using alcohol and different kinds of other drugs, which have become a conspicuous part of the social landscape. The shifting pattern of use by young people and the possible links to trends in mental health problems are the subject of this chapter.

The interface between adolescence and substance use is particularly salient. To start with, adolescence is generally when people begin using substances. It is thus a particularly interesting period with respect to the natural history of substance use; when and how people start is, we know from research, important to their later outcomes, so adolescence constitutes a critical period (Mirza and Mirza, 2008).

Second, brain and hormonal changes in adolescence have special significance when we are considering the impact of drugs. Recent research on adolescent brain development points out how much basic building work is still being undertaken during the teenage years, and mind–altering substances could potentially have different effects at this stage compared with other age groups (Morris and Wagner, 2007; Windle et al, 2008). There is some evidence that adolescent brains show increased sensitivity to immediate rewards and different perspectives on risk taking, making drug use potentially more dangerous (Spear and Varlinskaya, 2005). Again, this is important to a consideration of trends and particularly to the potential for a relationship with mental health symptoms.

Third, the social challenges of identity development, the establishment of autonomy and the particular focus on peer groups may also all create a period of extra vulnerability to drug and alcohol use in adolescence. The social structures that, in their own ways, shape the initiation of young people into the world of substance use may have changed over time.

Research questions

Despite the existence of quite a lot of data, and much commentary, it still seemed that there was a need for an objective evaluation of the long-term time trends in substance use with a clear focus on the adolescent years, and also an evaluation of the extent of any potential causal relationship with adolescent mental health symptoms. The specific research questions for this chapter included:

- What is the evidence for *time trends* in patterns of substance use by UK adolescents over the last 30 years? What were the changes in the amounts and types of substances used? How about key indicators such as age at first use, intoxication and binge use? How does the UK fare in international comparisons?
- Moving beyond averages, is there any evidence of *different trends for subgroups* within the UK population, particularly for those in situations of disadvantage?
- What do we know about the *implications* of these time trends, with respect to adolescent mental health outcomes? Is there an association, and if so, any evidence that this is causal?

As part of the Changing Adolescence Programme's work, we funded a research team from the University of Manchester to assess the available evidence on the topic. This chapter draws in part on their scoping review of the available literature and data. The team was led by Dr Michael Donmall, and included Dr Tim Millar, Dr Judith Aldridge, Dr Petra Meier. We have summarised and highlighted some particular findings from their searches, and also supplemented their material with other research and data from surveys. Copies of their full scoping review are available from Professor Donmall (see Appendix I for more details).

What do we mean by 'substance use'?

The whole topic of young people's drug use is rife with inconsistencies, contradictions and issues of incomparability in the use of definitions and cut-offs. Words that are used to indicate type of engagement with substances range from 'use', 'non-problematic', 'recreational' and 'normative', through 'heavy', 'harmful', 'problematic' and 'binge', to 'dependence', 'misuse', 'abuse' and 'addictive', to offer just a selection. In many instances writers assume shared understanding of what these terms mean without giving concrete definitions.

As these words suggest, it is possible to view substance use as a continuum with one end representing a non-problematic 'lifestyle' choice potentially resulting in little or no harm, and the other end representing a dependent, addictive or compulsive activity with consequent detrimental health and social effects Harm may depend on a range of factors such as individual age, vulnerability and the situation in which the use is taking place. It is not possible to predict harm from regularity or quantity of use alone and there are many examples of heavy-end use resulting in little or no long-term harm and, conversely, of opportunistic one-off situations that result in severe damage or even death. Indeed, as we have already indicated, harm may be particularly difficult to detect and define in adolescence, when physiological reactions to drugs may be different to those in other age groups (Spear and Varlinskaya, 2005). The USA National Institute of Alcohol Abuse and Alcoholism's Underage Drinking Initiative recently evaluated the particular risks associated with underage drinking in a special issue of *Pediatrics* (Masten et al, 2008; Windle et al, 2008). Furthermore, particularly with regard to alcohol, most societal harm, including violence and anti-social behaviour, as well as the many adverse health consequences, result from non-dependent use. Rather than pre-empt a judgement about harm, we have opted to use the convention of usually referring simply to substance use, rather than suggesting when it is and is not problematic through terms such as 'problem use' or 'abuse'. Where we can, we have tried to rely on concrete indicators of what is being used, how it is being used, and what the consequences may be.

Further complications are added by the wide range of substances that can be included in 'substance use'. UK adolescents engage in the use of a wide variety of substances, including alcohol, volatile substances such as solvents, inhalants and glue, Class A drugs such as ecstasy, LSD, cocaine, crack, heroin, magic mushrooms and methadone, Class B drugs such as amphetamines and cannabis, and Class C drugs such as tranquilisers, some painkillers, Gamma hydroxybutyrate GHB and Ketamine (UK Drugs Act 2005). In practical terms the main focus in general population adolescent research is on alcohol and cannabis, with some reference to cocaine, ecstasy and amphetamines. The remit for this review excluded tobacco (see Fuller, 2009, for more information on trends in smoking).

Methodological considerations

Undertaking the review

The literature search undertaken by the Donmall team from the University of Manchester focused on published studies examining time trends in adolescent substance use, explanations for time trends and relationships among adolescent substance use and mental health and behavioural correlates. Studies were assessed for their methodological rigour and UK relevance. Searching took place of electronic databases (for example, Medline, ISI Web of Science, PsycINFO, Scopus, LexisNexis), specialist libraries (for example, DrugScope), government publications and international organisations such as the European Monitoring Centre on Drugs and Drug Addiction. Bibliographies of identified core articles were also used as leads to other relevant sources.

The search particularly looked for large, robust surveys, especially if repeated at different time points, and for comprehensive reviews of the evidence. Searches for primary material were limited to English language documents (with, where possible, a focus on the UK), and years of publication restricted from 1980 to 2009, although for this chapter reviews of trends before this time were evaluated, to allow us to piece together the longer history. As with the other chapters in this volume, we have been primarily interested in the trends for young people in their second decade of life (ages 10 to 20).

We also present a series of graphs in this chapter, which bring together previously published data from surveys, but in new ways. The data we draw on come from reports of the Smoking, Drinking and Drug Use survey (SDDU), the Health and Behaviour of School-aged Children survey (HBSC), the European School survey Project on Alcohol and other Drugs (ESPAD) and data provided to us by the Schools Health Education Unit (SHEU), from their schools survey. We have given citations to the original reports; these can be checked for full descriptions of samples and methodology (see Appendix II at the end of this book).

Methodological challenges in the substance use literature

It quickly transpires that, whereas concern about drug and alcohol use by young people is longstanding, good, repeated surveys on the topic across our time period are not. We start with a quick overview of the methodological considerations faced when unpicking this literature. Some are common to all kinds of substance use research; others are specific to either the drugs or the alcohol field. Most reviews give this topic reasonably thorough consideration, for example, particular issues in alcohol research, and especially understanding trends, were recently reviewed by Smith and Foxcroft (2009), and Goddard (2001, 2007).

The first relates to the strengths and weaknesses of *self-report measures* of drug use. The most common way of finding out about drug and alcohol use is, of course, through direct questions to the users, and it is fair to say that the self-report methodology has been found to be reasonably robust for general household samples. However, young people may exaggerate their drug/alcohol use (false positive reporting) or, conversely, may not disclose it (false negative reporting). It is possible that both of these remain fairly constant across time, but it is equally possible that they do not. Reporting tendencies may change in the face of health promotion messages, school/educational policies and sanctions designed to discourage use. Although big population surveys are considered to provide the best available picture of lower level substance use, they may be less suitable when considering more extreme or unusual behaviour. To counter this, official administrative data about users in contact with the health or criminal justice authorities can be used as complementary information. However, shifts in *reporting practices* may hinder use of official data too, driven by changes in policy and practice that affect how they are collated.

How the questions are asked can also be a problem. Surveys typically ask about recent use (in past month and/or past year) and/or lifetime use of substances. However, many published sources focus on lifetime use, which will include one-off experimentation as well as regular use. A lot of what purports to be comparative (among countries, primarily) throws up further questions about using the same survey instruments within different cultures, or assuming comparability among different questions and instruments used in different countries but intended to measure the same thing. These issues can, of course, also apply to comparisons across time (the past being a foreign country for these purposes). Even using the same instrument at two different time points does not mean that the survey is comparing like with like.

In addition, Smith and Foxcroft (2009) usefully outlined the difficulties in comparing alcohol consumption across time given the changes in the strength of alcohol and the measurement of a 'unit'. This is a particularly UK-based problem, as the official definition of a unit changed in the mid-2000s to reflect larger serving sizes and stronger drinks. This made sense from a public health perspective, but represents something of a nightmare from a repeated survey point of view.

Then there are issues of how different studies decide to provide information on different *age groupings*. Depending on the historical origins of different surveys, they may base themselves around groups that make sense to education, or to eligibility for different kinds of service provision, or for other purposes entirely. In drugs research arising from criminology, children are often grouped up to age 16 and then from age 16 into the mid 20s, whereas we might be more interested in a split at age 18, if we are thinking about transitions out of the world of education. Potentially interesting surveys can become incomparable if the age bandings cannot be regrouped to align with each other.

There is also a huge issue concerning the *difficulties of ensuring representative samples*. Household or school surveys may under-represent the groups most likely to be involved in serious or problematic use (school exclusions, drop-outs or truants, or the homeless), leading to under-estimates of prevalence. Even the larger surveys cited later, such as the World Health Organization's (WHO) HBSC survey, have some sample size limitations, and this means that studies of important and interesting subgroups are rare.

Finally, we need to refer to the *challenges of establishing causality* when thinking about drug trends, their causes and how they impact on other outcomes. Much of the cross-sectional work is of limited use in revealing causal mechanisms, although it can be useful in plotting trends. Longitudinal data, where the same samples are followed for a period of time, animal studies and human experimental studies can all help with causality if they are well-designed, but may be limited in shedding light on trends. However, it is fair to say that all the evidence suggests that individual substance use is predicted by a range of different factors and the same is likely to be true of time trends. These are all issues to be born in mind when evaluating the evidence summarised in this chapter.

National trends

Increase in alcohol consumption by adolescents after the Second World War

Industry statistics show that in the late Victorian and early Edwardian years alcohol consumption was very high across the population as a whole (IAS, 2010). For all sorts of social and economic reasons drinking then steadily fell over the early years of the 20th century (Rutter, 1979;

Smith and Foxcroft, 2009; IAS 2010). Rates of per capita consumption more than halved by the middle of the Second World War, and dropped to an all time low in 1948 (IAS, 2010).

From this baseline in the middle of the century, the 1950s witnessed the beginning of a dramatic and sustained upturn in consumption that continued to pick up speed through the 1960s and went on rising for another three decades, right through our period of interest. The data sources are a little bit of a mixed bag, compiled from a range of official, industry and administrative statistics. They include information on deaths from cirrhosis of the liver, arrests for drunkenness, admissions to hospital for alcoholism and data on alcohol–induced psychosis. The most widely used graph to represent the time trends for this period is based on the British Beer and Pub Association's estimates of per capita alcohol consumption for the population (BBPA, 2005). These data have been collated since 1900, and it is almost traditional to include a version of the graph in reviews on the topic. It appears, for example, in Silbereisen et al (1995), Plant and Plant (2006), the British Medical Association (2008) and Smith and Foxcroft (2009). Our version in Figure 7.1 is tailored to our period of interest, and illustrates the trends described above.

There is no reason to think that these trends did not apply as much to young people as to the rest of the population, but we have not found any data for the earlier decades that concentrate on people under 16 years old. A series of reliable and thorough previous reviews have already attempted to collate evidence on these trends in relation to young people (Rutter, 1979; May, 1992; Silbereisen et al, 1995; Gilvarry, 2000; Blocker et al 2003; Essau, 2006; Smith and Foxcroft, 2009) and all draw similar conclusions, although in all cases there are scant data to draw on until around 1980. These preceding reviews have concluded that alcohol use has long been a major problem for a small proportion of young people, but that between 1945 and 1980 alcohol consumption rose in the general population of young people. This is based on (a) evidence for the general population as a whole, (b) evidence on populations of USA high school students, and (c) evidence from rises in criminal and hospital statistics on indicators of alcohol abuse for UK young people. The rises seem likely to have been steepest in the 1960s and 1970s.

Figure 7.1: Per capita consumption of alcohol in the UK from 1956 to 2006

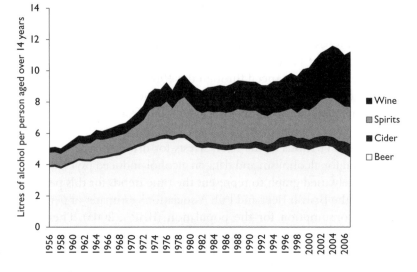

Source: IAS (2010)

More recent trends in adolescent alcohol use since 1980

As Essau (2006) has commented, the negative impact of rises in substance use across Europe up to the 1980s meant that large-scale surveys started to be put in place as a way of keeping track of what was going on. As a result, it seems that the surveys followed the trends, rather than clearly demarking them. In the UK these surveys include the SDDU survey administered by the National Centre for Social Research on behalf of the Department of Health (11- to 15-year-olds), with most indicators from 1985. We also have the SHEU surveys from 1987 (11- to 15-year-olds), ESPAD from 1995 and the WHO HBSC from 1986, but with useful alcohol data for England only from 1997. There are also several other surveys that are worth mentioning, including the British Crime Survey (but only for age 16 upwards, until 2009 when 10- to 15-year-olds were included), the Health Survey for England (11- to 15-year-olds from 1995), and some within-UK nation specific data such as the Scottish Schools Adolescent Lifestyle and Substance Use Survey (SALSUS) and the Young People's Behaviour and Attitudes Surveys in Northern Ireland.

All of these sources give information on more recent adolescent alcohol consumption trends. But what is noticeable is that all this more detailed information only addresses the last decade or so of our time scale. All are of limited use in determining the longer-term trends.

Virtually all of them were initiated at or after what turned out to have been the peak of the steepest rises. Studying the data they have generated can thus give the impression of a general decline, and the more dramatic picture of the steady rise with a small recent plateau can be somewhat missed.

Generally, as the right-hand side of Figure 7.1 shows, the picture from 1980 onwards is that UK per capita alcohol consumption temporarily peaked at that point, dropping back for a few years before starting to rise again. There was a further drop back in the early 1990s, but again a rise afterwards up to the mid-2000s. Average total of alcohol consumed per head of population rose overall from 9.25 litres in 1980, to 11.59 in 2004 (IAS, 2010). Much of the increase was in wine, and to a lesser extent, cider. Against this background, the self-report surveys for young people have shown trends for experimentation slightly rising and falling in the years since 1988. For example, the SDDU survey estimated that 65 per cent of boys and 59 per cent of girls aged 11-15 claimed to have ever had a proper alcoholic drink in 1988. The respective proportions in 1998 were 62 and 58 per cent, and in 2007 they were 54 and 54 per cent (Fuller, 2008).

The estimates for experimentation may not have risen overall in the last 20 years, but it is important to look separately at some key indicators of problematic use. These indicators include first use at an early age, very frequent use and drunkenness/binge drinking. For data points in the late 1990s and early 2000s, ESPAD reports that around 35 to 40 per cent of the sample report that they first stated drinking at age 13 or younger. This sounds high, but we have nothing to compare it to back in the 1970s and 1980s. We do know, however, that early onset is a particular indicator of later poorer outcomes both in drinking habits, later drug use and other sequelae (Brook et al, 2002; Odgers et al, 2008; Shiner, 2009), so this is an important indicator to watch. The USA National Institute on Alcohol Abuse and Alcoholism highlighted the dangers of underage drinking (see www.niaaa.nih.gov), and noted that it had only fallen slightly in the USA over the last decade. Age of onset is, however, a fairly crude measure; it could include both drinking in controlled settings under parental supervision and drinking with peers in unsupervised settings, although these are likely to have different meanings. The SHEU survey goes beyond age at first drinking to report proportions who said they had drunk at least once in the previous week. In 1990, 41 per cent of 12- to 13-year-olds said this was the case, compared with 24 per cent in 2000 and 21 per cent in 2008. Figures for the 14- to 15-year-olds were 50 per cent in 1990, 32.5 per cent in 2000 and 31.5 per cent in 2008.

Figure 7.2 presents the rates for 'drunkenness' in UK adolescents aged 11, 13 and 15, for the period from 1985 to 2008. Comparability across measures is a problem; we have included being drunk once or more (ESPAD), twice or more (HBSC) or drinking more than 10 units in the previous week (SHEU), and we should note that 'Have you been drunk?' is probably the most subjective of the self-report questions asked in these surveys. The graphs show that the regular UK data from the SDDU show a range of peaks and troughs over the last 20 years. Given the ups and downs, it would seem that neither ESPAD nor HBSC yet offer enough data points for us to tell which way the trends are going.

Figure 7.2: Trends in adolescent self-reported drunkenness in UK-based surveys, 1985–2008

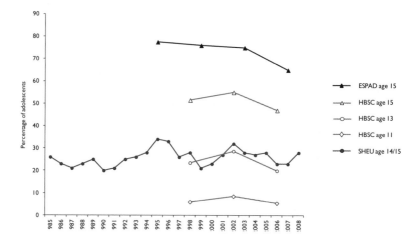

Notes:
SHEU, England: 14- to 15-year-olds who had drunk more than 10 alcohol units during the previous week.
HBSC, England: Have been drunk two or more times.
ESPAD, UK: Have been drunk one or more times.

Sources: See Appendix II at the end of the book for a list of data sources from each survey at different time points

Martin Plant and colleagues have reported reanalysis of ESPAD looking specifically at binge drinking (see Plant, 2000; Plant and Plant, 2006). They suggest that where there have been rises lately this is in relation to binge drinking by UK 15- to 16-year-old girls (binge drinking being defined as five or more drinks at one time, three or more times in the last month). It is notable that estimates of average consumption of units for those who do drink have also risen. In their analysis of trends in drinking by young people, Smith and Foxcroft (2009) drew on the SDDU to show that for those aged 11-15 who *had* drunk alcohol in the last week, the units consumed by boys increased from 5.7 to 12.3, and by girls from 4.7 to 10.5 units, from 1990 to 2006.

The fact that we have these recent data suggesting a plateau in overall participation by this age group is encouraging, but the subgroups showing more serious alcohol abusing behaviour may still be showing some rises. Certainly, looking at the broader range of evidence over a longer time period back to the 1960s and 1970s, the evidence points to significant increases over the long term.

Increase in drug use by adolescents after the Second World War

It is even more difficult to get reliable statistics for illicit drug use than alcohol across the early part of the period that we are interested in. Drug use is something of a moving target, in that the drugs being used can change, introducing even more measurement and comparability issues. The history of drug use by young people only tends to start mid-century. Drugs were used before that, of course, but substances and trends were pretty much unrelated to the patterns established after the Second World War. There is virtually no information of the epidemiological kind prior to the 1960s, and in the two decades after that the information comes largely from studies of the student population who are not, particularly at this time, representative of the general population. Shiner (2009), in a history of social drug use by young people, notes that the first British self-report survey containing questions on drug use was administered in 1969 by the Office of Population Censuses and Surveys on behalf of the Home Office, but this was an isolated event, and regular surveys did not get going for another couple of decades. As far as we are aware, it also did not include young people.

What evidence that does exist from other sources suggests that between 1945 and 1960 there was a slow increase in the use of illicit drugs in the UK (mostly cannabis), and that this speeded up in the 1960s and 1970s (Institute for the Study of Drug Dependence, 1993; Silbereisen et al, 1995), mirroring the trends for alcohol use. By the late 1970s, when the UK peak was still to come, Rutter (1979) concluded:

- Young adults in the student population were starting to use illegal drugs more regularly. In the USA it was estimated that between 20 and 60 per cent of college and university students had used marijuana at some time. Use in the UK was lower, between 10 and 40 per cent having experimented. Other estimates of lifetime use of drugs in USA samples reported only around 9 per cent in those aged over 45, but as high as 65 per cent in those aged 18-29 (Anthony and Helzer, 1991). Six per cent of UK students were reported to be regular or heavy users of cannabis.

• Students were also reporting the use of hallucinogens: North American surveys from the 1970s suggested that around 4 to 12 per cent of college students had tried them. This was more widespread at this time in white middle-class samples than lower socioeconomic and minority ethnic groups. Comparable figures for the UK were not available, but were assumed to be lower.

• Usage by school children (up to 16-18 years) was 'much less' but not quantified. There was far less information available about this age group than college students.

• Opiate (heroin) use in the UK was very rare until the 1960s. There were no records of heroin addicts under 20 years old in the UK in 1959. New cases of heroin addiction went up tenfold in the next 10 years but adolescents remained a 'tiny proportion' of notified addicts – by 1977, around 1 to 2 per cent.

More recent trends for drug use by young people since 1980

The thorough review of substance use trends undertaken by Silbereisen et al (1995) provided evidence on time trends in illicit drug use up to the early 1990s. The focus was on international comparisons and relatively few data are presented specifically for the UK. However, based on their review of the available evidence, the authors concluded that by this stage substance use was becoming a relatively common phenomenon among adolescents in Europe and the USA. Silbereisen et al's (1995) conclusions included:

• Up to about 25 per cent of all young people were engaging in occasional recreational use of illicit drugs.

• Rises in the post-war period could now be seen to have taken place across the whole spectrum of use, from occasional use to drug abuse and dependency.

• There were modest increases in cocaine and 'crack' use in the 1980s, mainly related to increases in use by young adults rather than the younger age group.

- There was possible evidence for a slight decline in use of some types of drugs after the mid-1980s, but there was evidence by the late 1980s for an increase (although not widespread) in other such as amphetamines and party drugs. Thus a mixed picture was beginning to emerge, with potentially different patterns for different drugs.
- USA data suggested a drop in age of high school students using drugs for the first time.

As mentioned, surveys have provided more detailed information from the mid-1980s onwards, and for drug use, they appear to capture the tail end of the most striking rises, which came a little after those for alcohol. Thus, Figure 7.3 presents UK-based data on those who have ever taken drugs from 1987 to 2008, and the bottom two lines representing the SHEU data suggest a rise in the prevalence of drug use over this period, mainly relating to cannabis, from the late 1980s, particularly among 14- to 15-year-olds. Taking a rough average, across surveys, we can estimate that in 1987, around one in twenty of this age group reported that they had ever used an illicit drug, but by the mid-1990s this had increased to around one in three. Taken in combination,

Figure 7.3: Trends in self-reported use of drugs ('ever') by UK adolescents, 1987–2008

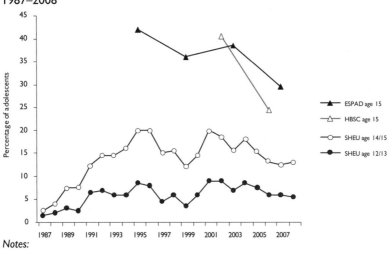

Notes:

SHEU, England: Have taken at least one of the listed drugs.

HBSC, England: Have ever used cannabis.

ESPAD, UK: Have ever used an illicit drug.

Sources: See Appendix II at the end of this book for a list of data sources from each survey at different time points

these suggest that the trends identified in Silbereisen continued for a few more years before peaking, although the estimates are not dissimilar.

Although use among the younger age group (12- to 13-year-olds) also increased during the same period, it has always been recorded as consistently much lower, never rising above 10 per cent during this period, perhaps indicating that most initiation continued to occur at around the age of 14 or 15.

All the surveys suggest considerable fluctuation in the late 1990s. ESPAD and SDDU suggest prevalence may have remained stable, or even declined slightly, since this time; the SHEU data are more equivocal on the trend, although the rates at the latest time point were lower than in 1996. The British Crime Survey also points to a levelling off or possible decline in youthful drug use (among 16- to 24-year-olds) from 1998 (Hoare and Moon, 2010).

Other trend indicators apart from self-report surveys

As we have commented, these sorts of surveys may all be subject to shared measurement errors (schools-based samples, relatively small samples, changes in the way alcohol and drugs are used, changes in the way units of alcohol are measured, etc). What other evidence on trends exists from alternative sources such as criminal statistics, hospital admissions and treatment facilities, that might elucidate these trends? In their scoping review for the Changing Adolescence Programme, Donmall et al summarised some of the key indicators on both alcohol and substance use from these alternative sources to assess whether they confirm or contradict the self-report data:

- *Official records of criminal offences* Trends in the number of offenders under the age of 17 or 17-21 convicted, cautioned, fined for offences under the Misuse of Drugs Act 1971 from 1973 onwards suggest that, after a period of relatively stability in the 1970s, the numbers started to increase during the early 1980s, became more pronounced during the late 1980s and continued throughout most of the 1990s (Police Foundation, 2000). These are individuals whose substance use has attracted legal sanction, but the trend in arrests also serves as an indicator of prevalence in the wider population. The trend will certainly, to some extent, have been inflated by changes in policing and recording practice, but it seems likely that the magnitude of the increase cannot be explained by these factors alone.

- *Official index of addicts* Between the mid–1970s and the late 1990s there was a marked increase in the number of young people (aged under 21) newly notified to the Home Office Addict's Index, from approximately 2,000 to over 40,000 (Corkery, 1997; Reuter and Stevens, 2007). The Index (1968-97) received notifications from doctors, of persons addicted to the opiates/cocaine. Although opiates and cocaine may not be typical components of a *young* drug user's repertoire, the increase in numbers of young users seeking medical attention suggests a much higher incidence of opiate or cocaine use by young people during the late 1990s than during the 1970s. Changes in incidence are likely to have pre-dated these statistics, because there is typically a delay between the drug use onset and treatment-seeking behaviour. It has been suggested that some of the increase in addicts in the 1980s at least was due to increased availability of Middle Eastern illicit heroin during this period (Lewis, 1994), which was picked up more by young people in deprived working-class neighbourhoods (Pearson et al, 1986; Pearson, 1987; Parker et al, 1988; Gilman and Pearson, 1991).
- *Treatment figures* Official records of the number of young people who started being treated for drug misuse were published in six-monthly bulletins from 1993-2001 by the Department of Health. These suggest a steady increase with signs of a plateau towards the end of the series (DH, 1994, 2004). It is likely that the trend has been driven by the development, during the late 1990s, of drug services specifically targeted at the needs of young people.
- *Drug fatality figures* Fortunately drug-related mortality among adolescents is relatively low, averaging around 50 per annum according to the Office for National Statistics (ONS) figures (ONS, 2009), currently representing around 3 per cent of drug-related deaths at all ages. What causes death has changed with time (opiates, or volatile solvents), and the chance of death has also changed with improved medical interventions. For opiates there was a significant *decline* between 1967-93 in drug-related deaths of 15- to 24-year-olds, and then fluctuation thereafter. On the other hand, solvent-related deaths showed a considerable increase from the 1970s to the early 1990s and subsequently a dramatic fall, particularly for young people (Field-Smith et al, 2008). This may well have been because of public health measures taken to restrict access to solvents.

Any evidence on particular trends for meaningful subgroups within the UK?

Do different subgroups of the youth population reflect different trend patterns in use of substances? Undoubtedly the answer to this question has to be yes, at least at some level, given the embeddedness of alcohol and drug use in different sectors of youth culture. However, the question of subgroup trends has not been well documented in the quantitative trends research.

Looking first at *poverty and disadvantage*, what analyses that do exist suggest that as more young people used substances, the differences among socioeconomic groups narrowed (Ramsay and Spiller, 1997; Forsyth and Barnard, 1999; Parker, 2005). Analyses of the Department of Health's SDDU survey in 2006 found income and social class to be unrelated to recent drug taking in school children (Hills and Li, 2007). The British Crime Survey, with an older sample (16-19 years), does find some socioeconomic markers, but again there is a suggestion that these are narrowing. Data addressing an interaction between poverty, disadvantage and some of the particularly problematic substance use behaviours is lacking for the adolescent age group, and this could do with more research focus.

Second, there are questions about whether the trends by *gender* reveal any interesting differences. Over the years of rising substance use, the gender gap (where girls used less) seemed to be closing, but good data on this do not pre-date the 1990s (for example, Parker et al, 1998). The British Crime Survey suggests that drug use by young women now stands at around two thirds of that by young men (Roe and Man, 2006). This relates to all kinds of use, but again the interesting question relates to more problematic behaviour. As we have seen, the Plant re-analysis of HBSC data suggest a particular rise in binge drinking by young women (Plant and Plant, 2006).

Third, we have not so far made any reference to ethnicity, but whether or not the trends vary by *ethnicity* is an important question. Again, good data do not really exist prior to the 1990s, and so drawing conclusions about trends is hard. The British Medical Association has noted that whereas 9 per cent of the White British population are non-drinkers, the comparable proportions for Black Africans and Pakistani/Bangladeshi people are 48 per cent and 90 per cent respectively (BMA, 2008). Other surveys have also usually shown lower rates of drug use among those describing themselves as Asian (Mott and Mirlees-Black, 1995; Parker et al, 1998), but whether the longer-term trends have been different for adolescents from these groups is less clear.

Finally, interesting questions potentially arise concerning subgroups based on participation in *education*. Do different educational tracks have different implications for trends in use of drugs and alcohol? Lower educational attainment and educational dissatisfaction have been found to be related to higher levels of use of cannabis and other drugs (Lynskey and Hall, 2000; Chatterji, 2006) However, results from re-analysis of the British Crime Survey suggest that illicit drug use is most widespread among those who *have* participated in higher education (or who were employed in professional, managerial or technical occupations) (Shiner, 2009); thus 'middle class bohemian youth cultures provided the major growth area for drug use during the mid to late 1960s' (Shiner, 2009, p 72). We should note that the rise in drug use came before the mass participation in higher education, so these patterns might be different now. Also, despite the links between earlier drug use and later drug use, it may be that the meaning, associations and health implications of school-age drug use are different to college student drug use. This also needs more attention.

International trends and comparisons

Are (a) *levels* of alcohol and other substance use and (b) *trends* in use different for young people in the UK to their counterparts in mainland Europe or in other countries around the world? A consensus has developed that British young people are very much more problematic in this regard than those in other countries. Is this true?

International comparison of alcohol use, 1970s-2000s

There are clearly national differences in how drugs are used, and this has particularly been noted for alcohol. In their review of the post-war period, Silbereisen et al (1995) concluded that most countries reflected higher levels of consumption of alcohol than they had in the 1930s, although there was less between-country variation by the 1990s than there had been 50 years previously. Europe was the continent with the highest alcohol consumption. They described some of the cultural differences (as they stood in 1995) as follows:

> The Nordic group (Denmark, Finland, Iceland, Norway, Sweden) has a relatively low level of alcohol consumption, interspersed with binge drinking, and the beverages used are mainly beer and spirits. Latin-Hellenic countries (France, Greece, Italy, Portugal, San Marino, Spain) show

the highest level of per capita consumption, dominated by wine. The Anglo-Germanic group vary somewhat in their levels of consumption, but are similar in their preference for beer. The mixed Germanic-Latin countries (Belgium, Luxembourg, Switzerland) mirror the drinking habits of their neighbours. Finally, the Eastern European group (... Bulgaria, Czechoslovakia, East Germany, Hungary, Poland, USSR) is known for very sporadic drinking of spirits. (Silbereisen et al, 1995, pp 499-500)

International comparative data specifically on alcohol consumption by young people within our age range again only really exist for the last decade of our time period, deriving from the two big international surveys previously mentioned (ESPAD and HBSC), but given that this is a relatively short time span, these data are not very useful for mapping trends. However, they do show that on most measures of consumption, the absolute levels by UK adolescents at all ages (11, 13 and 15) continue to be higher than those in other countries (see, for example, Currie et al, 2004; Hibell et al, 2004). Most countries show some kind of levelling or slight decline in alcohol consumption by young people across this more recent period. As with the UK data evaluated above, it remains the case that without comparative statistics from representative samples of young people in the 1970s, it is impossible to say with confidence how much higher rates are now than they were then, but the consistently higher levels of consumption by UK adolescents are notable.

Looking at our indices of problematic use – early starting, more frequent/heavy use and drunkenness or binging – these more recent data also continue to show higher rates of these behaviours in UK samples. Figure 7.4 shows that, for the period from 1995 to 2007, the UK's 15-year-olds more frequently reported having been drunk before they were 13 years old than all other groupings of countries in the ESPAD study.

Figure 7.5 shows rates of drunkenness for 15-year-olds across this period from 1995 to 2007, again drawing on the ESPAD survey. At all points the UK rates are higher than those for other countries.

Recent indicators thus confirm a continuation in the trend that sees adolescents in the UK getting drunk more often, and from an earlier age, than those in other European countries or in the USA.

Figure 7.4: International trends in self-reported recall of drinking by age 13 or younger, 1995–2007

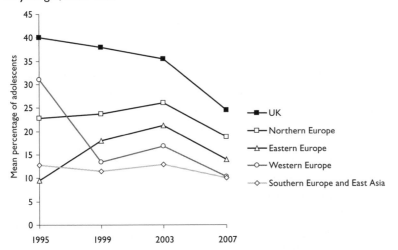

Notes: Data from ESPAD. UK scores are the average scores for samples from England, Wales and Scotland, using United Nations (UN) Statistical Division country classifications (as outlined by Currie et al, 2008). HBSC data not displayed as these are only available for one time point. The standard deviations for each UN division are large.

Sources: See Appendix II at the end of the book for a list of data sources from each survey at different time points

Figure 7.5: International trends in being drunk one or more times as reported at age 15, 1995–2007

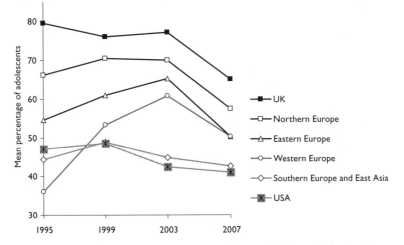

Notes: Data from ESPAD. UK scores are the average scores for samples from England, Wales and Scotland, using UN Statistical Division country classifications (as outlined by Currie et al, 2008).

Sources: See Appendix II at the end of the book for a list of data sources from each survey at different time points

International comparison of drug use, 1970s-2000s

International comparative data on drug use are almost non-existent for the longer-term trends. As Pirkis et al (2003) remind us, we should beware of international cross-national comparisons unless they use standard, uniform approaches. By comparing several different surveys of adolescents from the USA and Australia, they found quite different estimates for prevalence of various drug-related behaviours. However, reviews up to the mid-1990s, covering the decades since the Second World War, reported widespread rises throughout Europe and North America (Silbereisen et al, 1995).

The recent survey data from ESPAD and HBSC are at least consistent in confirming the UK's high levels of illicit drug when compared with other countries in the 1990s and 2000s, at least for the age 15 year group (earlier age groups were not asked the question). Although the data are better than for earlier time periods, they are still fairly restricted and, depending on the question, sometimes only relate to cannabis. In 1995, the UK had the highest reported level of lifetime use of any illicit drug (42 per cent), although by 2003, at 35 per cent, this had fallen to the fifth highest (after the Czech Republic, Switzerland, Ireland and the Isle of Man). The 2007 ESPAD data for cannabis use in the last 30 days show approximately a fifth of 15-year-olds in the UK (and the USA and Canada) saying 'yes' compared with around a tenth of most other countries in Europe. ESPAD also asked 15-year-olds to report on whether they started using at age 13 or younger, and again on these ratings the UK had the highest absolute level.

Thus, the data for long-term international comparisons are not strong, but they suggest steep rises occurred across Europe and North America over the beginning of our period of interest, as well as in the UK. More recent data, collected specifically for international comparative purposes, suggest more varied trend lines in recent years, with some movement up and some down, but the absolute levels on all indicators for UK adolescents remain high. In both the ESPAD and HBSC the samples are intended to be representative (although they are school-based), and whereas there is weighting to adjust back to population estimates in both surveys, there has not been, to our knowledge, any attempt to control for other variables that may influence rates in reporting such as, for example, proportions of the samples living in different family situations or family income level, so it is not clear how much of what looks like national variation is due to variations in demographics and how much relates to something more immeasurable about culture. But, methodological questions aside, it does appear that the UK has a high level of substance abuse among the young, with evidence for an early start as well.

We turn in the next section to an evaluation of the research on links between substance use and mental health problems, as the first part in an attempt to link cohort changes in drug and alcohol use to trends in other measures of well-being for this age group.

Overlap and relationship with mental health outcomes

We know that using substances is associated with a range of poor outcomes. There are short-term risks of intoxication which can impair both motor and cognitive functions and there are long-term risks of regular use that can lead to dependence and addiction. Other outcomes can include problems with employment and the quality of relationships with friends and family (Newbury-Birch et al, 2009). Several of the defining characteristics of the British trends – early onset, higher volume of intake – play an important role in determining whether substance use is likely to become problematic (Gilvarry, 2000; Brook et al, 2002; Odgers et al, 2008). As we have already noted, there is also growing evidence that adolescents may be more vulnerable than adults to the detrimental effects of substances (Spear, 2002).

In this section, we want to look at how these trends in adolescent substance use relate specifically to the trends in mental health problems described at the start of this volume, and to evaluate whether there are causal links between the two. Are the trends in alcohol and drug use part of the explanation of the increase in depression, anxiety and other mental health symptoms that we have described in British adolescents? These questions were a particular focus of Professor Donmall's scoping review for the Changing Adolescence Programme.

They are difficult questions, and the research does not often address them directly. Many reviews do not draw out distinctions between types of substances use and different kinds of mental health problems. We need to be careful that we are not just grouping things together and missing some of the picture in the process. The same problems that we have identified before about age ranges also apply in this section, in that research often treats the adolescent age range as one block, when there is a great deal of difference between being an 11-year-old user, and being one aged 16. In addition, reports of associations tend to be presented in different ways depending on the key index variable – if the interest is in substance use, then the proportions with mental health problems are reported. If the primary interest is in mental health problems, then the proportions are reported the other way around. Few studies look at the issue from both perspectives at the same time.

Are alcohol and drug use in adolescence associated with psychiatric disorder?

There is lots of evidence from large-scale surveys of this age group showing an association between heavy substance use and psychiatric disorder. A large international review reported that some 60 per cent of adolescents who meet a formal diagnosis of substance use disorder (that is, as defined in the widely used *Diagnostic and Statistical Manual*, DSM III-R) have co-occurring psychiatric disorders (Armstrong and Costello, 2002). A comprehensive survey of a representative sample of 11- to 15-year-olds in England, Scotland and Wales found that almost a quarter of those who frequently consumed alcohol had a mental illness using similar international diagnostic criteria (International Classification of Diseases, 10th revision, and DSM-IV; Meltzer et al, 2000). Approximately 50 per cent of heavy cannabis users in this age group had a psychiatric disorder.

These estimates provide a starting point, but we need to scratch below the surface to explore associations separately for the broad groups of problems that might arise (depression and anxiety, conduct disorder and attention deficit hyperactivity disorder [ADHD], and psychosis), and we need to distinguish between formal diagnoses and lower levels of symptomatology. We also need to ask about causality, rather than association.

Does alcohol and substance use lead to depression and anxiety?

There are several reasons to think that heavy use of alcohol and other drugs might cause depression. To start with, drugs like alcohol and cannabis affect the chemistry of the brain, and specifically some of the same chemicals and systems that control mood and anxiety. In adults the National Epidemiologic Survey on Alcohol and Related Conditions in the USA found associations between DSM-IV substance use disorders and independent mood and anxiety disorders that were 'overwhelmingly positive and significant' (Grant et al, 2004, p 807). Particularly in selected samples of high-risk groups, the overlaps seem obvious, with high proportions of heavy substance users reporting depression, anxiety, loneliness, low self-esteem, and so on (Miller and Plant, 2002; Best et al, 2004, 2006). Self-harm and suicides are much more common in people with alcohol problems (Windle et al, 1992; Fombonne, 1998; Kelly et al, 2004).

But is the link causal? Evidence is building to suggest that it is. For example, in one study approximately half of men who drank heavily had depressive symptoms, and if they stopped drinking this proportion dropped to around 6 per cent with a matter of weeks (Brown and Schuckit, 1988). A prospective study of two cohorts of 11- to 12-year-olds and 13- to 14-year-olds in East London found that substance use during the baseline data collection period was associated with higher psychological distress and depression scores during a two-year follow-up after adjusting for prior psychological distress (Clark et al, 2007). Fergusson et al (2009) provided a recent test of the causal links between alcohol abuse and major depression for young people. Using data from the Christchurch Health and Development Study the researchers explored causal pathways from age 17/18 to age 24/25 in a sample of 1,270 young people. At all ages alcohol abuse or dependence was associated with a 1.9 times increased risk of major depression. After controlling for a range of confounding factors there was still a significant prediction from earlier alcohol abuse to later depression, and the authors suggested that alcohol may trigger genetic markers (a gene or specific DNA sequence) that cause an increase in the risk of major depression. Silberg et al (2003) drew similar conclusions from the follow up of a general population twin sample, suggesting a shared genetic liability that led from substance use to later drug use (see also Lynskey et al, 2004). Looking at the neurobiological effects, Brady and Sinha (2005) made some interesting suggestions including the possibility that both psychiatric disorder and substance use might be underpinned by certain prefrontal cortex and frontal context features that predisposes to both.

There are some limitations to this body of research. First, more research has been done on depression than anxiety, so it is less clear what the contribution is to the types of symptoms of anxiety that were described earlier in Chapter Two as being part of the trends in mental health that we were interested in explaining. Second, there are some equivocal findings if we look below the level of serious problems to evidence for links with less frequent substance use. Some large-scale surveys of nationally representative samples have failed to demonstrate a strong association between regular or low level substance use and mental health problems (see, for example, Maxwell et al, 2007; Goodman, 2010), although other general population surveys do show a link (Boys et al, 2003). Third, we do not know whether there is still a direct effect from substance use to depression/anxiety once any shared genetic and environmental liability has been taken into account. It could be that the same liability is causing both problems. In addition, it seems unlikely that changes to genetic or neuropsychological features can explain the time trends changes over the last few decades. But clearly there is sufficient evidence to hypothesise that rising levels of substance misuse may play some part in explaining rising levels of depression and anxiety. We are just not sure yet whether this applies to low level symptomatology as well as to full-blown diagnostic categories of disorder, but it is definitely something that warrants further consideration.

Does substance use lead to conduct disorder and attention deficit hyperactivity disorder?

One of the mental health outcomes that we were interested in was conduct disorder, which had risen in adolescents since the 1970s. Could this be due to increased use of alcohol and other drugs? There are clear associations between behaviour problems such as conduct disorder and ADHD, and with substance use problems (see, for example, Weinberg et al, 1998; White et al, 1999; Wilens, 2004). This is hardly surprising as some of the same behaviours underlie both: risk taking, rule breaking etc. The 1999 UK-wide mental health survey found that a third of 11- to 14-year-olds who used cannabis were identified as having a conduct disorder (Meltzer et al, 2000). The large Scottish school survey SALSUS found that both regular drinking and regular drug use were associated with much increased rates of conduct problems, with stronger associations in 13-year-olds compared to 15-year-olds, and in girls compared to boys (Maxwell et al, 2007). Using a different index of behaviour problems, UK estimates of drug and alcohol use and youth offending support this pattern (Best et al, 2006) – excessive drinking and substance use in 14- to 16-year-olds was linked to a two- to three-fold risk of being involved in all types of delinquent acts including theft, joyriding and contact with the police (see also Richardson and Budd, 2003; Wilson et al, 2006).

Which comes first? Several large-scale studies (mostly not British) have addressed the question in waves across adolescence (see, for example, Measelle et al, 2006; Mason et al, 2007; Roberts et al, 2007). The patterns are not clear; associations across time have been shown with virtually all of the key variables. The most likely explanation seems to be that where there are pre-existing problems or vulnerability to psychiatric symptomatology and behaviour problems, and then the overlayering of substance misuse entrenches these problems, this leads to worse outcomes in both kinds of difficulties (Roberts et al, 2007).

Hayatbakhsh et al (2008) added a test of whether the predictions were different depending on whether the adolescent behaviour was part of a longer-term externalising problem, or adolescence-limited (cf Moffitt, 1993), and concluded that the links between both kinds of anti-social behaviour and problematic drug use at 18 and 26 were both strong (see also Odgers et al, 2008). Patterns were similar in the Dunedin Multidisciplinary Health and Development Study between the age 15 to age 18 sweeps – mental disorder at age 15 predicted elevated cannabis use at age 18, and elevated cannabis at age 18 led to higher risk of mental disorder at age 21 (McGee et al, 2000). In the British Cambridge Study of Delinquent Development, White et al (1999) also concluded that there were associations over time in both directions – substance use led to violence and vice versa, even when controlling for various shared risk factors. The links are perhaps less clear for ADHD on its own, without conduct problems (Pardini et al, 2007; also in the UK, Danckaerts et al, 2000), and the symptoms of ADHD are usually evident long before young people start using drugs.

Rises in alcohol and drug use may thus have made some contribution to increases in conduct disorder although this would be as part of a complicated, bidirectional model where the behaviours share the same causes and reinforce each other, rather than a simple and direct effect. It is possible that rises in conduct disorder have been part of the underlying causes of rises in substance use. This seems to be an issue of shared liability, rather than straightforward causal effect.

Does substance use lead to psychosis?

Strictly speaking, psychosis (schizophrenia and bipolar disorder) is so rare in the adolescent age group that it is unlikely to be driving the overall trends in mental health problems for the age group as a whole. However, whether or not psychosis is caused by substance use has been the target of much discussion, and as such might raise some interesting questions.

The focus has tended to be on the role of cannabis. Although obviously the majority of cannabis users do not develop schizophrenia, and psychosis is rare in this age group, there is evidence that that psychosis is more prevalent in young cannabis users than non–users (Macleod et al, 2004; Henquet et al, 2005). A recent systematic review by Moore et al (2007) concluded that people who used cannabis were at an increased risk of psychosis even after accounting for confounding factors and report evidence for a dose–response relationship, with the greatest psychosis risk observed in young people who used cannabis most frequently. Arseneault et al (2004), in a review of the link between cannabis and psychosis, only identified five robust studies for inclusion, and from these concluded that cannabis use doubled the relative risk for later schizophrenia. This is from a very low baseline, however. It is increasingly clear, from reviews of the evidence on gene and environment interactions, that the risks are substantially greater in those with a pre-existing genetic liability (Henquet et al, 2008). The combination of these genetic risks together with environmental factors such as stress may precipitate the problem, and early use of drugs also increases the risk (Henquet et al, 2008). During adolescence some young people will thus be more at risk than others.

Overall, looking at the evidence for the role of adolescent alcohol and substance use in predicting mental health problems, we have summarised in Box 7.1 the main messages where we feel fairly confident that the balance of evidence suggests these are valid conclusions.

Box 7.1: Summary of findings on the relationship between adolescent substance use and mental health symptoms

- We know that heavy, early and dependent drug use is not good for children. On the basis of what we know about adolescent hormonal and brain development, there are good reasons for hypothesising that no drug use is good for children; however, there are few robust data on the implications of low levels of use in the general population.

- There is good evidence on a causal link between alcohol/substance use and depression and anxiety. This is stronger in relation to full-blown diagnoses of disorder than lower level symptoms. Data specifically on anxiety seem much less available.

- For behaviour problems, on the other hand, the associations are strong across the range of symptoms, present both in general population and in those with full-blown diagnoses. Conduct disorder seems to be the main 'actor' here; the overlap with hyperactivity is usually accounted for once conduct disorder is controlled. Causally, however, the picture is very complicated, suggesting a complex 'ratcheting up' of problems when conduct disorder is associated with substance use, which is then established with further behaviour problems and more psychiatric symptomatology later down the line.

- Data on psychosis is of limited relevance for the general population of adolescents in whom we are interested – psychosis in this age group is extremely rare. However, there is convincing evidence for an independent causal role for cannabis, over and above just exacerbating pre-existing symptoms.

Conclusion

This chapter has set out to investigate the nature of changes in substance use by young people in the UK over the past 50 years, and to set these beside increases in behavioural and mental health problems. In our original research questions, we asked (a) what is the evidence for time trends in patterns of substance use, (b) is there evidence on different trends for subgroups, and (c) what do we know about the implications particularly in relation to mental health outcomes for young people? Our answers to these questions were informed by scoping work undertaken by Professor Donmall's research team.

It is clear from the available evidence that there was a striking and sustained rise in adolescent alcohol and substance use in the UK over the period from the mid-1970s until the early 2000s. Recent levels of almost all indicators remain much higher in the 2000s than they were in the 1970s, although in the last few years there have been some signs that some aspects of these trends are starting to level off. The methodological limitations of the available information make it difficult to quantify the exact magnitude of the increase in prevalence that has occurred since the 1970s. It is easier once the large national surveys start to appear in the 1980s and 1990s, but just concentrating on these data can give the impression of static or declining trends, rather than the more accurate long-term picture of significant long-term rises.

International comparisons show the UK to have a high level of adolescent alcohol consumption and substance use than other countries. It has to be emphasised that reviews in this area often draw on the same information, and this information comes from, essentially, two sources, the HBSC and ESPAD. Widespread media coverage and large numbers of column inches have been given in recent years to international comparisons which are based on analyses of these two international surveys, neither of which have country sample sizes of much over 2,000 young people, both of which draw on school-based samples, and only one of which was specifically designed to look at drug use. The studies are innovative and interesting, but they have limitations in their reach. These may well mask some very meaningful inter- and intra-country variations that might lead us to think rather differently about what was going on for different subgroups of the population. In writing this volume we have frequently been reminded to consider the 'tyranny of the mean' (Linn, 1994), the tendency of averages to conceal more interesting patterns underneath, and given the use of country averages that dominate substance use research and result in cross-sectional 'league tables', this seems to be an area with a particular shortfall in this regard. Our attempts to look at the literature on more interesting subgroups were not particularly rewarded because of the scarcity of good data. This deserves a great deal more attention with a particular eye to time trends.

There has been little in the way of a serious attempt to explain the trends, and by this we mean actually trying to test data as well as suggesting possible causes. There is a body of research on the risk factors for substance use and misuse, arising mainly in the child psychiatric and psychological literatures around the large-scale longitudinal studies on both sides of the Atlantic and in New Zealand. These explain individual risk. There is much less on explanations for group or cohort trends, either upwards or downwards. Many of the possible explanations suggested by Silbereisen et al (1995) still stand as unanswered questions, including changes in income inequality, economic growth and increased affluence, changes in the youth employment market with shift from manufacturing and manual work to service industry and knowledge society (and subsequent decline in occupational opportunities), extension of adolescence period so that markers of adulthood come later than previously and decline in informal social controls.

Others have added to these. Possibilities may also include changes to family formation and to parenting, but this seems unlikely to be a large part of the picture, as discussed in Chapter Five in this volume, on parenting. Changes in drug supply and legal and cost constraints and, relatedly, increased disposable income are, however, likely to play a part in some way, although it is hard to pin down the relevant evidence (Rutter, 2002). The Academy of Medical Sciences (2004) reviewed the evidence on the effects of changes in the law and cost and called for an increase in taxes to restore alcohol pricing to 1970 levels (when it was less affordable), and tighter drink-driving regulations, as well as a review of advertising effects. Changes to shared cultural views on the acceptability substance use might have played a role – cultural mores – but this presents a chicken-and-egg conundrum as these are likely to shift as a result of behaviour, as well as cause a behaviour shift. And, with regard to the recent levelling in the trends, the role of government drugs and alcohol interventions, and the introduction and intensification of public health and well-being interventions in the school curriculum in England may be having a positive impact, although the fact that the levelling is an international trend suggests something not specific to the UK.

Some of the sociological literature is more developed at least with respect to the development of hypotheses, around, for example, changes in licensing laws, changes in youth *mores* and fashions, or changes in drugs trafficking and availability. For example, it has been proposed that drug use is a meaningful, goal-directed behaviour that is linked to other leisure-related activities. With changes to leisure time options and more free time, a youth culture with an emphasis on pubs and night clubs, more people spending time as students at colleges and universities, and increasingly affordable drugs on the market, it is perhaps not surprising that there has been an increase in consumption (Shiner, 2009, p 119). However, these kinds of explanations are more focused on the older adolescent age group rather than on those still in their secondary school years, where the habits seem to be setting in. Operationalising and measuring changes in social contexts and structures is a field in its infancy within the UK, at least in relation to this age group and these kinds of behaviours, but more development on this front would seem very important if we are to understand the reasons behind the trends.

Wherever they have come from, what are the implications of these rises in substance use for this age group? We noted that the substance use literature is rarely focused on the specific developmental aspects of use in adolescence, and that we possibly have to think differently about harm in adolescence, being careful not to make assumptions about similarities with harm in adults. What looks like less harm may still be very damaging. In this context, certain aspects of UK adolescents' patterns of substance use give particular cause for concern, particularly if the long view is taken from the 1970s onwards. Concern especially relates to evidence that UK adolescents (or at least subgroups of them) have a long-term tendency to start using earlier, and use more of, both alcohol and cannabis, than young people in the UK several decades ago, or young people in other countries.

Our review of the relationship between substance use and mental health outcomes indicated preliminary evidence that there may be links between the rising trends in both sets of indicators. It is interesting to note that both have seen a levelling off in the trends in recent years. Interestingly, we found no research that included a direct test of an association between trends in adolescent drug use and psychiatric symptoms at the population level over recent decades in the UK. There was no concrete evidence that trends in substance use had contributed to overall trends in mental health symptoms, but that was largely because this had been untested. There was some evidence, particularly from research on depression, that allowed us to develop a hypothesis that it is possible that increasing alcohol and cannabis use may have contributed in part to increasing depression and anxiety. But as we say, this is untested at the population level.

Several areas for further research seem to present themselves. First, it was clear from our brief look at evidence on trends in notable subgroups that this is where there is a particular lack of data. For example, is alcohol use polarising within the youth population, with general use declining but particular subgroups drinking more? Is there more than one distribution operating? There is more regular and detailed information available from within UK surveys than in the international studies, but they still remain self-report surveys of school children, and without good comparisons and some triangulation of data they do not take us much further forward in understanding what may be unique about the UK situation. They were not designed to look at subgroups and cannot be easily turned to address the more sophisticated questions about sub-trends.

Second, along similar lines, is it possible to do more fine grading of some of the patterns for meaningful groups of young people on different study/work/training/unemployment trajectories, moving on from just using age as a meaningful banding? Have we conflated age with adolescent life stage? Drugs research on the normal population has tended to come originally from sociology and criminology. As a result, much of it suffers from a lack of consideration of developmental changes occurring within adolescence – to a developmentalist with an eye to social structures, lumping together 16- to 25-year-olds seems to waste interesting data and gives rise to potentially misleading conclusions about adolescent lives. The lives of 16- to 18-year-olds in the UK are now more like those of 11- to 15-year-olds (see the time use in Chapter Four); those of university students, casual workers and the unemployed (making up the bulk of those aged 19-25) are quite different. The numbers of people on these different tracks has shifted considerably in the last 30 years. On the other hand, the big, repeated, quantitative surveys tend to focus mostly on secondary school-aged children and do not include the 16-18 age group and so tell us little about the group for whom we think there may have been most social change. There are several problems as a result. One is a tendency to generalise from these school-based surveys to the lives of all adolescents including those aged 16 and above who might be in quite different circumstances. A focus more on young people's social context (comprehensive school? sixth form college? unemployed? modern apprenticeship?) may be more informative than a focus on their chronological age in understanding trends in substance use.

Third, there seems to be little that we have discovered that looks at the trends for alcohol and drug use in relation to each other. Surveys consider both, but consider them separately, which is probably not how it feels to young people in the 'real world'. There is work, of course, on drugs 'careers', and on whether alcohol acts as a gateway to use of other substances. There is work on sequencing of substance use. But as far as we know this kind of work has not been extended to look at how the cohort trends in the use of substances interact, intersect and possibly diverge. For example, there has been some discussion about the changes in the licensing laws in the UK which have lifted many of the restrictions that previously restricted the availability of alcohol (BBPA, 2005). Is this a reason why the trends in alcohol are a bit different to those of cannabis use? Do the trends for young women to continue to binge drink more than (a) they used to and (b) their compatriots in mainland Europe bear any relation to what these same young women are doing with other substances?

Fourth, should we be moving beyond measures of frequency of consumption to indicators of problems that are especially tailored for the adolescent age group? Over-reliance on a measure of alcohol use based solely on consumption levels may be missing some of the implications for the lives of young people. Along these lines, a RAND study in the late 1990s showed that the quantity–frequency index usually used in surveys may in fact under-estimate potentially damaging levels of use. Rates of problems from drinking (missing school, feeling really sick, being in a fight, getting arrested), and high-risk drinking (combining alcohol and drugs, getting drunk) and any misuse affected more children than were given a 'high' rating on frequency–consumption alone (Ellickson et al, 1996). We could add, perhaps, age of first unsupervised drinking episode. Even a little may thus be problematic to some children in some circumstances. What do we know about these kinds of indices for UK young people?

Fifth, should research be thinking in new ways about what alcohol and drug use *mean* to young people, and how this has changed? Why do they use in the way that they do? As Plant and Plant note (2006, p 35), 'the great majority of teenagers expected that their drinking would be enjoyable, enhancing their leisure and their lives'. Hays and Ellickson (1996) reported that measures of alcohol use and misuse were more strongly associated with social activities such as dating and partying than with delinquent and related behaviours such as theft, burglary and running away from home. The opposite was true of drug use. Some attempts have been made since the peak of consumption in the mid-1990s to speculate in particular about how alcohol consumerism (as opposed to absolute levels of consumption) has changed. Kevin Brain's provocative and interesting paper for the Institute of Alcohol Studies in 2002 attempted to outline contemporary youth drinking patterns, based on an understanding of patterns in the big surveys, and results from qualitative interviews with children drinking on the street. In addition he provided some frankly terrifying quotations from people in the drinks industry illustrating how they tried to make alcohol more appealing to children, concluding that 'the brewing industry had understood and sought to exploit and encourage the fact that young people were drinking alcohol in more consumerist ways than their predecessors' (Brain, 2002, p 7).

Brain distinguished between young drinkers who drank to excess and expected some trouble as a result, but who did this as calculating hedonists (who could easily stop during the week to do their homework), and those who had dropped out of the structures that bounded behaviour in this way. This latter group lacked educational success, careers and ways of constructing meaningful identities, until 'the drinking event becomes inseparable from a general lifestyle of street consumption and a quest for excitement' (Brain, 2002, p 10), and takes over as a way of constructing an identity in its own right. This is part of a small literature exploring these sorts of issues and one that might generate some interesting and nuanced hypotheses that could potentially be tested empirically.

Terry Honess and colleagues undertook a similar qualitative study, but of school children, in *The social contexts of underage drinking*, for the Home Office in 2000, exploring the ways in which alcohol is used for a purpose (relaxation, bonding), and the role of local culture in determining young people's views about alcohol consumption even if they themselves did not drink (Honess et al, 2000). In 2005, the Trust for the Study of Adolescence published results from 64 interviews on motives for underage risky drinking, suggesting that first drunkenness was now more likely to be unsupervised, and potentially thus more harmful, than previously (Coleman and Cater, 2005). Fiona Measham has also written in this area on binge drinking and 'the new culture of intoxication' (see, for example, Measham et al, 2001; Measham, 2004, 2008). These types of discussions about changes in the way in which young people are directly (by family, peers and the drinks industry) and indirectly (although complicated societal norms and structures) encouraged to consume alcohol and drugs are more compelling than older debates over 'normalisation' or deviant subcultures. This is all, of course, about how drug use has changed and about what might lie behind recent trends. It does not directly relate to the question about whether trends in drug use might be behind trends in depression, anxiety or conduct disorder. However, one can see that some hypotheses could be generated from some of this material, if we think about indirect links.

Finally, a number of surveys and studies assert that family attitudes towards drinking are an important factor that moderates the probability of adolescent alcohol use occurring. They also suggest that there are other changes in the context of young people's drinking as they grow older. Younger drinkers are more likely to drink at home and with parents or other family members, where there are, presumably, opportunities for supervision. Older teenagers are more likely to drink with friends and in unsupervised settings away from home, such as at parties, friends' houses or outdoors. But again, these considerations are not extended to cohort change. Did this aspect of the context of adolescent substance use change in the 1980s and early 1990s? The proportion of adults who drank went up over this time, and is also showing a levelling off, but binge drinking among adult women increased (Smith and Foxcroft, 2009[1]). Are the same factors causing both trends, or are teenage drinking trends a consequence of changes in adult behaviours?

Thus, to sum up, the trends are looking reasonably clear at the broad, average level for those in their mid-teens. There is no doubt that one of the main social changes of the last 30 years has been the increase in alcohol and other drug use by this age group. There continue to be especially high rates in the UK of particularly worrying indicators such as starting younger, and consuming more heavily. But far more work needs to be done to dig below this surface to more interesting sub-trends, and more thinking needs to be done about what is driving these changes.

As Plant and Plant ask, 'Is this just a moral panic?' (2006, p 27), by which they mean, are we regarding these trends as overly deviant or menacing? The answer from our review of the literature would seem to be no, it is not just a moral panic, it is a real problem. Increased substance use over recent decades may well explain a proportion of the trends in anxiety and depression, although we have no hard and fast data to support this. The latter may also explain the former. It is likely that the two things are wrapped up together. The trends are likely also to relate to time use, to changes in patterns of peer group socialisation, and perhaps to the development of an extended and expanded school/college/student culture that has a different emphasis from working youth culture in the 1960s and 1970s. Drug use is both a social change in itself, and also a reflection of other more fundamental social changes.

Note

[1] 'For women the overall level of binge drinking has almost doubled from 8 per cent in 1998 to 15 per cent in 2006, with the increase most pronounced in women aged 25 years and older' (Plant and Plant, 2006, p 6).

EIGHT

Some thoughts on the broader context: neighbourhoods and peers

Ann Hagell, Sarah Curtis, Shari Daya, Yasmin Khatib, Rachel Pain, Catherine Rothon, Stephen Stansfeld and Sara Fuller

Introduction

In this section, we briefly raise three topics that are part of the broader context of adolescent development, specifically with a view to establishing what we know about their importance in adolescent mental health outcomes and also – as with the other chapters in this volume – with a view to assessing evidence for social change in these areas over recent decades. Our aim here, as with the other chapters in this volume, was to highlight key findings and identify interesting avenues for further research, although in this instance we have chosen to present brief introductions to these topics with pointers to fruitful areas for future research, rather than full summaries of these complex research topics. We identify the key challenges, and also the interesting new developments in these fields that will undoubtedly keep them at the forefront of work on young people's well-being in coming years.

Young people spend a great deal of time in their neighbourhoods, possibly more than anyone else except perhaps mothers with young children. Young people often go to school locally, and spend a great deal of time unsupervised in their local areas. How do neighbourhoods affect young people's well-being? There may be direct effects, and there may also be indirect effects that are mediated through families and schools. Given the different ways in which they spend time in their local area, we cannot assume that the demonstration of neighbourhood effects (or lack of demonstration) with adult samples means the same thing in adolescent samples. We have to be careful about generalising from any other age group. Taken together, this means taking the social structure outside the family seriously, and looking for measures of its importance specifically for young people.

As part of the Changing Adolescence Programme, a team led by Professor Sarah Curtis at Durham University undertook a scoping review of research on neighbourhood effects on adolescent mental health for the Nuffield Foundation, which has informed the first part of this chapter in particular. We draw partly on the studies identified in that review, and also on other work, in order to highlight some of the key findings. There are clear overlaps with the material covered in the time use review, substance use review and the schools review, and we return later to the need to link these areas.

Neighbourhoods and adolescent mental health

Defining neighbourhoods

Neighbourhoods is a term that can mean different things to different disciplines, but in this context we mean the social and geographical network of local streets, houses, shops, schools and parks that young people might regard as their 'territory'. Neighbourhoods are sometimes called 'areas' or 'places of residence', or just 'spaces', but 'neighbourhood' suggests something more than geographical area, indicating an area with some cohesion and boundaries that distinguish it from other neighbourhoods (Cummins et al, 2007). However, it suggests something less socially coherent (and more geographically delineated) than 'communities'. It is difficult to define neighbourhood (a) in a way that makes sense given the way people lead their lives, and (b) in a way that is measurable. The two are not always aligned. It is relatively easy to say that neighbourhood is the sum total of various characteristics of the social and physical environment, but much less easy to give a functional definition that includes how children *use* places. Definitions often arise from administrative boundaries, such as the areas set in various population censuses, but these boundaries often need some kind of local confirmation of validity for the people living in them if they are going to be meaningful in social research terms.

Building on this, in their review Curtis et al drew attention to the relevance of research on 'children's geographies', representing a way of looking at daily use of space, which may be relevant for understanding neighbourhood effects. Adolescents *appropriate* parts of public space, so that they have domains that are known to their group and where they can meet and share time, outside adult control, providing settings for unstructured and structured activities. Qualitative and ethnographic studies have explored how they do this in environments such as the Rhonda in South Wales (Skelton, 2000), Belfast (Leonard, 2010) and suburban California (Childress, 2004).

We need to note at the outset that one key issue is that, despite some UK based research, much of the neighbourhood and peers literature is drawn from the USA. This raises real questions of generalisability: North American neighbourhoods are generally far less heterogeneous than those in the UK. We have very few areas that are anything like as ethnically segregated as African–American ghettos in the USA, for example (Peach, 2010). There are also very different urban transport systems and the way that people use their local space is likely to be different. So one of the underlying themes of this chapter is how little we know about UK neighbourhoods and their effects on adolescents, as there are reasons to think that analyses from the USA may not be accurate representations of the situation in the UK.

Ways of thinking about the role of neighbourhoods

In a recent review, Leventhal et al (2009) provided a useful summary of the main ways of operationalising the various components of the overall construct of 'neighbourhood'. They clarify a difference between (a) neighbourhood *structure*, which relates to, for example, sociodemographic features such as poverty, unemployment rates and 'race' demographics, and (b) neighbourhood *processes*, which refer to the things that go on within neighbourhoods such as education, healthcare, recreation and issues of social norms and social control together with signs of disorder and decay. Research has generally focused on the effects of these two broad domains on physical health, academic achievement, and on anti-social behaviour (including crime) and, to a lesser extent, on mental health outcomes.

In a similar way, in their research review for the Foundation, Curtis et al (2004) suggested an overarching set of three themes relating to the material, social and 'stressful events' aspects of neighbourhood, which partly map on to the components suggested by Leventhal et al (2009). We look at each of these in brief.

Material aspects of neighbourhoods (partly including what Leventhal et al, 2009, called 'structure') include the effects of local poverty and poor quality environments. A number of studies confirm that measures of disadvantage map onto measures of children's emotional and conduct problems (see, for example, Dubow et al, 1997; Leventhal and Brooks-Gunn, 2000; Beyers et al, 2001; Curtis et al, 2004; Boardman and Saint Ong, 2005; Dupere et al, 2009). Xue et al (2005) focused particularly on the associations between neighbourhood residence and problems of depression, anxiety and withdrawal, using the large Project on Human Development in Chicago Neighbourhoods. The percentages of children (up to the age of 11) scoring over the cut-off on the Child Behaviour Checklist were 21.5 per cent in poor neighbourhoods, 18.3 per cent in medium socioeconomic status neighbourhoods and 11.5 per cent in high socioeconomic status neighbourhoods. By 'material aspects', researchers generally mean amounts of garbage, graffiti, public drinking, public drug use or broken windows and abandoned buildings in the area (see, for example, Sampson and Raudenbush, 2004; Fagg et al, 2006). The physical quality of environments is part and parcel of poverty and material disadvantage, and may have an individual contribution to mental health outcomes; this might include, for example, factory emissions, lead pollution, housing quality, noise and crowding (see, for example, Evans, 2004; Stansfeld et al, 2005; Clark and Uzzell, 2006).

But is neighbourhood poverty just a proxy for individual poverty? The two are clearly linked in complicated ways that go beyond individual disadvantage; families make up neighbourhoods and neighbourhoods attract different types of families. In addition, there is good evidence that families translate the effects of outside poverty into impacts on individuals and are part of the causal chain (Conger et al, 1994). Some North American studies have concluded that there is an association between material poverty and adolescent mental health that is independent of family effects, but others (including UK studies) have either not addressed the question or have found different patterns (see, for example, Fagg et al, 2006, 2008).

Studies of adolescents who have moved out of poor areas may help to untangle the selection effects (the issue about certain groups of people being attracted into certain neighbourhoods), and Box 8.1 summarises two of the best known of these quasi-experiments. There is some evidence that moving from very poor areas to less deprived neighbourhoods is associated with better mental health, and, conversely, that there may be a cumulative negative effect of staying in deprived settings. Some studies have shown less effect in older youth (Leventhal and Brooks-Gunn, 2003). However, there is more going on here than simply removal from poverty; for example, moving itself may be a separate risk factor for continuing problems for older youth (Fauth et al, 2005), or it may be the severance or continuity of links with 'influential' peer groups that is the issue rather than geographical area. The picture is complicated and, to date, not terribly clear (Jackson et al, 2009). Leventhal et al (2005, p 933) concluded that 'From a policy point of view, the complexity of enhancing low-income minority children's educational outcomes is underscored by the multiple dynamics involved – family, neighbourhood, housing and school'.

Box 8.1: Experiments in moving adolescents out of poor neighbourhoods

Over the last 10 years, research teams from Columbia University and Johns Hopkins Bloomberg School of Public Health in the USA have recorded the results of two natural experiments on the effects of moving out of poor neighbourhoods. The results have been mixed, reflecting the complexity of the issues involved.

The Yonkers Project: low-income black and Latino families, including 147 youth aged 8-18, living in poor and segregated neighbourhoods, were selected by lottery to move to middle-class, predominantly white neighbourhoods. For the younger children the effects were positive – less victimisation, disorder and access to illegal drugs. For those aged 16-18, however, there were more problems *after* the move (Fauth et al, 2005).

Moving to Opportunity (MTO): initiated by the USA Department of Housing and Urban Development in 1994, this randomised controlled trial compared families from high-poverty areas who were moved into private housing in less poor neighbourhoods with families who did not move. Five sites were included: Baltimore, Boston, Chicago, Los Angeles and New York City. Analyses of the New York City results showed programme effects on educational outcomes at 2.5 years, but these were not sustained for youths aged 14-20 years at the five-year follow-up (Leventhal and Brooks-Gunn, 2003; Leventhal et al, 2005).

Despite the difficulties of demonstrating positive benefits for moving, there are still clearly associations between material disadvantage and youth outcomes that need explaining. Apart from family poverty and direct effects of poor physical environments, what else might be driving the link? Other suggested mediators have included peer group factors (development of negative attitudes and behaviour arising from the lack of care of the local environment); restricted employment (and thus restricted opportunities for developing self-esteem and sense of purpose); lack of resources that support health promotion (such as leisure centres); residential instability as a result of people leaving poor areas; or stigma effects.

The second aspect that Curtis et al's review for the Foundation highlighted as important concerned the *social aspects of neighbourhood* (what Leventhal et al, 2009, call 'processes'), the importance of which had already started to emerge above. In particular, social capital and social fragmentation have been the focus. Social capital generally refers to the value of social networks – the social obligations and bonds that shape our relationships with others, incorporating shared norms and values. Social fragmentation can be conceptualised as the other side of the coin – a *lack* of social networks, measured by, for example, high levels of social mobility, privately rented households, single-person households and numbers of unmarried people (see, for example, Allardyce et al, 2005), all contributing to reduced social capital.

Evidence is accumulating on the importance of these aspects of neighbourhood life. For example, there are correlations between various measures of social capital and behaviour problems and crime rates (Sampson et al, 1997, 2002; Fazel and Stein, 2002), and between social fragmentation and hospital admissions for psychosis (Allardyce et al, 2005), even after controlling for deprivation and urban/rural status, although not all of these studies focused on adolescents. Aneshensel and Sucoff (1996) found lower levels of depression and anxiety for young people living in areas where people knew their neighbours. However, Curtis et al's review suggested that social capital is less well conceptualised as it relates to children and young people (see, for example, Morrow, 2000), and that it is very sensitive to the differences in neighbourhood features and meanings between the USA and the UK, resulting in problems of generalisation, as mentioned above. In addition, high levels of social capital may not always be a positive feature, if they are provided by strong bonds between for example, youth gang members. In this case they may act as a barrier to social inclusion in the wider community, facilitate crime and divide communities.

The final aspect of neighbourhoods suggested by Curtis et al's review as potentially important was the extent of *stressful events* experienced in the area. Children in poor neighbourhoods witness more violence than other children (Richters and Martinez, 1993). In this context, Aneshensel and Sucoff (1996) describe what they term 'ambient hazards' such as crime, shootings, property damage, drug dealing and police harassment. Self-report of these events were correlated with mental health outcomes including anxiety, depression and conduct disorder (see also Margolin and Gordis, 2000; Sampson et al, 2002; Clark and Uzzell, 2006; Fowler et al, 2009). There is a particular strand of research on victimisation, and reasonable evidence that being a victim is associated with depression (see, for example, Kilpatrick et al, 2003; Buckner et al, 2004; Fitzpatrick et al, 2005), anger and anxiety (Singer et al, 1995), aggression (Schwartz et al, 1998) and conduct disorder (McCabe et al, 2005). A significant part of the victimisation considered here takes the form of bullying by peers and may be influenced by conditions in schools as well as the wider neighbourhood.

However, in studies that look at these relationships at one point in time, it is difficult to establish what comes first: psychological disorders or stressful experiences. Sweeting et al (2006) commented on the fact that those with poorer mental health will be more at risk from community stressful events and, again, there is more research on younger children than adolescents. In a similar vein, some literature now suggests that those with common mental disorders are also more likely to be bullies (see, for example, van Hoof et al, 2008; Sourander et al, 2009; Fitzpatrick et al, 2010). One explanation for this might be that post-traumatic stress arising from exposure to violence leads to bullying behaviour (Ruchkin et al, 2007). There is clearly much more work to be done to sort out the mechanisms underlying the impacts of stressful events.

Issues raised by neighbourhood research

Thus, the Curtis review and other evidence in this area have demonstrated that the quality of neighbourhoods as rated by social cohesion and support, better resources and fewer stressful events, is associated with lower levels of adolescent internalising and externalising problems. The associations might be direct, but might also be mediated by family, peers and school.

However, there are some methodological issues raised that still pose some challenges for understanding what is going on in these studies. First, very few studies tackle the importance of the length of time that children are exposed to different types of neighbourhoods (Timberlake, 2003), and so we know less about the importance or otherwise of cumulative effects as opposed to experiences at, for example, specific turning points in adolescence, yet timing and 'dose' are likely to be very important (Wheaton and Clarke, 2003). Second, it is sometimes hard to tell exactly what it is about neighbourhoods that may matter: in the British RELACHS study (Fagg et al, 2006), neighbourhood differences in adolescents' mental health were not accounted for by variables measuring area poverty, social disorder or fragmentation. It was not clear *what* was generating the effect in this instance and this may be because the right things are not yet being measured. However, this is an area of research witnessing the development of increasingly sophisticated ways of analysing data at different levels of effect – untangling neighbourhood effects requires multilevel analysis of individual-level data nested within different neighbourhoods, and this work is promising.

Third, as we have noted, people may choose to move in and out of areas. This has been variously referred to as migration and immigration, selection effects and social drift. In particular, family selection effects into and out of neighbourhoods is a problem for conceptualising neighbourhood effects and for understanding causal chains, and this poses one of the largest challenges in this literature: if parents are worried about the effect their neighbourhood may have on their children, they may seek to move. This is, of course, a constrained choice: not everyone can move. But it does mean that over time neighbourhoods may change and reflect social change that has occurred precisely because parents were worried, and thus studies of people left behind might misrepresent the 'effect'. The studies that have created an opportunity to move have shown mixed results suggesting something quite complicated is going on here. Indeed, Sampson (2008) has suggested 'reconceptualising selection bias as a fundamental social process worthy of study in its own right rather than a statistical nuisance' (p 189).

Fourth, and related to the point above, another challenge to our ability to untangle causality relates to the overreliance on 'cross-sectional' designs (using information collected at one point of time) where the individual is the unit of analysis. As a result, neighbourhood processes are not well understood, nor are the objective features of neighbourhoods (rather than subjective perceptions). Yet some of the most innovative methods of data collection are being developed in some aspects of neighbourhoods research, and we hope that these will grow to have a longitudinal and repeated element in the future so that we can track change. Descriptions of Sampson and Raudenbush's study of data collection in Chicago neighbourhoods illustrate this (Sampson and Raudenbush, 1999), employing what they term 'systematic social observation', involving the videotaping and coding of various aspects of the social and physical environment. The main point is that multimethod assessments from different sources (over and above the family or individual of interest) must be attempted in order to get objective ratings of both local resources and local neighbourhood processes. In their review, Curtis et al drew attention to the use of trained observers to record neighbourhood features, or participatory photographic techniques that involve researchers or neighbourhood residents recording the environment. Electronic positioning devices may also be useful in recording how people are using space.

Fifth, there are very few studies that have specifically tested associations between neighbourhood poverty and children's mental health in the UK context, despite the evidence that suggests this would be a useful avenue to pursue. Also, effects will undoubtedly be different on different segments of society. As Sampson (2008) points out, the sample in the MTO study represented only about 5 per cent of the general population – the most deprived – and that generalising from this even within the USA might be unwise.

Finally, as with other topics in this volume, effects tend to be small, although they are larger in experimentally controlled studies where families were randomly assigned to different kinds of neighbourhoods (Leventhal and Brooks-Gunn, 2003). However, virtually all 'real world' 'manipulability' social changes show modest effects, and much of the interest may be in the additive and multiplicative effects they have with other factors such as family effects. For example, there is a growing body of research on the 'buffering' effects of family in difficult neighbourhoods. The chapter in this volume on parenting (Chapter Five) suggested that single parents in poor neighbourhoods may in fact be supervising their children more than their counterparts in safer areas, and may have moved over time to being more supervisory because of a sense of greater dangers to the children (whether these are real or not).

Have young people's neighbourhood experiences changed over recent decades?

The previous section discussed ways in which neighbourhood characteristics might be important for young people and their mental health, and summarised what we know, much of it from the USA. But in our search for ways that young people's lives might have changed over the past 30 years to bring about the large changes to adolescent well-being that sparked this inquiry, we need to consider time trends, and whether neighbourhoods have changed in ways that might make them a plausible cause, at least in part, for the time trends we observed in anxiety, depression and conduct disorders. How much neighbourhood change has there been? Have these been changes that might be less good for young people? Have the uses of spaces changed over time? Are there differences in relation to gender and socioeconomic status?

Curtis et al's review concluded that there were no studies that were concerned with area poverty in the UK and adolescent mental health which were repeated in similar areas, but at different points in time, with different generational cohorts of young people. Few studies date back before 1990, and there is not even much indirect evidence of longer-term trends. However, as we noted, there is a growing interest in 'children's geographies', describing how children use place on a day-to-day basis, and in the extent and range of children's autonomy in their local geographical area – how far they are allowed to roam (see, for example, Mackett et al, 2007). Some of this work has looked at social change in these aspects. It is clear that parents in the UK are now less likely to let younger children go out and about on their own than they used to, and that children's exposure to the outside world is mediated by adults who accompany them everywhere during the primary school years (see, for example, Hillman, 2006). Autonomy does come, but in a rush with the transfer to secondary school, when it becomes unfeasible for parents to carry on protecting to the same degree and children often experience a 'crash course' in managing journeys on public transport on their own at this point. These shifts do represent change in how young people interact with and learn from their local neighbourhoods, but the implications for their adjustment are not clear.

Have the neighbourhoods themselves changed? If key characteristics of neighbourhoods themselves have changed this might also be important for adolescent mental health. For example, Shaw et al (1999) and Dorling et al (2007) have demonstrated increasing inequalities in local economic conditions across England in recent decades. Area disparities in household income, in numbers of people claiming Jobseeker's Allowance, and in housing wealth have increased. Exeter et al (2011) showed that in Scotland the increasing gap between richer and poor areas was accompanied by a growing disparity in general (all age) mortality, and that while in most areas mortality has fallen over time, in the most deprived areas it actually increased. Such growing geographical disparities in the social determinants of health at local level have not so far been linked to trends in mental health of adolescents, but future research could usefully address this issue.

Although there are good reasons for thinking neighbourhoods are important, albeit with a small contribution to the overall effect (but that goes for most social factors), there is no evidence that experiences have changed. That is not to say that there have not been changes; it just reflects the limitations of the research.

The role of peers in neighbourhood effects

Peers and friendship groups might provide an important mediating link between neighbourhoods and children's mental health. The peers with whom young people associate are affected by where they live, and the prevalence of deviant peer groups may be higher in some more disadvantaged areas (Fauth et al, 2005). This is not a review of the role of peer groups in adolescent developmental outcomes (see, for example, Bradford Brown and Larson, 2009), because the literature linking adolescent peer relations to individual psychosocial adjustment is huge, and includes research on bullying and victimisation. What we intend to do here is raise some useful questions that relate directly to the neighbourhood issues.

As Levanthal et al describe in their review of neighbourhood effects (2009), peer group effects have generally been conceptualised and researched as being negative, related to the enhancement of risky behaviour when community norms and institutions are weak. From the literature, the impression is that they may be more salient in more disadvantaged neighbourhoods, although this may be as much a reflection of the fact that less research has been focused on their positive contributions in other settings. One way in which their negative and mediating effect has been explored is through the role of gangs. For example, Bellair and McNulty analysed data from the USA National longitudinal Survey of Youth in conjunction with neighbourhood data from the USA Census, and concluded that involvement in violence was higher for those involved in gangs and highest for those in gangs dealing in drugs. Neighbourhood disadvantage exacerbated the associations (Bellair and McNulty, 2009). Qualitative and quantitative work has shown how enmeshed gangs are with neighbourhood geography and identity, and that there are potential effects on children in the area who are not members, as well as those who are (see, for example, Bannister and Fraser, 2008; Bellair and McNulty, 2009).

But in the UK gangs in the formal North American sense are much rarer, and not widely applicable to the broader group of young people that this research programme has focused on, perhaps with the exception of some inner-city areas. Robust research on British adolescent involvement in gangs is not extensive. Evidence from the Edinburgh Study of Youth Transitions and Crime (ESYTC) concluded that around 5 per cent of 17-year-olds said they were part of a gang, and that this was associated with living in deprived neighbourhoods (Smith and Bradshaw, 2005), although definitions of 'gang' clearly varied from loose associations to more formal groups. A similar statistic (around 6 per cent of 10- to 19-year-olds) was reported in the UK Offending, Crime and Justice Survey (Roe and Ashe, 2008). It is clear, however, from USA research and the ESYTC that involvement in delinquent gangs predisposes to changes in criminal activity; David Smith (2010) reviewed the evidence as part of the Independent Commission on Youth Crime and Anti-social Behaviour (also funded by the Nuffield

Foundation), and concluded that gangs were an important factor in exacerbating offending behaviour.

The key question from our point of view is, is there any evidence for social change in peer group composition? Do British young people spend more time with their own age group than they used to? Are they more likely than in the past to have interactions with gangs? Are the contexts in which they mix the same as they have always been, or have they changed alongside the shifts to elongation of education and prolongation of entry to the workforce? Do they do different things with their peers? Indeed, the research on activity patterns and structured and unstructured activities, and the elongation of adolescence and the years spent studying, would suggest that time spent with peers *is* likely to have changed in meaningful ways. It is also possible that the time spent with adults – informal socialisation in the workplace, for example – may also have changed. However, there are no repeated studies of these kinds of peer contacts for this age group that we are aware of in the UK. In addition, we need more UK studies for different groups of young people, from different socioeconomic groups and on different educational tracks.

Despite the lack of trend data, this is an area showing promise of methodological advances. Social network analyses, for example, although an old idea, are experiencing resurgence because of the possibilities of using more sophisticated computer simulations and models to explore their extent and meaning (Fleisher, 2005). But overall we are left with the impression that changes over time in aspects of peer group socialisation for mid-adolescents is a somewhat neglected research area.

Conclusion

The point of this section was to find out what research there might be on how broader social structures and environments provide shape for everyday life for young people, routineising and organising social constraints and behaviours, and providing spatial constraints. Our concern here was with community-level social processes. We asked if there was research that would tighten up our conceptual thinking in this area, helping to produce more sophisticated models of how the broader social context shapes adolescent experiences in ways that may or may not be positive. We drew on Curtis et al's review, funded as part of the Foundation's Changing Adolescence Programme, which covered some of this ground.

What we found was that there was evidence on cross-sectional associations, particularly between structural aspects of neighbourhood (indicators of poverty, restriction of resources) and certain outcomes such as behaviour problems, but that the problem of 'selective' movement between areas had not been conquered. Important aspects of peer group relations are likely to have an effect on adolescent outcomes, but there is no time trend information available for the UK that has enough detail and power to allow us to conclude that these patterns have changed in recent decades. We found that there is a tendency to focus on the potentially negative outcomes in neighbourhood research rather than taking a rounded view. We also found a tendency in some of the literature to discuss young people or adolescents as if they were all of the same age, when the meaning of some of the same social contexts will be quite different for an 11-year-old versus an 18-year-old. We hope that one of the contributions of this programme of work will be to encourage a more nuanced discussion about young people so that we do not expect too much of 11-year-olds and not enough of 18-year-olds, recognising that they have different needs even if they are all in education. With the exception of a few longitudinal studies, many of these from outside the UK, the research reviewed does not allow us to establish how much of the 'effect' on mental health of neighbourhood conditions is already established in childhood, before children reach adolescence.

Findings on neighbourhood factors and social capital effects need to be taken alongside findings on school-level effects and research on out-of-school activities, both of which have been discussed elsewhere in this volume, but which are rarely brought together. Both schools and out-of-school activities are a key part of the lives of adolescents in their communities, whether they spend much time in them or not – getting to and from school, hanging out in the neighbourhood with people from school, learning about out-of-school events from other school peers are all part of the local life for people in this age group. In much of the UK's cities and suburbs, a whole part of adolescent life is lived on local buses on the way to and from all these various neighbourhood activities. Yet work on these topics tends to be taken in different disciplinary strands.

Questions remain, of course, about the extent to which the community and overall social environment can be changed or affected by policy. We have not addressed this, as establishing the main research messages seemed an important first step before jumping ahead to policy. However, it is worth saying that there are very few examples of actually

NINE

Reflections and implications

Ann Hagell and Sharon Witherspoon

The chapters in this volume summarise and integrate the results from a series of research reviews funded by the Nuffield Foundation in the late 2000s, with a view to shedding light on what we do and what we do not know about some key changes in the lives of young people over the last three decades in the UK, and the relevance of these changes for symptoms of mental health. The work has brought together a range of topics that are not normally considered in the round. It aimed to test what we knew in the way of substantive findings across these topics, and also to set an agenda for further research.

It is not easy to chart a clear line through the various results and non-results that we uncovered. We want to make some general points, and highlight some specific implications arising from particular topic reviews. Some counter-intuitive facts are interesting in their own right. There is, however, a need to remember what we can and cannot say with these kinds of data. First, the extent of information available was, we found, often surprisingly limited, even at the basic descriptive level. This was itself an interesting finding, given the strident assertions in the general media and by various stakeholders about how things have changed for young people. Second, although we started with work showing clear time trends in adolescent mental health, it seems clear that the implications may be different for different groups of adolescents. Yet very little work in our selected topics focused on group comparisons, showing how different subgroups of young people diverge in their experiences. In this chapter, then, we reflect on some of the broader implications of the work as a whole for our thinking on social structures and young people's everyday experiences, given these two limitations. Of course more research is needed, as all researchers almost invariably conclude, and this chapter will make some concrete suggestions about where we need to know more. But we also think that some issues are clear enough to warrant some substantive observations, or at the very least some hypotheses that might usefully inform public discussion. We have tried to be clear where these are more or less firmly founded.

Our starting point

Stephan Collishaw's tracking (in Chapter Two) of emotional and behavioural problems of young people in their mid-teens demonstrated at the outset that rates of these remain at historically high levels. These long-term trends do represent grounds for concern, despite the evidence of recent levelling out. In particular, Collishaw drew attention to increases in common emotional problems such as anxiety, worry and depression, and non-violent behaviour problems, such as lying and stealing, noting that these increases were not just artefacts of changes in how we measure these things. That these symptoms had actually increased in the UK was the starting point for our concern for understanding why, and what, this might mean.

We should of course note that this does not require a moral panic, even in the face of the current concern about the riots in England of the summer of 2011, which happened as the final draft of this book was being completed. For example, the proportions of young people aged 15-16 who were reported by their parents to be generally worried increased between 1986 and 2006 from 5 to 9 per cent in boys and from 7 to 12 per cent in girls, and the proportions with irritable moods went from 10 to 14 per cent in boys and from 12 to 17 per cent in girls (Collishaw et al, 2010). Overall, only a relatively small proportion – perhaps one or two out of ten – of all young people have potentially diagnosable mental health symptoms at any given time, with much of the variation due to the different measures being used. But the important points are that whether the diagnoses are more or less formal, represent individual symptoms or complex syndromes, or are based on different survey measures, the proportions are higher than they used to be and represent a fair number of young people who have had a variety of problems. The most likely explanation for such long-term secular trends is social change. Our interest was in the proportion of young people who may be particularly vulnerable, and in seeking possible explanations for these trends, looking particularly at some social changes that might be causing them.

The assembled evidence

Some commentary on the topic has tended to use the evidence of rising levels of anxiety and depression as evidence that stress has risen for this age group, even using the constructs as if they were synonymous. But in Chapter Three we asserted that we need to be more precise about what we mean by stress, and to separate it out from mental health problems. Rather than saying stress has gone up, it is more useful to look at whether the things that *cause* stress have risen, and whether the *response* to stressful events is more acute now. In both cases, it turned out that there were in fact no trend data. There is a consensus over what it is that adolescents find stressful in their lives (school work and examinations, friendships and relationships, future opportunities and physical appearance), and a consensus that adolescence is a period of particular importance when thinking about stress, because biological and social mechanisms make stress at this life period potentially more powerful. But we do not know if stress has increased, either with respect to increases in stressors or increases in sensitivity to stress. Any simple view that the lives of today's adolescents are more 'stressful' than those of their counterparts of 30 years ago would be hard to substantiate.

In an attempt to unpick more concrete ways in which social change might have affected young people, Chapter Four assessed the evidence about whether young people were spending their time in different ways now compared with the 1970s. Although there is a growing body of research on the importance of supervised and structured constructive activities for positive youth outcomes, much of it is focused on rather narrow (although important) issues like youth clubs. There is much less basic information about non-discretionary use of time, which for this age group is often set within social institutions such as schools and further education colleges. Secondary analysis of the British time use surveys was undertaken to look at the issue, which supported the now widely held view that the elongation of adolescence into early adulthood is important in shaping the nature of everyday experiences throughout adolescence. Time use for 16- to 18-year-olds, in particular, looked quite different from that of their peers some 30 years earlier, as a result of the increased participation in various kinds of education and the virtual disappearance of the youth labour market.

In Chapter Five we turned to look at the evidence that family life for teenagers had changed in significant ways. The research suggested that parents were adapting and responding to social change themselves: spending more time with their children, exerting increasing levels of supervision and control and demonstrating warm and positive relationships. Despite widening income inequality and declining social mobility over parts of our time period, there was no evidence that parenting quality as a whole had declined, or that it had declined more in the most disadvantaged subgroups in society. There remains, however, a social gradient, in that lone parents reported more difficulties in supervising and parenting their adolescents than two-parent families. However, further examination showed that the growing proportion of one-parent families could only account directly for about a fifth of the rise in problem behaviours that we were concerned about in this chapter: enough to warrant some concern but not the most important part of the story. But within families in general there were indications that perhaps parenting was itself becoming more stressful; it certainly seems to go on for longer with the extension in financial dependence generated by the expansion of further and higher education and the collapse of the youth labour market.

Chapter Six revealed a series of major changes in the basic structure of school experiences for adolescents over the last three decades. More attention is now being paid to attainment and examinations, applying widely across the ability and socioeconomic range. There has been a significant increase in examination participation and 'success', an increase in the proportions staying on in education at 16 years, and more participation in a variety of non-school, post-16 educational routes than in previous decades. The expansion of educational opportunity is to be welcomed, of course, as it brings greater social advantages and choices to most of those who carry on. However, the chapter raised a number of concerns, including the possibility that the higher rate of 'staying on' represents in part the lack of alternatives within the rather unique English and Welsh education system, which still (unlike most other continental European systems) has a significant break point at age 16. But we noted that research evidence linking the extension of time in education to wider aspects of adolescent well-being and emotional adjustment — that is, to social and psychological development and not just educational attainment — was lacking. This seems a particular gap in the research literature and one that we believe needs urgent attention.

Chapter Seven focused on trends in the use of drugs and alcohol. It was clear that there was a striking and sustained rise in adolescent alcohol and substance use in the UK across our period of interest. Recent levels of use and abuse remained much higher in the 2000s than they were in the 1970s, although in the last few years there have been welcome signs that trends in both drug and alcohol use are levelling off. This does not apply to all indicators or all groups — some groups of young people continue to have particularly problematic alcohol and substance use. This seems to be an area where the UK may be distinctive, and where more subgroup analysis would be revealing. Underage alcohol use is particularly noteworthy in the UK. Evidence on the links with mental health outcomes demonstrated a probable role for alcohol and drug use in the development of anxiety and depression and behaviour problems. But this is not a straightforward, one-way link. Instead the chapter showed a picture of 'ratcheting up' of problems, where pre-existing difficulties or vulnerabilities leads to more problematic alcohol and substance use, which in turn causes other difficulties. Each kind of difficulty makes another kind more likely regardless of the order in which they occur.

Finally, in Chapter Eight, it was clear that research on adolescent outcomes and their experiences of their neighbourhoods was a field that needed real investment and invigoration in coming years. Adolescence is, after all, the time when young people start looking outside the home and peer groups become more influential, so network-based studies of behaviour in schools and neighbourhoods (and the connections between them) are substantively important. There is certainly evidence that structural aspects of neighbourhood (indicators of poverty, restriction of resources) are associated with particular outcomes such as behaviour problems, and may play a role in shaping peer group behaviour. Yet it was especially notable that in this area there was not much good and robust evidence that was directly relevant to our questions. As with other domains we looked at, establishing causal effects was tricky, and little evidence was collected on these issues 30 years ago, so it is hard to establish whether young people's experiences of their neighbourhoods and broader communities have changed over time.

Some integrating themes

We would be the first to admit that the reviews contained within this volume represented a particular collection of topics, with some important omissions. However, they did begin a process of considering adolescent lives in the round. This has not always been obvious in research and policy in the UK, where we have a weaker culture of considering the age group in a joined-up way than, it could be argued, the USA or mainland Europe. Both of these have, for example, societies for researchers working on adolescence, generating networks for sharing learning across domains, and with a focus more on adolescent development than on adolescent problems. Adolescence research in the UK tends to be bounded by disciplinary allegiances (to education, psychology, sociology or child psychiatry etc), and to focus more on deficits and challenges rather than on normal development. This contributes to a history of rather under-developed support for practitioners working with adolescents, and limited consideration of social policy initiatives for this age group.

Yet adolescence is critical. While the focus on 'early years' is obviously important, it is clearly not the case that everything is decided by the time a young person hits their teenage years. Thinking about the way we structure the lives of young people and whether our institutions have kept up with the challenges of a changing world is as important as consideration of earlier childhood experiences. The evidence we gathered challenged us to consider what can be done to improve the life chances and well-being of the groups of young people who might be more likely to be depressed, have conduct problems or simply be at a loose end in the world, a group that seems to have grown in the last 30 years.

As the reviews developed, we were drawn first to thinking about the particular importance of the 16-18 age group, partly as a result of the peculiarities of the English and Welsh education system. It can be argued that it is within these mid- to late-teen years that the impact of social change is being felt most acutely. In particular this highlights the growing importance of education as a conduit for longer-term life chances. There are three sets of implications here: for those who are on A-level tracks who might not have been in the past, for those who are in parallel post-16 courses that are less academic, and for those who are not in any kind of post-16 education.

Much of the structure of our post-16 world remains from the previous elite model provided by A-levels, taken as little as 30 years ago by only around 18 per cent of the relevant age group, but now started (at least) by over 40 per cent (Bassett et al, 2009). In the 1970s, for those on the academic track, a certain amount of independent study was built into the day – school days were short, and the school year relatively short too. The structure has not changed much in the intervening years but, given the larger proportion of the age group taking this route, we might ask whether the assumptions underlying the structure of the school day and year is optimal even for those on this most academic track For example, the A-level curriculum is not as wide as in other secondary models, as it is built on an assumption that young people have clear ideas of what they want to study at university; it seems unlikely that this is as true now as it was when a much smaller proportion of the age cohort went to university. And timetabling for A-levels builds in fewer contact hours, and shorter school days, than systems in many other countries even for the university-bound. It might be useful to examine these issues not just from the perspective of educational effects but bearing in mind the move to a mass education system.

In addition to those staying on to do A-levels, a much larger proportion of young people than previously are now on non-academic alternatives at further education colleges and in post-16 courses at other educational institutions, where again the content and structure of the day may vary considerably but which are unlikely to be provide more structured timetables or more contact hours than A-levels. We think an important priority should be to look at the way days and weeks are organised for this group in the UK compared to similar groups or academic streams in the USA and Western Europe. For example, how do these experiences compare with those doing a North American high school diploma? How do they compare to trajectories for the non-university-bound in continental Europe? We suspect that comparable pathways in the UK provide less structured days, and less structured working years, than elsewhere.

This is not simply an issue of educational training. Apprenticeships and vocational education provide not only skills and pathways to further opportunity, but also interaction between young people and a mixed world of adults and young people, and the sense of doing something useful and productive; they are a means of socialisation into an adult world. Beyond considering only educational qualifications or labour markets, we need to see educational institutions as transitions to a wider adult world. As it stands now, the fairly rigorous organisation of the school day pre-16 can fall away into a great deal of unstructured time even for young people who remain in post-16 education, especially for those who are not on A-level courses. This was a theme of the recent Nuffield Foundation review of 14-19 education and training (Pring et al, 2009), but here we want to push consideration of the implications of different post-16 trajectories into an examination of wider issues than just occupational consequences. One of these issues is how young people find their way onto these trajectories. For those not doing A-levels evidence suggests there is relatively little counselling, and few automatic routes after GCSEs. This is unlike the notion of a North American 'high school' or many continental systems with clear streaming and vocational paths. We suspect that having clear and structured paths for those who are not university-bound would have wider benefits for young people and those around them, and believe this issue warrants further consideration in the round, looking at the lack of clear paths not only as an educational issue but as a factor in young people's social and emotional development.

But in addition to this, the UK has a relatively high proportion of young people over 16 who are *not* in any education, employment or training, the so-called NEETs). Other countries do better with vocational qualifications and in providing clear pathways for young people who are not bound for university but who do not necessarily know what they want to do, and, importantly, for whom few jobs now exist. Several authors have noted (in different contexts) that the expansion of the higher and further education sectors can exacerbate rather than reduce inequalities (see, for example, Heath, 2009), as those who opt out (or are pushed out) are progressively disadvantaged. The general question of whether social change might be more problematic for some groups than for others is not, of course, a new question, and is regularly raised in discussions about this age group (see, for example, Furlong, 2009; Smith, 2010; Coleman, 2011). But our questions relate not only to the longer-term outcomes of educational pathways, but to the structuring of how time and activities are organised on those paths. For so-called NEETS, these problems are at their most extreme.

Indeed, the Rathbone/Nuffield Engaging Youth Enquiry (Hayward et al, 2008) into young people classified as 'NEET' alerted our attention to a 'prospective NEET' group for whom no statistics were available, of people under 16 who were becoming disengaged from education even before GCSEs. Again we stress that these are not just educational issues, but issues of socialisation and development.

One final set of educational questions relates to neighbourhoods and younger adolescents, rather than pathways for 16- to 18-year-olds. While the chapter on educational transitions (Chapter Six) suggests that for many young people, the move directly from primary to secondary school may cause few problems, there still remains a question about interactions between challenging neighbourhoods and underperforming local secondary schools; disengagement from education at a very early stage after transition to secondary school can be an issue here, and concerns over recruitment of the youngest pupils into gangs are part of this. Research into whether different models of schools, perhaps with narrower age ranges, could more safely protect younger adolescents in difficult neighbourhoods and facing other social problems might be worthwhile. This may be an area where moving beyond modal patterns and looking at the differing effects of social institutions for different groups of young people living in different contexts could be especially helpful, although this is more speculative than some other suggestions we make, and this kind of research is technically and practically complex.

On a different topic, the review programme raised familiar questions about the role of families in parenting adolescents, but drew particular attention to the challenges of doing so at a time of extended dependency on the family of origin. While changing family structures, particularly the increase in lone-parent (and step-parent) families, were directly responsible for only modest changes in young people's mental health outcomes, family form and parental support are clearly important. Reassuringly, the secondary data analysis showed that, on average, parental quality and attentiveness has actually improved over the past 30 years although there are subgroups of concern, especially where mothers and fathers are themselves showing signs of stress and anxiety. We have not been able to explore the reasons why some parents are showing more signs of strain but it reminds us of the importance of supporting families in order to support young people.

We also need a better dynamic understanding of how family relationships interact with other aspects of changing adolescence experiences. For instance, one of the salient features of adolescence is that young people look outside their families to their friends, peer groups and others for cues about behaviour. In the chapter on peer groups (Chapter Eight) we asked whether there is more teenage age segregation nowadays at this point in their lives, as young people interact less in the mixed-age world of work. Over time too different groups of young people set norms for others, and it may be that children from less supervising families are setting norms for others in a dynamic way. But the sorts of evidence we have to rely on, such as large-scale surveys, are unable to capture that sort of dynamic effect. Helping families compensate for and influence these social norms may well repay some thought.

One example of changes in behaviour is the issue of underage drinking and binge drinking where there is worrying evidence about the consumption patterns of young people in the UK. While the average trends in drug and alcohol use show a levelling off or reduction in usage, levels are still far too high, and some groups show a worsening in behaviour, with higher levels of consumption among those who do start drinking, and more frequent binge drinking. As a society, we seem more tolerant of this behaviour than other countries. A more robust public health policy response (involving regulation, taxation and building public support for change) might help parents feel confident in setting norms, especially for younger adolescents. A series of recent projects by the Joseph Rowntree Foundation on youth drinking have emphasised the critical role of parents and the need for policy to support them (see, for example, Bremner et al, 2011). Enforcing underage drinking laws and considering the benefits of minimum alcohol pricing on child purchasing behaviour might be a start, but we are likely to need a systematic, multipronged approach, all the elements of which work in the same direction, to effect real change among the groups we are most worried about.

In a different way, we have also been struck throughout the course of the programme by the way that some of the research had rather a 'myth busting' role, challenging or complicating the commonsense assumptions about this age group and social change. The finding about increased supervision of adolescents by parents is an example. This demonstrates for us the importance of robust tracking data that can plot changes (or lack of them) over time in areas that we know are important for young people's outcomes – such as parenting, risky health behaviours and peer group dynamics. There is plenty of commentary about these issues, but much less in the way of robust quantitative explorations using imaginative research designs. As a result, we struggled – the literature struggled – to reveal much about causality in relation to social change and outcomes for young people. The programme did, however, reveal the usefulness of descriptively mapping key variables over time.

The programme has also led us to interesting questions about whether previously established associations between key variables are changing over time. After all, social science is not like physics: relationships that held at one time, when the buttressing social conditions were very different, may not work in the same way now. We should not assume that research results from the 1980s and early 1990s will necessarily hold true now. For example, teenage pregnancies are now stronger markers of social disadvantage than they were in eras where more people from all social and educational groups became pregnant before their 25th birthdays (Randall et al, 2009). This means we need to look beyond analyses based simply on individual-level data to include an examination of the social context. It also explains why we have tried to exercise caution generalising from USA or continental European data to the UK, since the wider social contexts are often so different.

Still on the theme of methodology, we noted throughout the reviews that while there is evidence for some effect in some places, even the strong causal factors virtually never account for all the effects we observe. In the sorts of social science and social interventions we have examined, effect sizes, even when significant, are generally modest, accounting for generally about 5 to 15 per cent of the variance in adolescent outcomes. Methodology gets better over time, and as a result effect sizes tend to go down, as more precision becomes possible and we account for other features. Causal effects are most difficult to demonstrate when they are small, and all the effects debated here are likely to be small in isolation. But it should not be assumed as a result that they are not important. A young person with several risk factors – poor parenting, poor school structure, deviant peer groups and so on – is more likely to demonstrate troubling behaviour; a corollary is that reducing more than one risk factor might bring about better than expected improvements.

Finally, a word about the omissions. We will return to the research gaps later, but there are some broad topic areas that readers will feel are missing from this collection. They include, for example, the importance of the transformation of the media and communication facilities available to young people, and the broadening of horizons, and especially important in the context of adolescence, a widening of the comparison groups that widespread use of the internet may bring. They may also include the rise of youth consumerism and materialism, changes in young people's sexual lives and experiences, deterioration in aspects of physical health and exercise, and any specific gender dimensions of many of the areas we have looked at. We agree that these are important, and would like to see more work done in these areas. However, we started with a focus on social structure, and we began by concentrating on the big frameworks guiding individual's lives, such as family and education. Our aim has been to set out some key themes, and to identify some questions that need addressing in the coming years. We hope this begins a process rather than defines it. The next section spells out what some of the 'next questions' might be.

Looking forward

As we have made clear, there turned out to be less evidence on any of these topics than one might have imagined at the outset. We were looking for information about associations, and if possible about causality, but it turned out that there were difficulties even in getting useful information that mapped out the basic features of social change. Some of the gaps related to data shortcomings; perhaps we forget how short the history of social research actually is. Others related to conceptual and theoretical weaknesses, about how to deal with different and potentially conflicting levels of effects, for example, or with multiple and additive risks. We highlight four particular areas where more investment in research needs to be made.

First, more empirical research on time use might help us to think more concretely about the extent and the implications of the social change in educational and other experiences into the late teens and early 20s. Such work might benefit from having an explicitly comparative design – comparing young people who are of similar characteristics but on different trajectories, or looking at those in different educational structures or even cross-national comparisons. Time use data is subject to some limitations with respect to what it can tell us, but detailed analysis of what the school day/college day/part-time working day in different countries actually looks like could be interesting, taken in the context of the whole day – and the whole week, or whole year. It would also help us understand the extent to which different groups of young people spend time in 'teen-only' groups, and others spend time in activities that involve adult supervision or interaction with adults.

Second, related to these questions about the patterning of time use are our questions about the implications for aspects of development. We have indicated that we think this is important for reasons beyond just educational and occupational trajectories, and that more cross-cutting work on adolescence is needed that sets education research within the broader context of adolescent development and social lives. Links need to be drawn across different domains; do changing educational experiences have an impact on peer group relationships and family relationships? How do they interact? Are these experiences important in understanding the development of identity and constructs of social status? If work is not a route open to some groups, and education is also not providing much sense of achievement, does this affect how they feel about themselves in ways that might be important for mental health?

Third, there is still a need for more longitudinal data and for analysis on subgroups. It is not the case that adolescent problems and challenges are evenly spread through the population, and because few of the reviews included secondary analysis, we were less able to explore this than we think is warranted. We think it particularly important to scratch below the surface of the overall group mean. Clearly, social change will have affected different subgroups in different ways. Numerous authors have asked important questions about the impacts of poverty and inequality, and in particular in relation to educational tracks and future employment prospects. Our suggestion is that this needs to be broader than just consideration of economic opportunities. Another issue along similar lines is the need to appreciate the vast difference between, for example, a 13-year-old and an 18-year-old in considering the adolescent age group. Too often in the research we read we found young people at very different stages of development grouped together into one category. We are also aware that little of the analysis we have carried out has said much about gender, yet gender has a different profile in depression and conduct disorder epidemiology and outcomes, and has a role in school experiences and peer group relations. Understanding the relevance of gender for the questions we have raised is essential. The same would be true of ethnicity, where there have, of course, been real population changes over the 30 years covered by the review.

But while more longitudinal data focusing on this age group is crucial, we suspect some of this needs to take place in the context of neighbourhood studies, like the ESYTC (McVie and Norris, 2006), or by looking at in ways pioneered by Rob Sampson (see, for example, Sampson and Raudenbush, 1999), to capture the more dynamic interplay between groups of young people in neighbourhoods, the way they form themselves into peer groups around place and school, and so on. We need far more methodological innovation, particularly for this age group, as they quite simply less 'household-based' than older adults.

Fourth, it would be useful to find out exactly what it is that is specific about adolescence within the trends we have identified, and the extent to which they form part of wider social phenomena. For example, this question was raised in part in relation to time trends in mental health symptoms and could be in relation to alcohol use: are these patterns specific to adolescents? Or have they been experienced in other age groups? Of course the results were mixed; the answer was partly yes and partly no – we highlighted the importance of trends in parental mental health as well as those of young people. But that still leaves us making a plea for more of an adolescence focus in the UK research field – what is it about this age group that is distinctive and important, both in developmental terms, and also in terms of social trends?

Conclusion

In this volume we have been interested in social change – in shifts in the experiences of young people – and the implications for well-being. The detective work undertaken by the review teams revealed many ways in which particular aspects of young people's changing social lives are likely to affect their mental health, while acknowledging the data shortfalls and the complications in establishing directions of effects. We think that further secondary analysis could address some of the questions about subgroups, and regret that we were not able to go further in this direction. But the missing longer-term data cannot be addressed retrospectively; only by thinking about data collection needs now can we hope to do better in future.

Overall, it is critical to stress the range of experiences of teenagers living in the late 20th and early 21st century in the UK. We do not support the assumption that adolescence is, by definition, a problematic and stressful time, nor would we assert that UK young people are, en masse, in a calamitous situation. Far from it. This book provides evidence on many positive advances in their lives, and a large proportion have more choices and opportunities than ever. However, a minority are doing less well than their peers in other countries, and some part of that is not an individualised problem but may be due to the social structures they live in. A focus on social structures allows rays of hope,

References

Academy of Medical Sciences (2004) *Calling time: The nation's drinking as a major health issue*, London: Academy of Medical Sciences.

Academy of Medical Sciences (2007) *Identifying the environmental causes of disease: How should we decide what to believe and when to take action?*, London: Academy of Medical Sciences.

Achenbach, T.M., Dumenci, L. and Rescorla, L.A. (2002a) 'Is American student behavior getting worse? Teacher ratings over an 18-year period', *School Psychology Review*, vol 31, no 3, pp 428-42.

Achenbach, T.M., Dumenci, L. and Rescorla, L.A. (2002b) 'Ten-year comparisons of problems and competencies for national samples of youth: self, parent and teacher reports', *Journal of Emotional and Behavioral Disorders*, vol 10, no 4, pp 194-203.

Achenbach, T.M., Dumenci, L. and Rescorla, L.A. (2003) 'Are American children's problems still getting worse? A 23-year comparison', *Journal of Abnormal Child Psychology*, vol 31, no 1, pp 1-11.

Adrian, C. and Hammen, C. (1993) 'Stress exposure and stress generation in children of depressed mothers', *Journal of Consulting and Clinical Psychology*, vol 61, no 2, pp 354-9.

Aggleton, P., McClean, C., Taylor-Laybourne, A., Waller, D., Warwick, I., Woodhead, D. and Youdell, D. (1995) *Young men speaking out*, London: Health Education Authority.

Allardyce, J., Gilmour, H., Atkinson, J., Rapson, T., Bishop, J. and McCreadie, R.G. (2005) 'Social fragmentation, deprivation and urbanicity: relation to first-admission rates for psychoses', *British Journal of Psychiatry*, vol 187, no 5, pp 401-6.

Allen, C. (2007) *Crime, drugs and social theory*, Aldershot: Ashgate.

Allen, J.L., Rapee, R.M. and Sandberg, S. (2008) 'Severe life events and chronic adversities as antecedents to anxiety in children: a matched control study', *Journal of Abnormal Child Psychology*, vol 36, no 7, pp 1047-56.

Alspaugh, J. (1998) 'Achievement loss associated with the transition to middle school and high school', *The Journal of Educational Research*, vol 92, no 1, pp 20-5.

Amato, P. (1993) 'Children's adjustment to divorce: theories, hypotheses and empirical support', *Journal of Marriage and Family*, vol 55, pp 23-38.

Anderson, S.E., Dallal, G.E. and Must, A. (2003) 'Relative weight and race influence average age at menarche: results from two nationally representative surveys of US girls studied 25 years apart', *Pediatrics*, vol 111, no 4, pp 844-50.

Aneshensel, C.S. and Gore, S. (1991) 'Development, stress and role restructuring: social transitions in adolescence', in J. Ecklenrode (ed) *The social context of coping*, New York: Plenum Press, pp 55-83.

Aneshensel, C.S. and Sucoff, C.A. (1996) 'The neighbourhood context of adolescent mental health', *Journal of Health and Social Behaviour*, vol 37, no 4, pp 293-310.

Anthony, J. and Helzer, J. (1991) 'Syndromes of drug abuse and dependence', in L.N. Robins and D.A. Reiger (eds) *Psychiatric disorders in America: The Epidemiologic Catchment Area Study*, New York: Free Press, pp 116-54.

Armstrong, C., Hill, M. and Secker, J. (1998) *Listening to children*, London: Mental Health Foundation.

Armstrong, T.D. and Costello, E.J. (2002) 'Community studies on adolescent substance use, abuse, or dependence and psychiatric comorbidity', *Journal of Consulting and Clinical Psychology*, vol 70, no 6, pp 1224-39.

Arnett, J.J. (1999) 'Adolescent storm and stress, reconsidered', *American Psychologist*, vol 54, no 5, pp 317-26.

Arnett, J.J. (2004) *Emerging adulthood: The winding road from late teens through the twenties*, Oxford: Oxford University Press.

Arseneault, L., Bowes, L. and Shakoor, S. (2009) 'Bullying victimization in youths and mental health problems: "Much ado about nothing?"', *Psychological Medicine*, vol 40, no 5, pp 717-29.

Arseneault, L., Cannon, M., Witton, J. and Murray, R. (2004) 'Causal association between cannabis and psychosis: examination of the evidence', *British Journal of Psychiatry*, vol 184, no 2, pp 110-17.

Atladottir, H.O., Parner, E.T., Schendel, D., Dalsgaard, S., Thomsen, P.H. and Thorsen, P. (2007) 'Time trends in reported diagnoses of childhood neuropsychiatric disorders. A Danish cohort study', *Archives of Pediatric Adolescent Medicine*, vol 161, no 2, pp 193-8.

Balding, J., Regis, D. and Wise, A. (1998) *No worries: Young people and mental health: A study of the worries and concerns that affect young teenagers in our society*, Exeter: School Health Education Unit.

Bandura, A. (1997) *Self-efficacy: The exercise of control*, New York: W.H. Freeman.

Bannister, J. and Fraser, A. (2008) 'Youth gang identification: learning and social development in restricted geographies', *Scottish Journal of Criminal Justice Studies*, vol 14, pp 96-114.

Barber, B.L. and Olsen, J. (2004) 'Assessing the transitions to middle and high school', *Journal of Adolescent Research*, vol 19, no 1, pp 3-30.

Barber, B.L., Eccles, J.S. and Stone, M.R. (2001) 'Whatever happened to the Jock, the Brain, and the Princess? Young adult pathways linked to adolescent activity involvement and social identity', *Journal of Adolescent Research*, vol 16, no 5, pp 429-55.

Bartko, T.W. and Eccles, J.S. (2003) 'Adolescent participation in structured and unstructured activities: a person-oriented analysis', *Journal of Youth and Adolescence*, vol 32, no 4, pp 233-41.

Bassett, D., Cawston, T., Thraves, L. and Truss, E. (2009) *A new level*, London: Reform.

Battistich, V., Solomon, D., Kim, D., Watson, M. and Schaps, E. (1995) 'Schools as communities, poverty levels of student populations, and students' attitudes, motives and performance: a multilevel analysis', *American Educational Research Journal*, vol 32, no 3, pp 627-58.

Baumrind, D. (1991) 'The influence of parenting style on adolescent competence and substance use', *The Journal of Early Adolescence*, vol 11, no 1, pp 56-95.

BBPA (British Beer and Pub Association) (2005) *Statistical handbook*, London: BBPA.

Bellair, P.E. and McNulty, T.L. (2009) 'Gang membership, drug selling and violence in neighbourhood context', *Justice Quarterly*, vol 26, no 4, pp 644-69.

Benn, C. and Chitty, C. (1996) *Thirty years on: Is comprehensive education alive and well or struggling to survive?*, London: David Fulton Publishers.

Benner, A.D. and Graham, S. (2007) 'Navigating the transition to multi-ethnic urban high schools: changing ethnic congruence and adolescents' school related affect', *Journal of Research on Adolescence*, vol 17, no 1, pp 207-20.

Benner, A.D. and Graham, S. (2009) 'The transition to high school as a developmental process among multi-ethnic urban youth', *Child Development*, vol 80, no 2, pp 356-76.

Berrington, A., Stone, J. and Falkingham, J. (2009) 'The changing living arrangements of young adults in the UK', *Population Trends*, vol 138, pp 27-37.

Best, D., Manning, V., Gossop, M., Gross, S. and Strang, J. (2006) 'Excessive drinking and other problem behaviours among 14-16 year old schoolchildren', *Addictive Behaviours*, vol 31, no 8, pp 1424-35.

Best, D., Manning, V., Gossop, M., Witton, J., Floyd, K., Rawaf, S. and Strang, J. (2004) 'Adolescent psychological health problems and delinquency among volatile substance users in a school sample in South London', *Drugs: Education, Prevention and Policy*, vol 11, no 6, pp 473-82.

Beyers, J.M., Loeber, R., Wikstrom, P.-O. and Stouthamer-Loeber, M. (2001) 'What predicts adolescent violence in better-off neighbourhoods?', *Journal of Abnormal Child Psychology*, vol 29, no 5, pp 369-81.

Biggart, A. (2009) 'Young people's subjective orientations to education', in A. Furlong (ed) *Handbook of youth and young adulthood: New perspectives and agendas*, London: Routledge, pp 114-20.

Blatchford, P. and Baines, E. (2008) *A Follow-up national survey of breaktimes in primary and secondary schools*, London: Institute of Education, University of London.

Blocker, J.S., Fahey, D.M. and Tyrrell, I.R. (2003) *Alcohol and temperance in modern history: A global encyclopaedia*, Santa Barbara, CA: ABC-Clio.

Blum, R. and Libbey, H. (2004) 'School connectedness – strengthening health and education outcomes for teenagers', *Journal of School Health*, vol 74, no 7, pp 229-99.

BMA (British Medical Association) (2008) *Alcohol misuse: Tackling the UK epidemic*, London: BMA.

Boardman, J. and Saint Ong, J. (2005) 'Neighbourhoods and adolescent development', *Children, Youth and Environments*, vol 15, no 1, pp 138-64.

Bowen, C. (1997) 'School survey highlights teenage problem area', *Nursing Times*, vol 93, no 11, pp 54-5.

Bowes, L., Arseneault, L., Maughan, B., Taylor, A., Caspi, A. and Moffitt, T.E. (2009) 'School, neighbourhood and family factors are associated with children's bullying involvement: a nationally representative longitudinal study', *Journal of the American Academy of Child and Adolescent Psychiatry*, vol 48, no 5, pp 545-53.

Boys, A., Farrell, M., Taylor, C., Marsden, J., Goodman, R., Brugha, T., Bebbington, P., Jenkins, R. and Meltzer, H. (2003) 'Psychiatric morbidity and substance use in young people aged 13-15 years: results from the Child and Adolescent Survey of Mental Health', *British Journal of Psychiatry*, vol 182, no 6, pp 509-17.

Bradford Brown, B. and Larson, J. (2009) 'Peer relationships in adolescence', in R. Lerner and L. Steinberg (eds) *Handbook of adolescent psychology, Volume 2: Contextual influences on adolescent development* (3rd edn), Hoboken, NJ: John Wiley & Sons Inc, pp 74-103.

Bradshaw, J. and Keung, A. (2011) 'Trends in child subjective well-being in the UK', *Journal of Children's Services*, vol 6, no 1, pp 4-17.

Brady, D. and Sinha, R. (2005) 'Co-occurring mental and substance use disorders: the neurobiological effects of chronic stress', *American Journal of Psychiatry*, vol 162, no 8, pp 1483-93.

Brain, K. (2002) *Youth, alcohol and the emergence of the post-modern alcohol order*, IAS Occasional Paper, London: Institute of Alcohol Studies.

Bremner, P., Burnett, J., Nunney, F., Ravat, M. and Mistral, W. (2011) *Young people, alcohol and influences: A study of young people and their relationship with alcohol*, York: Joseph Rowntree Foundation.

Brewer, M., Browne, J. and Joyce, R. (2011) *Child and working age poverty and inequality in the UK: 2010*, London: Institute for Fiscal Studies.

British Academy (2010) *Social science and family policies*, Working Group Report, London: British Academy Policy Centre.

Brook, D., Brook, J.S., Zhang, C., Cohen, P. and Whiteman, M. (2002) 'Drug use and the risk of major depressive disorder, alcohol dependence and substance use disorders', *Archives of General Psychiatry*, vol 59, no 11, pp 1039-44.

Brown, G.W. and Harris, T.O. (1978) *The social origins of depression: A study of psychiatric disorder in women*, London: Tavistock Publications.

Brown, G.W. and Harris, T.O. (1986) 'Establishing causal links: the Bedford College studies of depression', in H. Katschnig (ed) *Life events and psychiatric disorders: Controversial issues*, London: Cambridge University Press, pp 107-87.

Brown, G.W. and Rutter, M. (1966) 'The measurement of family activities and relationships', *Human Relations*, vol 19, no 2, pp 241-63.

Brown, S. and Schuckit, M. (1988) 'Changes in depression amongst abstinent alcoholics', *Journal of Studies in Alcohol*, vol 52, pp 37-43.

Buckner, J.C., Beardslee, W.R. and Bassuk, E.L. (2004) 'Exposure to violence and low-income children's mental health: direct, moderated and mediated relations', *American Journal of Orthopsychiatry*, vol 74, no 4, pp 413-23.

Bynner, J. and Parsons, S. (2002) 'Social exclusion and the transition from school to work: the case of young people not in education, employment or training (NEET)', *Journal of Vocational Behaviour*, vol 60, no 2, pp 289-309.

Bynner, J., Elias, P., McKnight, A., Pan, H. and Pierre, G. (2002) *Young people are changing routes to independence*, York: Joseph Rowntree Foundation.

Cabinet Office (2008) *Families in Britain: An evidence paper*, London: Cabinet Office, The Strategy Unit and Department for Children, Schools and Families.

Cairns, E. and Lloyd, K. (2005) *Stress at 16: Research update from data collected in Young Life and Times Survey 2004*, Belfast: ARK (Access, Research, Knowledge) (www.ark.ac.uk).

Carrion, V.G., Weems, C.F., Ray, R.D., Glaser, B., Hessl, D. and Reiss, A.L. (2002) 'Diurnal salivary cortisol in pediatric posttraumatic stress disorder', *Biological Psychiatry*, vol 51, no 7, pp 575-82.

CDC (Center for Disease Control) (2008) *Physical activity and good nutrition: Essential elements to prevent chronic diseases and obesity*, Atlanta, GA: CDC (www.cdc.gov/nccdphp/publications/aag/pdf/dnpa.pdf).

Chamberlain, T., George, N., Golden, S., Walker, F. and Bengon, T. (2010) *Tellus4 national report*, London: National Foundation for Educational Research, Department for Children, Schools and Families (www.education.gov.uk).

Champion, L.A., Goodall, G.M. and Rutter, M. (1995) 'Behavioural problems in childhood and stressors in early adult life: a 20-year follow-up of London school children', *Psychological Medicine*, vol 25, no 2, pp 231-46.

Chapman, C., Laird, J. and Kewal Ramani, A. (2010) *Trends in high school dropout and completion rates in the United States: 1972-2008*, Washington, DC: National Center for Education Statistics.

Chatterji, P. (2006) 'Illicit drug use and educational attainment', *Health Economics*, vol 15, no 5, pp 489-511.

Chen, E. and Hanson, M. (2005) 'Perceptions of threat; understanding pathways between stress and health in adolescents', *The Prevention Researcher*, vol 12, no 3, pp 10-12.

Cheng, S.-L., Olsen, W., Southerton, D. and Warde, A. (2007) 'The changing practice of eating: evidence from UIK time diaries, 1975 and 2000', *The British Journal of Sociology*, vol 58, no 1, pp 39-61.

Chenu, A. (2003) 'Trends in adolescent time use: France 1986 to 1998', Paper presented at the International Association for Time Use Research Conference, Brussels, Belgium, 17-19 September.

Childress, H. (2004) *Landscapes of betrayal, landscapes of joy: Curtisville in the lives of its teenagers*, Albany, NY: State University of New York.

Chitty, C. (2002) *Understanding schools and schooling*, London: Routledge.

Clark, C., Haines, M.M., Head, J., Klineberg, E., Arephin, M., Viner, R., Taylor, S.J., Booy, R., Bhui, K. and Stansfeld, S.A. (2007) 'Psychological symptoms and physical health and health behaviours in adolescents: a prospective 2-year study in East London', *Addiction*, vol 102, no 1, pp 126-35.

Clark, C. and Uzzell, D. (2006) 'The socioeconomic affordances of adolescents' environments', in C. Spencer and M. Blades (eds) *Children and their environments: Learning, using and designing spaces*, Cambridge: Cambridge University Press, pp 176-99.

Coleman, J. (2011) *The nature of adolescence* (4th edn), Abingdon: Routledge.

Coleman, L. and Cater, S. (2005) *Underage 'risky' drinking: Motivations and outcomes*, York: Joseph Rowntree Foundation.

Coleman. J, Brooks, F. and Threadgold, J. (2011) *Key data on adolescence*, London: Association for Young People's Health.

Coleman, K., Eder, S. and Smith, K. (2011) 'Homicide', in K. Smith, K. Coleman, S. Eder and P. Hall (eds) *Homicides, firearm offences and intimate violence 2009/10. Supplementary Volume 2 to Crime in England and Wales 2009/10*, London: Home Office, pp 11-43. (www.homeoffice. gov.uk).

Collishaw, S. (2009) 'Trends in adolescent depression: a review of the evidence', in W. Yule (ed) *Depression in childhood and adolescence: The way forward*, Occasional Paper No 28, London: Association for Child and Adolescent Mental Health, pp 7-18.

Collishaw, S., Goodman, R., Pickles, A. and Maughan, B. (2007) 'Modelling the contribution of changes in family life to time trends in adolescent conduct problems', *Social Science & Medicine*, vol 65, no 12, pp 2576-87.

Collishaw, S., Maughan, B., Goodman, R. and Pickles, A. (2004) 'Time trends in adolescent mental health', *Journal of Child Psychology and Psychiatry*, vol 45, no 8, pp 1350-62.

Collishaw, S., Maughan, B., Natarajan, L. and Pickles, A. (2010) 'Trends in adolescent emotional problems in England: a comparison of two national cohorts twenty years apart', *Journal of Child Psychology and Psychiatry*, vol 51, no 8, pp 885-94.

Collishaw, S., Gardner, F., Maughan, B., Scott, J. and Pickles, A. (2011) 'Do historical changes in parent–child relationships explain increases in youth conduct problems?', *Journal of Abnormal Psychology* (www. springerlink.com/content/4605243851065382/).

Colman, I., Murray, J., Abbott, R.A., Maughan, B., Kuh, D., Croudace, T.J. and Jones, P.B. (2009) 'Outcomes of conduct problems in adolescence: 40 year follow-up of national cohort', *British Medical Journal*, vol 338, a2981.

Compas, B.E. (1995) 'Promoting successful coping during adolescence', in M. Rutter (ed) *Psychosocial disturbances in young people*, Cambridge: Cambridge University Press, pp 247-73.

Compas, B.E., Orosan, P.G. and Grant, K.E. (1993) 'Adolescent stress and coping: implications for psychopathology during adolescence', *Journal of Adolescence*, vol 16, no 3, pp 331-49.

Compas, B.E., Connor-Smith, J.K., Saltzman, H., Thomsen, A.H. and Wadsworth, M.E. (2001) 'Coping with stress during childhood and adolescence: problems, progress, and potential in theory and research', *Psychological Bulletin*, vol 127, no 1, pp 87-127.

Compton, W.M., Conway, K.P., Stinson, F.S. and Grant, B.F. (2006) 'Changes in the prevalence of major depression and comorbid substance use disorders in the United States between 1991-1992 and 2001-2002', *American Journal of Psychiatry*, vol 163, no 12, pp 2141-7.

Conger, R.D., Ge, X., Elder, G.H., Lorenz, F.O. and Simons, R.L. (1994) 'Economic stress, coercive family process, and developmental problems of adolescence', *Child Development*, vol 65, no 2 (special no), pp 541-61.

Corkery, J. (1997) *Statistics of drug addicts notified to the Home Office, UK, 1996*, Home Office Statistical Bulletin 22/97, London: Home Office Research and Statistics Directorate.

Costello, E.J., Erkanli, A. and Angold, A. (2006) 'Is there an epidemic of child or adolescent depression?', *Journal of Child Psychology and Psychiatry*, vol 47, no 12, pp 1263-71.

Costello, E.J., Mustillo, S., Erkanli, A., Keeler, G. and Angold, A. (2003) 'Prevalence and development of psychiatric disorders in childhood and adolescence', *Archives of General Psychiatry*, vol 60, no 8, pp 837-44.

Côté, J. and Bynner, J. (2008) 'Changes in the transition to adulthood in the UK and Canada: the role of structure and agency in emerging adulthood', *Journal of Youth Studies*, vol 11, no 3, pp 251-68.

Craig, L. (2006) 'How employed mothers in Australia find time for both market work and childcare', *Journal of Family and Economic Issues*, vol 28, no 1, pp 69-87.

Cross-National Collaborative Group (1992) 'The changing rate of major depression', *Journal of the American Medical Association*, vol 268, no 21, pp 3098-105.

CSDH (Commission on Social Determinants of Health) (2008) *Closing the gap in a generation: Health equity through action on the social determinants of health*, Final Report of the CSDH, Geneva: World Health Organization.

Cuffe, S.P., McKeown, R.E., Addy, C.L. and Garrison, C.Z. (2005) 'Family and psychosocial risk factors in a longitudinal epidemiological study of adolescents', *Journal of the American Academy of Child and Adolescent Psychiatry*, vol 44, no 2, pp 121-9.

Cuijpers, P. and Smit, F. (2002) 'Excess mortality in depression: a meta-analysis of community studies', *Journal of Affective disorders*, vol 72, no 3, pp 227-36.

Cummins, S., Curtis, S.E., Diez-Roux, A.V. and McIntyre, S. (2007) 'Understanding and representing "place" in health research: a relational approach', *Social Science & Medicine*, vol 65, no 9, pp 1925-38.

Currie, C., Roberts, C., Morgan, A., Smith, R., Settertobulte, W., Samdal, O. and Barnekow Rasmussen, V. (2004) *Young people's health in context*, Copenhagen: World Health Organization Regional Office for Europe.

Currie, C., Gabainn, S., Godeau, E., Roberts, C., Smith, R., Currie, D., Picket, W., Richter, M., Morgan, A. and Barnekow, V. (eds) (2008) *Inequalities in young people's health: HBSC international report from the 2005/2006 survey*, Copenhagen: World Health Organization Regional Office for Europe.

Curtis, L.J., Doolley, M.D. and Phipps, S.A. (2004) 'Child well-being and neighbourhood quality: evidence from the Canadian National Longitudinal Survey of Children and Youth', *Social Science & Medicine*, vol 58, no 10, pp 1917-27.

D'Imperio, R.L., Dubow, E.F. and Ippolito, M.F. (2000) 'Resilient and stress-affected adolescents in an urban setting', *Journal of Clinical Child Psychology*, vol 29, no 1, pp 129-42.

Danckaerts, M., Heptinstall, E., Chadwick, O. and Taylor, E. (2000) 'A natural history of hyperactivity and conduct problems: self-reported outcome', *European Child Adolescent Psychiatry*, vol 9, no 1, pp 26-38.

DCSF (Department for Children, Schools and Families) (2007a) *The Children's Plan: Building brighter futures*, London: The Stationery Office.

DCSF (2007b) *Children and young people today: Evidence to support the development of The Children's Plan*, London: DCSF.

Derbyshire, J. (1996) 'The feel-bad factor', *Young People Now*, October, pp 20-1.

DfE (Department for Education) (1994) *Bullying: Don't suffer in silence*, London: HMSO.

DfE (1999) *National Healthy Schools Standard*, London: The Stationery Office.

DfE (2011) *Participation in education of 16-18 year olds by institution type, England, 1985 onwards*, London: DfE (www.education.gov.uk/rsgateway/DB/SFR/s000551/sfr03-2005tables.xls#'B13'!A1).

DH (Department of Health) (1994) *Drug misuse statistics*, Statistical Bulletin 3/94, London: DH.

DH (2004) *Statistics from the regional drug misuse databases for six months ending March 2001*, Statistical Bulletin 2002/07, London: DH.

Dishion, T., McCord, J. and Poulin, F. (1999) 'When interventions harm: peer groups and problem behavior', *American Psychologist*, vol 54, no 9, pp 755-64.

Dodge, K.A., Pettit, G.S., Bates, J.E. and Valente, E. (1995) 'Social information-processing patterns partially mediate the effects of early physical abuse on later conduct problems', *Journal of Abnormal Psychology*, vol 104, no 4, pp 632-43.

Dohrenwend, B.P. (2006) 'Inventorying stressful life events as risk factors for psychopathology: toward resolution of the problem of intracategory variability', *Psychology Bulletin*, vol 132, no 3, pp 477-95.

Doi, Y., Roberts, R.E., Takeuchi, K. and Suzuki, S. (2001) 'Multiethnic comparison of adolescent major depression based on DSM-IV criteria in a US–Japan study', *Journal of the American Academy of Child and Adolescent Psychiatry*, vol 40, no 5, pp 1308-15.

Dorling, D., Rigby, J., Wheeler, B., Ballas, D. Thomas, B., Fahmy, E., Gordon, D. and Lupton, R. (2007) *Poverty, wealth and place in Britain, 1968-2005*, Bristol: The Policy Press.

Dubas, J.S. and Snider, B.A. (1993) 'The role of community-based youth groups in enhancing learning and achievement through nonformal education', in R.M. Lerner (ed) *Early adolescence: Perspectives on research, policy, and intervention*, Hillsdale, NJ: Lawrence Erlbaum Associates, pp 150-74.

Dubow, E.F., Edwards, S. and Ippolito, M.F. (1997) 'Life stressors, neighbourhood disadvantage and resources: a focus on inner-city children's adjustment', *Journal of Clinical Child Psychology*, vol 26, no 2, pp 130-44.

Duchesne, S., Ratelle, C.F., Poitras, S.-C. and Drouin, E. (2009) 'Early adolescent attachment to parents, emotional problems, and teacher–academic worries about the middle school transition', *Journal of Early Adolescence*, vol 29, no 5, pp 743-66.

Duda, J.L. and Ntounumis, N. (2005) 'After-school sport for children: implications of a task involving motivational climate', in J. Mahoney, R. Larson and J.S. Eccles (eds) *Organized activities as contexts of development: Extracurricular activities, after-school and community programs*, Mahwah, NJ: Lawrence Erlbaum Associates, pp 311-30.

Dupere, V., Leventhal, T. and Lacourse, E. (2009) 'Neighbourhood poverty and suicidal thoughts and attempts in late adolescence', *Psychological Medicine*, vol 39, no 8, pp 1295-306.

Durlak, J.A. and Weissberg, R.P. (2007) *The impact of after-school programs that promote personal and social skills*, Chicago, IL: Collaborative for Academic, Social, and Emotional Learning.

East, K. and Campbell, S. (1999) *Aspects of crime. Young offenders 1999*, London: Home Office (www.npia.police.uk).

Eccles, J.S. (1983) 'Expectancies, values and academic behaviors', in J.T. Spence (ed) *The development of achievement motivation*, Greenwich, CT: JAI Press, pp 283-331.

Eccles, J.S. and Barber, B.L. (1999) 'Student council, volunteering, basketball, or marching band: what kind of extracurricular involvement matters?', *Journal of Adolescent Research*, vol 14, no 1, pp 10-43.

Eccles, J.S. and Gootman, J.A. (2002) 'Features of positive developmental settings', in J.S. Eccles and J.A. Gootman (eds) *National Research Council and Institute of Medicine, Community programs to promote youth development, Committee on Community-level Programs for Youth, Board on Children, Youth, and Families*, Washington, DC: National Academy Press, pp 86-118.

Eccles, J.S. and Templeton, J. (2002) 'Extracurricular and other after-school activities for youth', *Review of Research in Education*, vol 26, no 1, pp 113-80.

Eccles, J.S., Midgley, C., Wigfield, A., Buchannan, C., Reuman, D., Flanagan, C. and MacIver, D. (1993) 'Development during adolescence: the impact of stage–environment fit on adolescents' experiences in schools and families', *American Psychologist*, vol 48, no 2, pp 90-101.

Eckersley, R. (2007) 'The health and well-being of young Australians: present, past and future challenges', *International Journal of Adolescent Medicine and Health*, vol 19, no 3, pp 217-27.

Eckersley, R. (2010) 'Commentary on Trzesniewski and Donnellan (2010): a transdisciplinary perspective on young people's well-being', *Perspective on Psychological Science*, vol 5, no 1, pp 76-80.

Elder, G. (1974) *Children of the Great Depression*, Boulder, CO: Westview Press.

Ellenbogen, M.A. and Hodgins, S. (2004) 'The impact of high neuroticism in parents on children's psychosocial functioning in a population at high risk for major affective disorder: a family-environmental pathway of intergenerational risk', *Development and Psychopathology*, vol 16, no 1, pp 113-36.

Ellickson, P., McGuigan, K., Adams, V., Bell, R. and Hays, R. (1996) 'Teenagers and alcohol misuse in the United States: by any definition, it's a big problem', *Addiction*, vol 91, no 10, pp 1489-503.

Essau, C.A. (2006) 'Epidemiological trends and clinical implications of adolescent substance abuse in Europe', in H.A. Liddle and C.L. Rowe (eds) *Adolescent substance abuse: Research and clinical advances*, Cambridge: Cambridge University Press, pp 129-47.

EURYDICE (2002) *Transition from primary to secondary education in European countries*, London: EURYDICE/National Foundation for Education Research.

Evangelou, M., Taggard, B., Sylva, K., Melhuish, E., Sammons, P. and Siraj-Blatchford, I. (2008) *What makes a successful transition from primary to secondary school?*, Research Report No 19, DCSF-RR019, London: Department for Children, Schools and Families.

Evans, G.W. (2004) 'The environment of childhood poverty', *American Psychologist*, vol 59, no 2, pp 77-92.

Exeter, D.J., Boyle, P.J. and Norman, P. (2011) 'Deprivation (im)mobility and cause-specific premature mortality in Scotland', *Social Science & Medicine*, vol 72, no 3, pp 389-97.

Fabio, A., Loeber, R., Balasubramani, G.K., Roth, J., Fu, W. and Farrington, D.P. (2006) 'Why some generations are more violent than others: assessment of age, period, and cohort effects', *American Journal of Epidemiology*, vol 164, no 2, pp 151-60.

Fagg, J., Curtis, S., Stansfeld, S.A. and Congdon, P. (2006) 'Psychological distress among adolescents, and its relationship to individual, family and area characteristics in East London', *Social Science & Medicine*, vol 63, no 3, pp 636-48.

Fagg, J., Curtis, S., Clarke, C., Congdon, P. and Standfeld, S.A. (2008) 'Neighbourhood perceptions among adolescents, relationships with their individual characteristics and with independently assessed neighbourhood conditions', *Journal of Environmental Psychology*, vol 28, no 2, pp 128-42.

Fauth, R., Leventhal, T. and Brooks-Gunn, J. (2005) 'Early impacts of moving from poor to middle-class neighborhoods on low-income youth', *Applied Developmental Psychology*, vol 26, no 4, pp 415-39.

Fazel, M. and Stein, A. (2002) 'The mental health of refugee children', *Archives of Diseases in Childhood*, vol 87, no 5, pp 366-70.

FBI (Federal Bureau of Investigation) (2009) *Crime in the United States*, Washington, DC: FBI (www2.fbi.gov/ucr/cius2009/data/table_01.html).

FDA (Food and Drug Administration) (2004) *Background on suicidality associated with antidepressant drug treatment (memorandum)*, FDA Center for Drug Evaluation and Research, Silver Spring: MD (www.fda.gov/ohrms/dockets/ac/04/briefing/4006B1_03_Background%20Memo%2001-05-04.htm).

Feinstein, L., Bynner, J. and Duckworth, K. (2006) 'Young people's leisure contexts and their relation to adult outcomes', *Journal of Youth Studies*, vol 9, no 3, pp 305-27.

Fergusson, D.M. and Horwood, L.J. (2001) 'The Christchurch health and development study: review of findings on child and adolescent mental health', *Australian and New Zealand Journal of Psychiatry*, vol 35, no 3, pp 287-96.

Fergusson, D.M., Boden, J. and Horwood, L.J. (2009) 'Test of causal links between alcohol abuse or dependence and major depression', *Archives of General Psychiatry*, vol 66, no 3, pp 260-6.

Fergusson, D.M., Horwood, L.J. and Lynskey M.T. (1992) 'Family change, parental discord and early offending', *Journal of Child Psychology and Psychiatry*, vol 33, no 6, pp 1059-75.

Fergusson, D.M., Woodward, L.J. and Horwood, L.J. (2000) 'Risk factors and life processes associated with the onset of suicidal behaviour during adolescence and early adulthood', *Psychological Medicine*, vol 30, no 1, pp 23-39.

Ferri, E., Bynner, J. and Wadsworth, M. (eds) (2003) *Changing Britain, changing lives: Three generations at the turn of the century*, London: Institute of Education.

Fichter, M.M., Xepapadakos, F., Quadflieg, N., Georgopoulou, E. and Fthenakis, W.E. (2004) 'A comparative study of psychopathology in Greek adolescents in Germany and in Greece in 1980 and 1998 – 18 years apart', *European Archives of Psychiatry and Clinical Neuroscience*, vol 254, no 1, pp 27-35.

Field-Smith, M., Butland, B., Ramsey, J. and Anderson, H. (2008) *Trends in death associated with abuse of volatile substances 1971-2006. Report 21*, London: Division of Community Health Sciences, St George's, University of London.

Finkelhor, D. and Jones, L. (2006) 'Why have child maltreatment and child victimization declined?', *Journal of Social Issues*, vol 62, no 4, pp 685-716.

Fisher, K. and Gershuny, J. (2009) *Diaries from children and young people: Supplement of the Multinational Time Use Study* Oxford: Centre for Time Use Research, University of Oxford (www.timeuse.org/files/cckpub/633/youth-supplement.doc).

Fisher, K., Gershuny, J. and Gauthier, A.H. (2009) *Multinational Time Use Study: User's guide and documentation* (3rd version), Oxford: Centre for Time Use Research, University of Oxford.

Fitzpatrick, K.M., Dulin, A. and Piko, B.F. (2010) 'Bullying and depressive symptomatology among low-income, African-American youth', *Journal of Youth and Adolescence*, vol 39, no 6, pp 634-45.

Fitzpatrick, K.M., Wright, D.R., Piko, B.F. and LaGory, M. (2005) 'Depressive symptomatology, exposure to violence and the role of social capital among African American adolescents', *American Journal of Orthopsychiatry*, vol 75, no 2, pp 262-74.

Flammer, A. and Schaffner, B. (2003) 'Adolescent leisure across European nations', *New Directions for Child and Adolescent Development*, vol 99, pp 65-77.

Fleisher, M. (2005) 'Fieldwork research and social network analysis: different methods creating complementary perspectives', *Journal of Contemporary Criminal Justice*, vol 21, no 2, pp 120-34.

Fombonne, E. (1998) 'Suicidal behaviours in vulnerable adolescents: time trends and their correlates', *British Journal of Psychiatry*, vol 173, pp 154-9.

Ford, T., Goodman, R. and Meltzer, H. (2003) 'Service use over 18 months among a nationally representative sample of British children with psychiatric disorder', *Clinical Child Psychology and Psychiatry*, vol 8, no 1, pp 37-51.

Forsyth, A.J.M. and Barnard, M. (1999) 'Contrasting levels of adolescent drug use between adjacent urban and rural communities in Scotland', *Addiction*, vol 94, no 11, pp 1707-18.

Fowler, P., Tomsett, C.J., Braciszewski, J.D., Jacques-Tiura, A.J. and Baltes, B.B. (2009) 'Community violence: a meta-analysis of the effect of exposure and mental health outcomes of children and adolescents', *Development and Psychopathology*, vol 21, no 1, pp 227-59.

Friedli, L. and Scheerzer, A. (1996) *Positive steps: Mental health and young people: Attitudes and awareness among 11-24 year olds*, London: Health Education Authority.

Fuller, E. (2008) *Smoking, drinking and drug use among young people in England in 2007*, London: National Health Service Information Centre for Health and Social Care.

Fuller, E. (2009) *Smoking, drinking and drug use among young people in England in 2008*, London: National Health Service.

Furlong, A. (2009) 'Reconceptualizing youth and young adulthood', in A. Furlong (ed) *Handbook of youth and young adulthood: New perspectives and agendas*, London: Routledge, pp 1-2.

Furlong, A. and Cartmel, F. (2007) *Young people and social change: New perspectives*, Maidenhead: McGraw Hill/Open University Press.

Furstenberg Jr, F.F., Rumbaut, R.C. and Settersten Jr, R.A. (2005) 'On the frontier of adulthood: emerging themes and new directions', in R.A. Settersten Jr, F.F. Furstenberg Jr and R.C. Rumbaut (eds) *On the frontier of adulthood: Theory, research and public policy*, Chicago, IL: University of Chicago Press, pp 3-27.

Gallagher, M. and Millar, R. (1996) 'A survey of adolescent worry in Northern Ireland', *Pastoral Care in Education*, vol 14, no 2, pp 26-31.

Gallagher, M. and Millar, R. (1998) 'Gender and age differences in the concerns of adolescents in Northern Ireland', *Adolescence*, vol 33, no 132, pp 862-76.

Gallagher, M., Millar, R., Hargie, O. and Ellis, R. (1992) 'The personal and social worries of adolescents in Northern Ireland: results of a survey', British *Journal of Guidance and Counselling*, vol 20, no 3, pp 274-90.

Galton, M. (2009) 'Moving to secondary school: initial encounters and their effects', *Perspectives in Education*, issue 2, *Primary-Secondary transfer in science*, London: Welcome Foundation, pp 5-21 (www.welcome. ac.uk/perspectives).

Galton, M. and Hargreaves, L. (2002) 'Transfer and transition', in L. Hargreaves and M. Galton (eds) *Transfer from the primary classroom: 20 years on*, London: RoutledgeFalmer, pp 1-28.

Galton, M. and Willcocks, J. (1983) *Moving from the primary classroom*, London: Routledge & Kegan Paul Ltd.

Galton, M., Gray, J. and Rudduck, J. (1999a) *The impact of school transitions and transfers on pupil progress and attainment*, Research Report No 131, Norwich: Department for Education and Employment.

Galton, M., Hargreaves, L., Comber, C., Pell, T, and Wall, D. (1999b) Inside the primary classroom: 20 years on, London: Routledge.

Galton, M., Gray, J., Rudduck, J., Berry, M., Demetriou, H., Edwards, J., Goalen, P., Hargreaves, L., Hussey, S., Pell, T., Schagen, I. and Charles, M. (2003) *Transfer and transitions in the middle years of schooling (7-14): Continuities and discontinuities in learning*, Research Brief No 443, London: Department for Education and Employment.

Gardner, F., Burton, J. and Klimes, I. (2006) 'Randomised controlled trial of a parenting intervention in the voluntary sector for reducing child conduct problems: outcomes and mechanisms of change', *Journal of Child Psychology and Psychiatry*, vol 47, no 11, pp 1123-32.

Garry, J.P. and Morrissey, S.L. (2000) 'Team sports participation and risk-taking behaviors among a biracial middle school population', *Clinical Journal of Sport Medicine*, vol 10, no 3, pp 185-90.

Gauthier, A.H., Smeeding, T.M. and Furstenberg, F. (2004) 'Are parents investing less time in children? Trends in selected industrialized countries', *Population and Development Review*, vol 30, no 4, pp 647-71.

Ge, X., Lorenz, F., Conger, R., Elder, G. and Simons, R. (1994) 'Trajectories of stressful life events and depressive symptoms during adolescence', *Developmental Psychology*, vol 30, no 4, pp 467-83.

Gershuny, J. (2000) *Changing times: Work and leisure in post-industrial society*, Oxford: Oxford University Press.

Gershuny, J. (2004) 'Time use', in *Taking the long view: The ISER report 2004/5*, Essex: Institute for Social and Economic Research.

Gershuny, J., Lader, D. and Short, S. (2006) *The Time Use Survey, 2005: How we spend our time*, London: Office for National Statistics.

Gill, T. (2007) *No fear: Growing up in a risk averse society*, London: Calouste Gulbenkian Foundation.

Gilman, M. and Pearson, G. (1991) 'Lifestyles and law enforcement', in D.K. Whynes and P.T. Bean (eds) *Policing and prescribing: The British system of drug control*, London: Macmillan, pp 95-124.

Gilvarry, E. (2000) 'Substance abuse in young people', *Journal of Child Psychology and Psychiatry*, vol 41, no 1, pp 55-80.

Gleave, J. (2008) *Risk and play: A literature review*, London: Playday Project, National Children's Bureau.

Glen, S., Simpson, A., Drinnan, D., McGuiness, D. and Sandberg, S. (1993) 'Testing the reliability of a new measure of life events and experiences in childhood: the Psychosocial Assessment of Childhood Experiences (PACE)', *European Journal of Child and Adolescent Psychiatry*, vol 2, no 2, pp 98-110.

Goddard, E. (2001) *Obtaining information about drinking through surveys of the general population*, National Statistics Methodological Series No 24, Newport: Office for National Statistics.

Goddard, E. (2007) *Estimating alcohol consumption from survey data: Updated method of converting volumes to units*, National Statistics Methodological Series No 37, Newport: Office for National Statistics.

Goldstein, H. and Noden, P. (2003) 'Modelling social segregation', *Oxford Review of Education*, vol 29, no 2, pp 225-37.

Gonzales, N., George, P., Fernandez, A. and Huerta, V. (2005) 'Minority adolescent stress and coping', *The Prevention Researcher*, vol 12, no 3, pp 7-9.

Goodman, A. (2010) 'Substance use and common mental health problems: examining longitudinal associations in a British sample', *Addiction*, vol 105, no 8, pp 1484-96.

Goodyer, I.M., Kolvin, I. and Gatzanis, S. (1985) 'Recent undesirable life vents and psychiatric disorder in childhood and adolescence', *British Journal of Psychiatry*, vol 147, pp 517-23.

Goodyer, I.M., Wright, C. and Altham, P.M.E. (1990) 'The friendships and recent life events of anxious and depressed school-age children', *British Journal of Psychiatry*, vol 156, no 5, pp 689-98.

Goodyer, I.M., Herbert, J., Tamplin, A. and Altham, P.M.E. (2000) 'Recent life events, cortisol, dehydroepiandrosterone and the onset of major depression in high-risk adolescents', *British Journal of Psychiatry*, vol 177, pp 499-504.

Goodyer, I.M., Herbert, J., Tamplin, A., Secher, S.M. and Pearson, J. (1997) 'Short term outcome of major depression II: life events, family dysfunction, and friendship difficulties as predictors of persistent disorder', *Journal of the American Academy of Child and Adolescent Psychiatry*, vol 36, no 4, pp 474-80.

Gordon, A. (2001) 'School exclusions in England: children's voices and adult solutions?', *Educational Studies*, vol 27, no 1, pp 69-85.

Gordon, J. and Grant, G. (eds) (1997) *How we feel: An insight into the emotional world of teenagers*, London: Jessica Kingsley Publishers.

Gore, S., Farrell, F. and Gordeon, J. (2001) 'Sports involvement as protection against depressed mood', *Journal of Research on Adolescence*, vol 11, no 1, pp 119-30.

Gottfredson, M. and Hirschi, T. (1990) *A general theory of crime*, Stanford, CA: Stanford University Press.

Grant, B., Stinson, F., Dawson, D., Chou, S., Dufour, M., Compton, W., Pickering, R. and Kaplan, K. (2004) 'Prevalence and co-occurrence of substance use disorders and independent mood and anxiety disorders: results from the National Epidemiologic Survey on alcohol and related conditions', *Archives of General Psychiatry*, vol 61, no 8, pp 807-16.

Grant, K.E., Compas, B.E., Stuhlmacher, A.F., Thurm, A.E., McMahon, S.D. and Halpert, J.A. (2003) 'Stressors and child and adolescent psychopathology: moving from markers to mechanisms of risk', *Psychological Bulletin*, vol 129, no 3, pp 447-66.

Grant, K.E., Compas, B.E., Thurm, A.E., McMahon, S.D., Gipson, P.Y., Campbell, A.J., Krochock, K. and Westerholm, R.I. (2006) 'Stressors and child and adolescent psychopathology: evidence of moderating and mediating effects', *Clinical Psychology Review*, vol 26, no 3, pp 257-83.

Gray, J. (2004) 'School effectiveness and the "other outcomes" of schooling: a reassessment of three decades of British research', *Improving Schools*, vol 7, no 2, pp 185-98.

Gray, J., Galton, M., McLaughlin, C., Clarke, B. and Symonds, J. (2011) *The supportive school*, Newcastle upon Tyne: Cambridge Scholars Publishing.

Green, H., McGinnity, A., Meltzer, H., Ford, T. and Goodman, R. (2005) *Mental health of children and young people in Great Britain, 2004*, London: Palgrave Macmillan.

Griffiths, M. (2005) 'Video games and health', *British Medical Journal*, vol 331, no 7509, pp 122-3.

Gross, E. (2004) 'Adolescent internet use: what we expect, what teens report', *Applied Developmental Psychology*, vol 25, pp 633-49.

Grossman, A.W., Churchill, J.D., McKinney, B.C., Kodish, I.M., Otte, S.L. and Greenough, W.T. (2003) 'Experience effects on brain development: possible contributions to psychopathology', *Journal of Child Psychology and Psychiatry*, vol 44, no 1, pp 33-63.

Gullone, E. and King, N.J. (1992) 'Psychometric evaluation of a revised fear survey schedule for children and adolescents', *Journal of Child Psychology and Psychiatry*, vol 33, pp 987-98.

Gunnar, M.R., Wewerka, S., Frenn, K., Long, J.D. and Griggs, C. (2009) 'Developmental changes in HPA axis activity over the transition to adolescence: normative changes and associations with pubertal stage', *Development and Psychopathology*, vol 21, no 1, pp 69-85.

Gustafsson, J.E., Allodi, M. Westling, A., Akerman, B., Eriksson, C., Eriksson, L., Fischbein, S., Granlund, M., Gustafsson, P., Ljungdahl, S., Ogden, T. and Persson, R. (2010) *School, learning and mental health: A systematic review*, Stockholm: The Health Committee, The Royal Swedish Academy of Sciences.

Hagell, A. and Shaw, C. (1996) *Opportunity and disadvantage at age 16*, London: Policy Studies Institute.

Hall, G.S. (1904) *Adolescence: Its psychology and its relation to physiology, anthropology, sociology, sex, crime, religion and education* (2 vols), New York: Appleton.

Hankin, B.J. and Abramson, L.Y. (2001) 'Development of gender differences in depression: an elaborated cognitive vulnerability-transactional stress theory', *Psychological Bulletin*, vol 127, no 6, pp 773-96.

Hankin, B.J., Mermelstein, R. and Roesch, L. (2007) 'Sex differences in adolescent depression: stress exposure and reactivity models', *Child Development*, vol 78, no 1, pp 279-95.

Harden, A., Rees, R., Shepherd, J., Brunton, G., Oliver, S. and Oakley, A. (2001) *Young people and mental health: A systematic review of research on barriers and facilitators*, London: EPPI-Centre, Social Science Research Unit, Institute of Education, University of London.

Harkness, K.L., Bruce, A.E. and Lumley, M.N. (2006) 'The role of childhood abuse and neglect in the sensitization to stressful life events in adolescent depression', *Journal of Abnormal Psychology*, vol 115, no 4, pp 730-41.

Hasebrink, U., Livingston, S., Haddon, L. and Olafsson, K. (2009) *Comparing children's online opportunities and risks across Europe: Cross-national comparisons for EU Kids Online*, London: EU Kids Online, London School of Economics and Political Science.

Hawker, D. and Boulton, M. (2000) 'Twenty years' research on peer victimization and psychosocial maladjustment: a meta-analytic review of cross-sectional studies', *Journal of Child Psychology and Psychiatry*, vol 41, no 4, pp 441-56.

Hayatbakhsh, M., Najman, J., Jamrozik, K., Al Mamun, A., Bor, W. and Alati, R. (2008) 'Adolescent problem behaviours predicting DSM-IV diagnoses of multiple substance use disorder', *Social Psychiatry and Psychiatric Epidemiology*, vol 43, no 5, pp 356-63.

Hays, R. and Ellickson, P. (1996) 'Associations between drug use and deviant behaviour in teenagers', *Addictive behaviors*, vol 21, no 3, pp 291-302.

Hayward, G., Wilde, S. and Williams, R. (2008) *Rathbone/Nuffield Engaging Youth Enquiry: Consultation report*, Manchester: Rathbone.

HEA (Health Education Authority) (1995) *Expectations for the future: An investigation into the self-esteem of 13 and 14 year old girls and boys*, London: HEA.

Heath, S. (2009) 'Young, free and single? The rise of independent living', in A. Furlong (ed) *Handbook of youth and young adulthood: New perspectives and agendas*, London: Routledge, pp 211-16.

Henquet, C., Di Forti, M., Morrison, P., Kuepper, R. and Murray, R. (2008) 'Gene-environment interplay between cannabis and psychosis', *Schizophrenia Bulletin*, vol 34, no 6, pp 1111-21.

Henquet, C., Krabbendam, L., Spauwen, J., Kaplan, C., Lieb, R., Wittchen, H.U. and van Os, J. (2005) 'Prospective cohort study of cannabis use, predisposition for psychosis, and psychotic symptoms in young people', *British Medical Journal*, vol 330, no 7481, p 11.

Hibell, B., Andersson, B., Bjarnason, T., Ahlström, S., Balakireva, O., Kokkevi, A. and Morgan, M. (2004) *The ESPAD report 2003: Alcohol and other drug use among students in 35 European countries*, Sweden: The Swedish Council for Information on Alcohol and Other Drugs (CAN), The Pompidou Group at the Council of Europe.

Hillman, M. (2006) 'Children's rights and adults' wrongs', *Children's Geographies*, vol 4, no 1, pp 61-7.

Hills, A. and Li, N. (2007) 'Smoking, drinking and drug use', in E. Fuller (ed) *Smoking, drinking and drug use among young people in England in 2006*, London: The Information Centre for Health and Social Care, National Centre for Social Research, pp 129-52.

Hirsch, B.J. and Rapkin, B.D. (1987) 'The transition to junior high school: a longitudinal study of self-esteem, psychological symptomatology, school life, and social support', *Child Development*, vol 58, no 5, pp 1235-43.

Hirschi, T. and Gottfredson, M. (1983) 'Age and the explanation of crime', *The American Journal of Sociology*, vol 89, no 3, pp 552-84.

Hoare, J. and Moon, D. (2010) *Drug misuse declared: Findings from the 2009/2010 British Crime Survey*, London: Home Office.

Holdsworth, C. (2000) 'Leaving home in Britain and Spain', *European Sociological Review*, vol 16, no 2, pp 201-22.

Home Office (2008) *Young people and crime: Findings from the 2006 Offending, Crime and Justice Survey*, London: Home Office Statistical Bulletin.

Home Office (2010) *Crime in England and Wales 2009/2010*, London: Home Office Statistical Bulletin.

Honess, T., Seymour, L. and Webster, R. (2000) *The social contexts of underage drinking*, London: Research Development and Statistics Directorate, Home Office.

Horwitz, A.V. and Wakefield, J.C. (2007) *The loss of sadness: How psychiatry transformed normal sorrow into depressive disorder*, New York: Oxford University Press.

Hsia, Y. and MacLennan, K. (2009) 'Rise in psychotropic drug prescribing in children and adolescents during 1992-2001: a population-based study in the UK', *European Journal of Epidemiology*, vol 24, no 4, pp 211-16.

Iacovou, M. (2001) *Leaving home in the European Union*, ISER Working Paper 2001-18, Colchester: Institute for Social and Economic Research.

IAS (Institute for Alcohol Studies) (2010) *IAS Factsheet: Alcohol consumption in the UK*, London: IAS (www.ias.org.uk/resources/factsheets/consumption-uk.pdf).

Institute for the Study of Drug Dependence (1993) *National audit of drug misuse in Britain, 1992*, London: Institute for the Study of Drug Dependence.

Ireson, J., Hallam, S., Mortimore, P., Hack, S., Clark, H. and Plewis, I. (1999) 'Ability grouping in the secondary school: the effects on academic achievement and pupils' self-esteem', Paper presented at the British Educational Research Association Annual Conference, University of Sussex at Brighton, 2-5 September.

Isacsson, G., Rich, C.L., Jureidini, J. and Raven, M. (2010) 'In debate: the increased use of antidepressants has contributed to the worldwide reduction in suicide rates', *British Journal of Psychiatry*, vol 196, no 6, pp 429-33.

Jackson, L., Langille, L., Lyons, R., Hughes, J., Martin, D. and Winstanley, V. (2009) 'Does moving from a high-poverty to lower-poverty neighborhood improve mental health? A realist review of Moving to Opportunity', *Health Place*, vol 15, no 4, pp 961-70.

James, A. (2010) *School bullying*, Research Briefing, London: NSPCC.

Jennings, K. and Hargreaves, D.J. (1981) 'Children's attitudes to secondary school transfer', *Educational Studies*, vol 7, no 1, pp 35-9.

Jose, P. and Huntsinger, C. (2005) 'Moderation and mediation effects of coping by Chinese American and European American adolescents', *Journal of Genetic Psychology*, vol 166, no 1, pp 16-43.

Jose, P. and Ratcliffe, V. (2004) 'Stressor frequency and perceived intensity as predictors of internalizing symptoms: gender and age differences in adolescence', *New Zealand Journal of Psychology*, vol 33, no 3, pp 145-54.

Juvonen, J., Le, V.-N., Kaganoff, T., Augustine, C. and Constant, L. (2004) *Focus on the wonder years: Challenges facing the American middle school*, Santa Monica, CA: Rand Corporation.

Kandel, D. and Davies, M. (1982) 'Epidemiology of depressive mood in adolescents', *Archives of General Psychiatry*, vol 39, no 10, pp 1205-12.

Kellam, S., Ling, X., Merisca, R., Brown, C. and Ialongo, N. (1998) 'The effect of the level of aggression in the first grade classroom on the course and malleability of aggressive behaviour into middle school', *Development and Psychopathology*, vol 10, no 2, pp 165-85.

Kelly, T.M., Cornelius, J.R. and Clark, D.B. (2004) 'Psychiatric disorders and attempted suicide among adolescents with substance use disorders', *Drug and Alcohol Dependence*, vol 73, no 1, pp 87-97.

Kessler, R.C., Berglund, P., Demler, O., Jin, R., Merikangas, K.R. and Walters, E.E. (2005) 'Lifetime prevalence and age-at-onset distributions of DSM-IV disorders in the National Comorbidity Survey Replication', *Archives of General Psychiatry*, vol 62, no 6, pp 593-602.

Kilpatrick, D., Ruggiero, K., Acierno, R., Saunders, B.E., Resnick, H.S. and Best C.L. (2003) 'Violence and risk of PTSD, major depression, substance abuse/dependence and comorbidity: results from the National Survey of Adolescents', *Journal of Consulting and Clinical Psychology*, vol 71, no 4, pp 692-700.

Kim, K.J. (2005) 'Interconnected accumulation of life stresses and adolescent maladjustment', *The Prevention Researcher*, vol 12, no 3, pp 13-15.

Kim-Cohen, J., Caspi, A., Moffitt, T.E., Harrington, H., Milne, B.J. and Poulton, R. (2003) 'Prior juvenile diagnoses in adults with mental disorder: developmental follow-back of a prospective-longitudinal cohort', *Archives of General Psychiatry*, vol 60, no 7, pp 709-17.

King, R.A., Schwab-Stone, M., Flisher, A.J., Greenwald, S., Kramer, R.A., Goodman, S.H., Lahey, B.B., Shaffer, D. and Gould M.S. (2001) 'Psychosocial and risk behavior correlates of youth suicide attempts and suicidal ideation', *Journal of the American Academy of Child and Adolescent Psychiatry*, vol 40, no 7, pp 837-46.

Kivel, B. (1998) 'Adolescent identity formation and leisure contexts: a selective review of literature', *Journal of Physical Education, Recreation and Dance*, vol 69, no 1, pp 36-40.

Kleiber, D. and Kirshnit, C. (1991) 'Sport involvement and identity formation', in L. Diamant (ed) *Mind-body maturity: Psychological approaches to sports, exercise and fitness*, New York: Hemisphere Publishing Corporation, pp 193-211.

Kleiber, D. and Powell, G. (2005) 'Historical change in leisure activities during after-school hours', in J. Mahoney, R. Larson, and J.S. Eccles (eds) *Organized activities as contexts of development: Extracurricular activities, after-school and community programs*, Mahwah, NJ: Lawrence Erlbaum Associates, pp 23-44.

Kosidou, K., Magnusson, C., Mittendorfer-Rutz, E., Hallqvist, J., Hellner Gumpert, C., Idrizbegovic, S., Dal, H. and Dalman, C. (2010) 'Recent trends in levels of self-reported anxiety, mental health service use and suicidal behaviour in Stockholm', *Acta Psychiatrica Scandinavica*, vol 122, no 1, pp 47-55.

Kotchick, B.A. and Forehand, R. (2002) 'Putting parenting in perspective: a discussion of the contextual factors that shape parenting practices', *Journal of Child and Family Studies*, vol 11, no 3, pp 255-69.

Kumpulainen, K. (2008) 'Psychiatric conditions associated with bullying', *International Journal of Adolescent Medicine and Health*, vol 20, no 2, pp 121-32.

Larson, R.W. (2000) 'Toward a psychology of positive youth development', *American Psychologist*, vol 55, no 1, pp 170-83.

Larson, R.W. and Kleiber, D. (1993) 'Free time activities as factors in adolescent adjustment', in P. Tolan and B. Cohler (eds) *Handbook of clinical research and practice with adolescents*, New York: Wiley, pp 125-45.

Larson, R.W. and Seepersad, S. (2003) 'Adolescents' leisure time in the United States: partying, sports, and the American experiment', *New Directions for Child and Adolescent Development*, vol 99, pp 53-64.

Larson, R.W. and Verma, S. (1999) 'How children and adolescents spend time across cultural settings of the world: work, play and developmental opportunities', *Psychological Bulletin*, vol 125, no 6, pp 701-36.

Larson, R.W., Jarrett, R., Hansen, D., Pearce, N., Sullivan, P., Walker, K., Watkins, N. and Wood, D. (2004) 'Organised youth activities as contexts for positive development', in P. Linley and S. Joseph (eds) *Positive psychology in practice*, New York: Wiley, pp 540-60.

Larson, R.W., Hansen, D.M. and Moneta, G. (2006) 'Differing profiles of developmental experiences across types of organized youth activities', *Developmental Psychology*, vol 42, no 5, pp 849-63.

Layard, R.W. and Dunn, J. (2009) *A good childhood: Searching for values in a competitive age*, London: Penguin.

Lazarus, R. and Folkman, S. (1984) *Stress appraisal, and coping*, New York: Springer.

Lefebvre, P., Merrigan, P. and Verstraete, M. (2008) *The effects of school quality and family functioning on youth math scores: A Canadian longitudinal analysis*, Cahiers de recherche 0822, Montreal: CIRPEE.

Leonard, M. (2010) 'Parochial geographies: growing up in divided Belfast', *Childhood*, vol 17, no 3, pp 329-42.

Leventhal, T. and Brooks-Gunn, J. (2000) 'The neighbourhoods they live in: the effects of neighbourhood residence on child and adolescent outcomes', *Psychological Bulletin*, vol 126, no 2, pp 309-37.

Leventhal, T. and Brooks-Gunn, J. (2003) 'Moving to Opportunity: an experimental study of neighbourhood effects on mental health', *American Journal of Public Health*, vol 93, no 9, pp 1576-82.

Leventhal, T., Fauth, R.C. and Brooks-Gunn, J. (2005) 'Neighbourhood poverty and public policy: a 5-year follow-up of children's educational outcomes in the New York City moving to opportunity demonstration', *Developmental Psychology*, vol 41, no 6, pp 933-52.

Leventhal, T., Dupere, V. and Brooks-Gunn, J. (2009) 'Neighbourhood influences on adolescent development', in R. Lerner and L. Steinberg (eds) *Handbook of adolescent psychology, Volume 2: Contextual influences on adolescent development* (3rd edn), Hoboken, NJ: John Wiley & Sons Inc, pp 411-43.

Lewinsohn, P.M., Rohde, P. and Seeley, J.R. (1998) 'Major depressive disorder in older adolescents: prevalence, risk factors, and clinical implications', *Clinical Psychology Review*, vol 18, no 7, pp 765-94.

Lewis, R. (1994) 'Flexible hierarchies and dynamic disorder: the trading and distribution of illicit heroin in Britain and Europe 1970-90', in J. Strang and M. Gossop (eds) *Heroin addiction and drug policy: The British system*, Oxford: Oxford University Press, pp 42-54.

Linn, M. (1994) 'The tyranny of the mean: gender and expectations', *Notices of the American Mathematical Society*, vol 41, no 7, pp 766-9.

Lipps, G. (2005) *Making the transition: The impact of moving from elementary to secondary school on adolescents' academic achievement and psychological adjustment*, Analytical Studies Branch Research Paper Series, Ontario: Statistics Canada, Family and Labour Studies Division.

Little, S.A. and Garber, J. (2004) 'Interpersonal and achievement orientations and specific stressors predict depressive and aggressive symptoms', *Journal of Adolescent Research*, vol 19, pp 63-84.

Loeber, R. (1990) 'Development and risk factors of juvenile antisocial behaviour and delinquency', *Clinical Psychology Review*, vol 10, no 1, pp 1-41.

Loeber, R. and Stouthamer-Loeber, M. (1986) 'Family factors as correlates and predictors of juvenile conduct problems and delinquency', in M. Tonry and N. Morris (eds) *Crime and justice: A review of research. Vol 7*, Chicago, IL: University of Chicago Press, pp 29-149.

Lohaus, A., Elben, C., Ball, J. and Klein-Hessling, J. (2004) 'School transition from elementary to secondary school: changes in psychological adjustment', *Educational Psychology*, vol 24, no 2, pp 161-73.

Lynskey, M.T. and Hall, W. (2000) 'The effects of cannabis use on educational attainment: a review', *Addiction*, vol 95, no 11, pp 1621-30.

Lynskey, M.T., Glowinski, A.L., Todorov, A.A., Bucholz, K.K., Madden, P.A., Nelson, E.C., Statham, D.J., Martin, N.G. and Heath, A.C. (2004) 'Major depressive disorder, suicidal ideation, and suicide attempt in twins discordant for cannabis dependence and early-onset cannabis use', *Archives of General Psychiatry*, vol 61, no 10, pp 1026-32.

Ma, J., Lee, K.V. and Stafford, R.S. (2005) 'Depression treatment during outpatient visits by US children and adolescents', *Journal of Adolescent Health*, vol 37, no 6, pp 434-42.

MacDonald, R. (2009) 'Precarious work: risk, choice and poverty traps', in A. Furlong (ed) *Handbook of youth and young adulthood: New perspectives and agendas*, London: Routledge, pp 167-75.

MacDonald, R. and Marsh, J. (2002) 'Crossing the rubicon: youth transitions, poverty, drugs and social exclusion', *International Journal of Drug Policy*, vol 13, no 1, pp 27-38.

MacDonald, R. and Marsh, J. (eds) (2005) *Disconnected youth? Growing up in Britain's poor neighbourhoods*, Basingstoke: Palgrave Macmillan.

McArdle, P., Prosser, J., Dickinson, H. and Kolvin, I. (2003) 'Secular trends in the mental health of primary school children', *Irish Journal of Psychological Medicine*, vol 20, no 2, pp 56-8

McCabe, K., Hough, R.L., Yeh, M., Lucchini, S.E. and Hazen, A. (2005) 'The relationship between violent exposure and conduct problems among adolescents: a prospective study', *American Journal of Orthopsychiatry*, vol 75, no 4, pp 574-84.

McCormick, C. and Mathews, I. (2007) 'HPA function in adolescence: role of sex hormones in its regulation and the enduring consequences of exposure to stressors', *Pharmacology, Biochemistry and Behaviour*, vol 86, no 2, pp 220-3.

McCrory, E., de Brito, S.A. and Viding, E. (2010) 'Research review: the neurobiology and genetics of maltreatment and adversity', *Journal of Child Psychology and Psychiatry*, vol 51, no 10, pp 1079-95.

McEwen, B. (2000) 'Stress, definition and concepts of', in G. Fink (ed) *Encyclopedia of stress* (vol 3), San Diego, CA: Academic Press, pp 508-9.

McGee, R., Williams, S., Poulton, R. and Moffitt, T. (2000) 'A longitudinal study of cannabis use and mental health from adolescence to early adulthood', *Addiction*, vol 95, no 4, pp 491-503.

McMahon, S., Grant, K., Compas, B., Thurm, A. and Ey, S. (2003) 'Stress and psychopathology in children and adolescents: is there evidence of specificity?', *Journal of Child Psychology and Psychiatry*, vol 44, no 1, pp 107-33.

McNeal, R. (1995) 'Extracurricular activities and high school dropouts', *Sociology of Education*, vol 68, no 1, pp 62-81.

McNeely, C., Nonnemaker, J. and Blum, R. (2002) 'Promoting school connectedness: evidence from the National Longitudinal Study of Adolescent Health', *Journal of School Health*, vol 72, no 4, pp 138-46.

McVicar, D. and Rice, P. (2001) 'Participation in further education in England and Wales: an analysis of post-war trends', *Oxford Economic Papers* (Oxford University Press), vol 53, no 1, pp 47-66.

McVie, S. and Norris, P. (2006) *Neighbourhood effects on youth delinquency and drug use*, Edinburgh Study of Youth Transitions and Crime (ESYTC) Research Digest No 10, Edinburgh: ESYTC.

Machin, S. and Vignoles, A. (2006) *Education policy in the UK*, London: Centre for the Economics of Education.

Mackett, R., Brown, B., Gong, Y., Kitazawa, K. and Paskins, J. (2007) 'Children's independent movement in the local environment', *Built Environment*, vol 33, no 4, pp 454-68.

Macleod, J., Oakes, R., Copello, A., Crome, I., Egger, M., Hickman, M., Oppenkowski, T., Stokes-Lampard, H. and Davey Smith, G. (2004) 'Psychological and social sequelae of cannabis and other illicit drug use by young people: a systematic review of longitudinal, general population studies', *Lancet*, vol 363, no 9421, pp 1579-88.

Mahoney, J.L. (2000) 'School extracurricular activity participation as a moderator in the development of antisocial patterns', *Child Development*, vol 71, no 2, pp 502-16.

Mahoney, J.L. and Cairns, R.B. (1997) 'Do extracurricular activities protect against early school dropout?', *Developmental Psychology*, vol 33, no 2, pp 241-53.

Mahoney, J.L., Cairns, B.D. and Farmer, T.W. (2003) 'Promoting interpersonal competence and educational success through extracurricular activity participation', *Journal of Educational Psychology*, vol 95, no 2, pp 409-18.

Mahoney, J.L., Larson, R.W. and Eccles, J.S. (eds) (2005) *Organized activities as contexts of development*, Mahwah, NJ: Lawrence Erlbaum Associates.

Mahoney, J.L., Stattin, H. and Lord, H. (2004) 'Unstructured youth recreation centre participation and antisocial behaviour development: selection influences and the moderation role of antisocial peers', *International Journal of Behavioral Development*, vol 28, no 6, pp 553-60.

Margo, J. and Dixon, M. (2006) *Freedom's orphans: Raising youth in a changing world*, London: Institute for Public Policy Research.

Margolin, G. and Gordis, E.B. (2000) 'The effects of family and community violence on children', *Annual review of Psychology*, vol 51, pp 445-79.

Marsh, H.W. and Kleitman, S. (2002) 'Extracurricular school activities: the good, the bad, and the nonlinear', *Educational Review*, vol 72, no 4, pp 464-514.

Mason, W.A., Hitchings, J.E. and Spoth, R.L. (2007) 'Emergence of delinquency and depressed mood throughout adolescence as predictors of late adolescent problem substance use', *Psychology of Addictive Behaviours*, vol 21, no 1, pp 13-24.

Masten, A.S. (2001) 'Ordinary magic: resilience processes in development', *American Psychologist*, vol 56, no 3, pp 227-38.

Masten, A.S. and Powell, J.L. (2003) 'A resilience framework for research, policy, and practice', in S.S. Luthar (ed) *Resilience and vulnerability: Adaptation in the context of childhood adversities*, New York: Cambridge University Press, pp 1-25.

Masten, A.S., Faden, V., Zucker, R. and Spear, L. (2008) 'Underage drinking: a developmental framework', *Pediatrics,* vol 121, Suppl, pp S235-S251.

Maughan, B. (2004) 'Schooling and psychosocial development', Unpublished manuscript, London: Institute of Psychiatry.

Maughan, B., Iervolino, A.C. and Collishaw, S. (2005) 'Time trends in child and adolescent mental disorders', *Current Opinion in Psychiatry*, vol 18, no 4, pp 381-5.

Maughan, B., Collishaw, S., Meltzer, H. and Goodman, R. (2008) 'Recent trends in UK child and adolescent mental health', *Social Psychiatry and Psychiatric Epidemiology*, vol 43, no 4, pp 305-10.

Maxwell, C., Kinver, A. and Phelps, A. (2007) *Scottish Schools Adolescent Lifestyle and Substance Use Survey (SALSUS), National report*, Edinburgh: ISD Scotland.

May, C. (1992) 'A burning issue: adolescent alcohol use in Britain 1970-1991', *Alcohol and Alcoholism*, vol 27, no 2, pp 109-15.

Mayhew, E., Finch, N., Beresford, B. and Keung, A. (2005) 'Children's time and space', in J. Bradshaw and E. Mayhew (eds) *The well-being of children in the UK* (2nd edn), London: Save the Children, pp 161-81.

Mayo, E. and Nairn, A. (2009) *Consumer kids: How big business is grooming our children for profit*, London: Constable and Robinson Ltd.

Measelle, J.R., Stice, E. and Hogansen, J.M. (2006) 'Developmental trajectories of co-occurring depressive, eating, antisocial, and substance abuse problems in female adolescents', *Journal of Abnormal Psychology*, vol 115, no 3, pp 524-38.

Measham, F. (2004) 'The decline of ecstasy, the rise of binge drinking and the persistence of pleasure', *Probation Journal*, vol 51, no 4, pp 309-26.

Measham, F. (2008) 'The turning tides of intoxication: young people's drinking in the 2000s', *Health Education, Special Edition: Drugs in the 21st century*, vol 108, no 3, pp 207-22.

Measham, F., Aldridge, J. and Parker, H. (2001) *Dancing on drugs: Risk, health and hedonism in the British club scene*, London: Free Association Books.

Meltzer, H., Gatward, R., Goodman, R. and Ford, T. (2000) *The mental health of children and adolescents in Great Britain*, London: The Stationery Office.

Miller, P. and Plant, M. (2002) 'Heavy cannabis use among UK teenagers: an exploration', *Drug and Alcohol Dependence*, vol 65, no 3, pp 235-42.

Minde, K., Eakin, L., Hechtman, L., Ochs, E., Bouffard, R., Greenfield, B. and Looper, K. (2003) 'The psychosocial functioning of children and spouses of adults with ADHD', *Journal of Child Psychology and Psychiatry*, vol 44, no 4, pp 637-46.

Mirza, K. and Mirza, S. (2008) 'Adolescent substance misuse', *Psychiatry*, vol 7, no 8, pp 357-62.

Mittendorfer-Rutz, E. and Wasserman, D. (2004) 'Trends in adolescent suicide mortality in the WHO European Region 2004', *European Child and Adolescent Psychiatry*, vol 13, no 5, pp 321-31.

Moffitt, T.E. (1993) 'Adolescence-limited and life-course-persistent antisocial behavior: a developmental taxonomy', *Psychological Review*, vol 100, no 4, pp 674-701.

Mohler, B. and Earls, F. (2001) 'Trends in adolescent suicide: misclassification bias?', *American Journal of Public Health*, vol 91, no 1, pp 150-3.

Monck, E. and Dobbs, R. (1985) 'Measuring life events in an adolescent population: methodological issues and related findings', *Psychological Medicine*, vol 15, no 4, pp 841-50.

Monroe, S., Rohde, P., Seeley, J. and Lewinsohn, P. (1999) 'Life events and depression in adolescence: relationship loss as a prospective risk factor for first onset of major depressive disorder', *Journal of Abnormal Psychology*, vol 108, no 4, pp 606-14.

Moody, J., Feinberg, M., Osgood, D., Gest, W. and Scott D. (2010) 'Mining the network: peers and adolescent health', *Journal of Adolescent Health*, vol 47, no 4, pp 324-6.

Moon, B. (1994) 'The national curriculum, origins, context and implementation', in B Moon, A.S. Mayes and S. Hutchinson (eds) *Teaching and learning in the secondary school*, London: RoutledgeFalmer, pp 245-60.

Moore, T.H., Zammit, S., Lingford-Hughes, A., Barnes, T.R., Jones, P.B., Burke, M. and Lewis, G. (2007) 'Cannabis use and risk of psychotic or affective mental health outcomes: a systematic review', *Lancet*, vol 370, no 9584, pp 319-28.

Morris, S. and Wagner, E. (2007) *Alcohol and substance use: Developmental considerations*, Florida Certification Board/Southern Coast ATTC Monograph Series #1, Tallahassee, FL: Florida Department of Children and Families.

Morrow, V.M. (2000) '"Dirty looks" and "trampy places" in young people's accounts of community and neighbourhood: implications for health inequalities', *Critical Public Health*, vol 10, no 2, pp 141-52.

Mortimer, J.T. and Larson, R.W. (eds) (2002a) *The changing adolescent experience*, Cambridge: Cambridge University Press.

Mortimer, J.T. and Larson, R.W. (2002b) 'Macrostructural trends and the reshaping of adolescence', in J.T. Mortimer and R.W. Larson (eds) *The changing adolescent experience: Societal trends and the transition to adulthood*, Cambridge: Cambridge University Press, pp 1-17.

Mott, J. and Mirrlees-Black, C. (1995) *Self-reported drug misuse in England and Wales: Findings from the 1992 British Crime Survey*, Home Office Research and Planning Unit Paper 89, London: Home Office.

MTUS, Versions World 5.5.3, 5.80 and 6.0 (released 26 March 2009) Created by Jonathan Gershuny and Kimberly Fisher, with Evrim Altintas, Alyssa Borkosky, Anita Bortnik, Donna Dosman, Cara Fedick, Tyler Frederick, Anne H. Gauthier, Sally Jones, Jiweon Jun, Aaron Lai, Qianhan Lin, Tingting Lu, Fiona Lui, Leslie MacRae, Berenice Monna, José Ignacio Giménez Nadal, Monica Pauls, Cori Pawlak, Andrew Shipley, Cecilia Tinonin, Nuno Torres, Charlemaigne Victorino, and Oiching Yeung, Centre for Time Use Research, University of Oxford (www.timeuse.org/mtus).

Mullins, E. and Irvin, J. (2005) 'Transition into middle school', *Middle School Journal*, vol 31, no 3, pp 57-60.

Murray, L. and Cooper, P.J. (1997) *Postpartum depression and child development*, New York: Guilford Press.

National Center for Education Statistics (2005) *Youth indicators, 2005: Trends in the well-being of American youth*, Washington, DC: US Government Printing Office.

Newbury-Birch, D., Walker, J., Avery, L., Beyer, F., Brown, N., Jackson, D., Lock, C., McGovern, R., Kaner, E., Gilvarry, E., McArdle, P., Ramesh, V. and Stewart, S. (2009) *Impact of alcohol consumption on young people: A systematic review of published reviews*, London: Department for Children, Schools and Families.

Nolen-Hoeksema, S., Wisco, B. and Lyubomirsky, S. (2008) 'Rethinking rumination', *Perspectives on Psychological Sciences*, vol 3, no 5, pp 400-24.

Nuffield Foundation (2009a) *Time trends in adolescent well-being*, Update December, London: Nuffield Foundation.

Nuffield Foundation (2009b) *Time trends in parenting and outcomes for young people*, Changing Adolescence Programme Briefing Paper, London: Nuffield Foundation.

O'Donnell, S., Sargent. C., Byrne. A. and White. E. with Gray, J. (2010) *International Review of Curriculum and Assessment Frameworks Internet Archive, November 2010 edition*, Coventry: Qualifications and Curriculum Development Agency.

Odgers, C.L., Caspi, A., Nagin, D.S., Piquero, A.R., Slutske, W.S., Milne, B.J., Dickson, N., Poulton, R. and Moffitt, T.E. (2008) 'Is it important to prevent early exposure to drugs and alcohol among adolescents?', *Psychological Science*, vol 19, no 10, pp 1037-44.

Ofsted (2007) *TellUs2 national report*, London: Ofsted.

Oldehinkel, A.J., Wittchen, H.U. and Schuster, P. (1999) 'Prevalence, 20-month incidence and outcome of unipolar depressive disorders in a community sample of adolescents', *Psychological Medicine*, vol 29, no 3, pp 655-68.

Olfson, M., Marcus, S.C., Druss, B., Elinson, L., Tanielian, T. and Pincus, H.A. (2002) 'National trends in the outpatient treatment of depression', *Journal of the American Medical Association*, vol 287, no 2, pp 203-9.

Olfson, M., Gameroff, M.J., Marcus, S.C. and Jensen, P.S. (2003) 'National trends in the treatment of attention deficit hyperactivity disorder', *American Journal of Psychiatry*, vol 160, no 6, pp 1071-7.

Olsson, G.I., and von Knorring, A.L. (1999) 'Adolescent depression: prevalence in Swedish high-school students', *Acta Psychiatry Scandinavica*, vol 99, no 5, pp 324-31.

ONS (Office for National Statistics) (1994) *Social focus on children*, London: ONS.

ONS (2002) *Social focus in brief: Children*, London: ONS.

ONS (2008) *Social Trends, 38,* Basingstoke: ONS/Palgrave Macmillan.

ONS (2009) *Social Trends, 39,* Basingstoke: ONS/Palgrave Macmillan.

Overmier, J.B. and Murison, R. (2005) 'Trauma and resulting sensitization effects are modulated by psychological factors', *Psychoneuroendocrinology*, vol 30, no 10, pp 965-73.

Page, R.M., Hammermeister, J., Scanlan, A. and Gilbert, L. (1998) 'Is school sports participation a protective factor against adolescent health risk behaviours?', *Journal of Health Education*, vol 29, no 3, pp 186-92.

Pallesen, S., Hetland, J., Sivertsen, B., Samdal, O., Torsheim, T. and Nordhus, I.H. (2008) 'Time trends in sleep-onset difficulties among Norwegian adolescents: 1983-2005', *Scandinavian Journal of Public Health*, vol 36, no 8, pp 889-95.

Pardini, D., Raskin White, H. and Stouthamer-Loeber, M. (2007) 'Early adolescent psychopathology as a predictor of alcohol use disorders by young adulthood', *Drug and Alcohol Dependency*, vol 88 (Suppl 1), S38-S49.

Parker, H. (2005) 'Normalization as a barometer: recreational drug use and the consumption of leisure by younger Britons', *Addiction Research and Theory*, vol 13, no 3, pp 205-15.

Parker, H., Aldridge, J. and Measham, F. (1998) *Illegal leisure. The normalisation of adolescent recreational drug use*, London: Routledge.

Parker, H., Bakx, K. and Newcombe R (1988) *Living with heroin: The impact of a drugs 'epidemic' on an English community*, Milton Keynes: Open University Press.

Parry-Langdon, N. (ed) (2008) *Three years on: Survey of the development and emotional well-being of children and young people*, Newport: Office for National Statistics.

Patrick, H., Ryan, A.M., Alfeld-Liro, C., Fredricks, J.A., Hruda, L. and Eccles, J.S. (1999) 'Adolescents' commitment to developing talent: the role of peers in continuing motivation for sports and the arts', *Journal of Youth and Adolescence*, vol 28, no 6, pp 741-63.

Patterson, G. (2002) 'The early development of coercive family processes', in J.B. Reid, G.R. Patterson and J. Snyder (eds) *Antisocial behaviour in children and adolescents: A developmental analysis and model for intervention*, Washington, DC: APA Press, pp 25-44.

Peach, C. (2010) 'Contrasts in US and British segregation patterns', in T. Clark, R. Putnam and E. Fieldhouse (eds) *The age of Obama: The changing place of minorities in the British and American societies*, Manchester: Manchester University Press (www.ageofobamabook.com/papers/CeriPeachPaper.pdf).

Pearson, G. (1987) *The new heroin users*, Oxford: Basil Blackwell.

Pearson, G., Gilman, M. and McIver, S. (1986) 'Young people and heroin: an examination of heroin use in the North of England', *Health Education Journal*, vol 45, pp 186-9.

Peck, S.C., Feinstein, L. and Eccles, J.S. (2008a) 'Pathways through education: why are some kids not succeeding in school and what helps others beat the odds?', *Journal of Social Issues*, Special Issue, vol 64, no 1, pp 227-33.

Peck, S.C., Vida, M. and Eccles, J.S. (2008b) 'Adolescent pathways to adulthood drinking: sport activity involvement is not necessarily risky or protective', *Journal of Addiction*, vol 103, Suppl 1, pp 69-83.

Pellegrini, A. and Blatchford, P. (2000) *The child at school: Interactions with peers and teachers*, London: Hodder Arnold.

Pellegrini, A. and Blatchford, P. (2002) 'Time for a break?', *The Psychologist*, vol 15, February, pp 60-82.

Piquero, A.R., Farrington, D.P., Welsh, B.C., Tremblay, R.E. and Jennings, W. (2008) *Effects of early family/parent training programmes on antisocial behaviour and delinquency*, Campbell Systematic Reviews 2008, Oslo: The Campbell Collaboration.

Pirkis, J., Irwin, C., Brindis, C., Patton, G. and Sawyer, M. (2003) 'Adolescent substance use: beware of international comparisons', *Journal of Adolescent Health*, vol 33, no 4, pp 279-86.

PISA (Programme for International Student Assessment) (2006) *PISA 2006 Science competencies for tomorrow's world*, Paris: OECD PISA.

Plant, M.A. (2000) 'Young people and alcohol abuse', in P. Aggleton, J. Hurry and I. Warwick (eds) *Young people and mental health*, London: Wiley, pp 13-28.

Plant, M.A. and Plant, M. (2006) *Binge Britain: Alcohol and the national response*, Oxford: Oxford University Press.

Police Foundation (2000) *Independent Inquiry into the Misuse of Drugs* (Runciman Report), London: Police Foundation.

Pring, R., Hayward, G., Hodgson, A., Johnson, J., Keep, E., Oancea, A., Rees, G., Spours, K. and Wilde, S. (2009) *Education for all: The future of education and training for 14-19 year olds*, Oxford: Routledge.

Rainey, C.J., McKeown, R.E., Sargent, R.G. and Valois, R.F. (1996) 'Patterns of tobacco and alcohol use among sedentary, exercising, nonathletic, and athletic youth', *Journal of School Health*, vol 66, no 1, pp 27-32.

Ramsay, M. and Spiller, A. (1997) *Drug misuse declared: Results of the 1996 British Crime Survey*, Home Office Research Study 172, London: Home Office.

Randall, M., Ekert-Jaffe, O., Joshi, H., Lynch, K. and Mougin, R. (2009) 'Universal versus economically polarized change at age at first birth: a French-British comparison', *Population and Development Review*, vol 35, no 1, pp 89-115.

Reuter, P. and Stevens, A. (2007) *An analysis of UK drug policy: A monograph prepared for the UK Drug Policy Commission*, London: UK Drug Policy Commission.

Richardson, A. and Budd, T. (2003) *Alcohol, crime and disorder: A study of young adults*, London: Home Office Research Unit, Home Office.

Richters, J.E. and Martinez, P. (1993) 'The NIMH Community Violence Project: 1. Children as victims of and witnesses to violence', *Psychiatry*, vol 56, no 1, pp 7-21.

Riggins-Caspers, K.M., Cadoret, R.J., Knutson, J.F. and Langbehn, D. (2003) 'Biology–environment interaction and evocative biology–environment correlation: contributions of harsh discipline and parental psychopathology to problem adolescent behaviors', *Behavior Genetics*, vol 33, no 3, pp 205-20.

Roberts, R., Roberts, C. and Xing, Y. (2007) 'Comorbidity of substance use disorders and other psychiatric disorders among adolescents: evidence from an epidemiologic survey', *Drug and Alcohol Dependency*, vol 88, Suppl 1, pp S4-13.

Robins, L.N. (1966) *Deviant children grown up: A sociological and psychiatric study of sociopathic personality*, Baltimore, MD: Williams & Wilkins.

Robins, L.N. (2001) 'Making sense of the increasing prevalence of conduct disorder', in J. Green and W.Yule (eds) *Research and innovation on the road to modern child psychiatry, Vol 1. Festschrift for Professor Sir Michael Rutter*, Glasgow: Gaskell, pp 115-28.

Robins L.N. and Regier, D.A. (eds) (1991) *Psychiatric disorders in America: The epidemiologic catchment area study*, New York: John Wiley & Sons.

Robson, K. and Feinstein, L. (2007) *Leisure contexts in adolescence and their associations with adult outcomes: A more complete picture*, London: Centre for Research on the Wider Benefits of Learning.

Roe, S. and Ashe, J. (2008) *Young people and crime: Findings from the 2006 Offending, Crime and Justice Survey*, London: Home Office.

Roe, S. and Man, L. (2006) *Drug misuse declared: Findings from the 2005/6 British Crime Survey: England and Wales*, Home Office Statistical Bulletin 15/06, London: Home Office.

Roeser, R., Eccles, J.S. and Freedman-Doan, C. (1999) 'Academic functioning and mental health in adolescence: patterns, progressions, and routes from childhood', *Journal of Adolescent Research*, vol 14, no 2, pp 135-74.

Roeser, R., Eccles, J.S. and Sameroff, A. (2000) 'School as a context of social-emotional development: a summary of research findings', *Elementary School Journal*, vol 100, no 5, pp 443-71.

Rojo, L., Conesa, L., Bermudez, O. and Livianos, L. (2006) 'Influence of stress in the onset of eating disorders: data from a two-stage epidemiological controlled study', *Psychosomatic Medicine*, vol 68, no 4, pp 628-35.

Rose, A., Carlson, W. and Waller, E. (2007) 'Prospective associations of co-rumination with friendship and emotional adjustment: considering the socioemotional trade-offs of co-rumination', *Developmental Psychology*, vol 43, no 4, pp 1019-31.

Ruchkin, V., Henrich, C.C., Jones, S.M., Vermeiren, R. and Schwab-Stone, M. (2007) 'Violence exposure and psychopathology in urban youth: the mediating role of posttraumatic stress', *Journal of Abnormal Child Psychology*, vol 35, no 4, pp 578-93.

Rudolph, K., Lambert, S., Clark, A. and Kurlakowsky, K. (2001) 'Negotiating the transition to middle school: the role of self-regulatory processes', *Child Development*, vol 73 no 3, pp 929-46.

Rutter, M. (1979) *Changing youth in a changing society*, London: Nuffield Provincial Hospitals Trust.

Rutter, M. (1983) 'Stress, coping and development: some issues and some questions', in N. Garmezy and M. Rutter (eds) *Stress, coping and development in children*, New York: McGraw-Hill, pp 1-41.

Rutter, M. (1985) 'Resilience in the face of adversity: protective factors and resistance to psychiatric disorder', *British Journal of Psychiatry*, vol 147, pp 598-611.

Rutter, M. (1989) 'Pathways from childhood to adult life', *Journal of Child Psychology and Psychiatry*, vol 30, no 1, pp 23-51.

Rutter, M. (2002) 'Substance use and abuse: causal pathways consideration', in M. Rutter and E. Taylor (eds) *Child and adolescent psychiatry*, Oxford: Wiley-Blackwell, pp 455-62.

Rutter, M. (2005) 'Environmentally mediated risks for psychopathology: research strategies and findings', *Journal of the American Academy of Child and Adolescent Psychiatry*, vol 44, no 1, pp 3-18.

Rutter, M. (2006a) 'The promotion of resilience in the face of adversity', in A. Clarke-Stewart and J. Dunn (eds) *Families count: Effects on child and adolescent development*, New York/Cambridge: Cambridge University Press, pp 26-52.

Rutter, M. (2006b) 'Implications of resilience concepts for scientific understanding', *Annals of the New York Academy of Sciences*, vol 1094, pp 1-12.

Rutter, M. (2007) 'Proceeding from observed correlations to causal inference: the use of natural experiments', *Perspectives in Psychological Science*, vol 2, pp 377-95.

Rutter, M. (In press) 'Gene-environment interdependence: background concepts, developmental perturbations, and epigenetics', *European Journal of Developmental Psychology*.

Rutter, M. and Maughan, B. (2002) 'School effectiveness findings 1979-2002', *Journal of School Psychology*, vol 40, no 6, pp 451-75.

Rutter, M. and Smith, D.J. (1995) *Psychosocial disorders in young people: Time trends and their causes*, Chichester: John Wiley & Sons.

Rutter, M., Giller, H. and Hagell, A. (1998) *Antisocial behaviour by young people*, Cambridge: Cambridge University Press.

Rutter, M., Maughan, B., Mortimore, P. and Ouston, J. (1979) *Fifteen thousand hours: Secondary schools and their effects on children*, London: Open Books.

Rutz, E.M. and Wasserman, D. (2004) 'Trends in adolescent suicide mortality in the WHO European Region', *European Child and Adolescent Psychiatry*, vol 13, no 5, pp 321-31.

Ryan, R.M. and Deci, E.L. (2000) 'Self-determination theory and the facilitation of intrinsic motivation, social development, and well-being', *American Psychologist*, vol 55, no 1, pp 68-78.

Ryan-Wenger, N., Sharrer, V. and Campbell, K. (2005) 'Changes in children's stressors over the past 30 years', *Paediatric Nursing*, vol 31, no 4, pp 282-8, 291.

Salmela-Aro, K., Kiuru, N. and Nurmi, J.-E. (2008) 'The role of educational track in adolescents' school burnout: a longitudinal study', *British Journal of Educational Psychology*, vol 78, pp 663-89.

Salmela-Aro, K., Savolainen, H. and Holopainen, L. (2009) 'Depressive symptoms and school burnout during adolescence: evidence from two cross-lagged longitudinal studies', *Journal of Youth and Adolescence*, vol 38, no 10, pp 1316-27.

Sampson, R. (2008) 'Moving to inequality: neighbourhood effects and experiments meet social structure', *American Journal of Sociology*, vol 114, no 1, pp 189-231.

Sampson, R. and Raudenbush, S. (1999) 'Systematic social observation of public spaces: a new look at disorder in urban neighborhoods', *American Journal of Sociology*, vol 105, no 3, pp 603-51.

Sampson, R. and Raudenbush, S. (2004) 'Seeing disorder: neighborhood stigma and the social construction of "broken windows"', *Social Psychology Quarterly*, vol 67, no 4, pp 319-42.

Sampson, R., Morenoff, J. and Gannon-Rowley, T. (2002) 'Assessing "neighbourhood effects": social processes and new directions in research', *Annual Review of Sociology*, vol 28, pp 443-78.

Sampson, R., Raudenbush, S. and Earls, R. (1997) 'Neighborhoods and violent crime: a multilevel study of collective efficacy', *Science*, vol 277, pp 918-24.

Sandberg, S. and Rutter, M. (2008) 'Acute life stresses', in M. Rutter, D. Bishop, D. Pine, S. Scott, J. Stevenson, E. Taylor and A. Thapar (eds) *Rutter's child and adolescent psychiatry*, Oxford: Blackwell Publishing, pp 394-408.

Sandberg, S., Rutter, M., Giles, S., Owen, A., Champion, L., Nicholls, J., Prior, V., McGuinness, D. and Drinnan, D. (1993) 'Assessment of psychosocial experiences in childhood: methodological issues and some illustrative findings', *Journal of Child Psychology and Psychiatry*, vol 34, no 6, pp 879-97.

Sandberg, S., McGuinness, D., Hillary, C. and Rutter, M. (1998) 'Independence of childhood life events and chronic adversities: a comparison of two patient groups and controls', *Journal of the American Academy of Child and Adolescent Psychiatry*, vol 37, no 7, pp 728-35.

Sandberg, S., Paton, J.Y., Ahola, S., McCann, D.C., McGuinness, D., Hillary, C.R. and Oja, H. (2000) 'The role of acute and chronic stress in asthma attacks in children', *Lancet*, vol 356, no 9234, pp 982-7.

Santalahti, P., Aromaa, M., Sourander, A., Helenius, H. and Piha, J. (2005) 'Have there been changes in children's psychosomatic symptoms? A 10-year comparison from Finland', *Pediatrics,* vol 115, e434-e442.

Savelsberg, H.J. and Martin-Giles, B.M. (2008) 'Young people on the margins: Australian studies of social exclusion', *Journal of Youth Studies*, vol 11, no 1, pp 17-31.

Schepman, K., Collishaw, S., Gardner, F., Maughan, B., Scott, J. and Pickles, A. (2011) 'Do changes in parent mental health explain trends in youth emotional problems?', *Social Science & Medicine*, vol 73, no 2, pp 293-300.

Schoon, I. (2006) *Risk and resilience: Adaptations in changing times*, Cambridge: Cambridge University Press.

Schoon, I. (2010) 'Planning for the future: changing education expectations in three British cohorts', *Historical Social Research*, vol 35, no 2, pp 99-199.

Schwartz, S., McFadyen-Ketchum, S.A., Dodge, K.A., Petit, G.S. and Bates, J.E. (1998) 'Peer group victimization as a predictor of children's behaviour problems at home and in school', *Developmental Psychopathology*, vol 10, pp 87-99.

Scott Porter Research and Marketing Ltd (2000) *Young people and mental well-being*, Edinburgh: Health Education Board for Scotland (HEBS).

Scott, J., Treas, J. and Richards, M. (2004) *The Blackwell companion to the sociology of families*, New York: Blackwell Publishing Ltd.

Scott, S., Knapp, M., Henderson, J. and Maughan, B. (2001) 'Financial cost of social exclusion: follow up study of antisocial children into adulthood', *British Medical Journal*, vol 323, no 7306, pp 191-4.

Scottish Government (2008) *Children's participation in culture and sport: Research findings*, Edinburgh: Scottish Government (www.scotland.gov.uk/).

Seiffge-Krenke, I. (1995) *Stress, coping and relationships in adolescence*, Mahwah, NJ: Lawrence Erlbaum Associates.

Selye, H. (1936) 'A syndrome produced by diverse nocuous agents', *Nature*, vol 138, July, p 32.

Shanahan, M. and Flaherty, B. (2001) 'Dynamic patterns of time use in adolescence', *Child Development*, vol 72, no 2, pp 385-401.

Shaw, M., Dorling, D., Gordon, G. and Davey-Smith, G. (1999) *The widening gap: Health inequalities and policy in Britain*, Bristol: The Policy Press.

Shea, A., Walsh, C., MacMillan, H. and Steiner, M. (2004) 'Child maltreatment and HPA axis dysregulation: relationship to major depressive disorder and post traumatic stress disorder in females', *Psychoneuroendocrinology*, vol 30, no 2, pp 162-78.

Shepherd, J. and Roker, D. (2005) *An evaluation of a 'transition to secondary school' project run by the National Pyramid Trust*, Brighton: Trust for the Study of Adolescence (now Focus on Adolescence).

Shields, D. and Bredemeier, B. (2001) 'Moral development and behavior in sport', in R. Singer, H. Hausenblas and C. Janelle (eds) *Handbook of sport psychology* (2nd edn), New York: Wiley, pp 585-603.

Shiner, M. (2009) *Drug use and social change*, Basingstoke: Palgrave Macmillan.

Shirtcliff, E.A., Granger, D.A., Schwartz, E. and Curran, M.J. (2001) 'Use of salivary biomarkers in biobehavioral research: cotton-based sample collection methods can interfere with salivary immunoassay results', *Psychoneuroendocrinology*, vol 26, no 2, pp 165-73.

Sigfusdottir, I.D., Asgeirsdottir, B.B., Sigurdsson, J.F. and Gudjonsson, G.H. (2008) 'Trends in depressive symptoms, anxiety symptoms and visits to healthcare specialists: a national study among Icelandic adolescents', *Scandinavian Journal of Public Health*, vol 36, no 4, pp 361-8.

Silbereisen, R.K., Robins, L. and Rutter, M. (1995) 'Secular trends in substance use: concepts and data on the impact of social change on alcohol and drug use', in M. Rutter and D. Smith (eds) *Psychosocial disorders in young people: Time trends and their causes*, Chichester: Wiley & Sons, pp 490-543.

Silberg, J., Rutter, M., D'Onofrio, B. and Eaves, L. (2003) 'Genetic and environmental risk factors in adolescent substance use', *Journal of Child Psychology and Psychiatry*, vol 44, no 5, pp 664-76.

Silberg, J., Pickles, A., Rutter, M., Hewitt, J., Simonoff, E., Maes, H., Carbonneau, R., Murrelle, L., Foley, D. and Eaves, L. (1999) 'The influence of genetic factors and life stress on depression among adolescent girls', *Archives of General Psychiatry*, vol 56, no 3, pp 225-32.

Simons, R., Whitbeck, L., Beaman, J. and Conger, R.D. (1994) 'The impact of mothers' parenting, involvement by non-residential fathers, and parental conflict on the adjustment of adolescent children', *Journal of Marriage and Family*, vol 56, no 2, pp 356-74.

Singer, M., Mender Anglin, T., Song, L.-Y. and Lunghofer, L. (1995) 'Adolescents' exposure to violence and associated symptoms of psychological trauma', *Journal of the American Medical Association*, vol 273, no 6, pp 477-82.

Singh, G.K. and Siahpush, M. (2006) 'Widening socioeconomic inequalities in US life expectancy, 1980-2000', *International Journal of Epidemiology*, vol 35, no 4, pp 969-78.

Skelton, T. (2000) 'Nothing to do, nowhere to go? Teenage girls and public space in the Rhondda Valleys, South Wales', in S. Holloway and G. Valentine (eds) *Children's geographies*, London: Routledge, pp 80-99.

Smetana, J.G., Campione-Barr, N. and Metzger, A. (2006) 'Adolescent development in interpersonal and societal contexts', *Annual Review of Psychology*, vol 57, pp 255-84.

Smith, D.J. (2004) *Parenting and delinquency at ages 12 to 15*, Edinburgh Study of Youth Transitions and Crime Research Digest No 3, Edinburgh: Centre for Law and Society, University of Edinburgh.

Smith, D.J. (2010) 'Changing patterns of youth', in D.J. Smith (ed) *A new response to youth crime*, Oxford: Willan Publishing, pp 17-53.

Smith, D.J. and Bradshaw, P. (2005) *Gang membership and teenage offending*, Edinburgh Study of Youth Transitions and Crime, Publication Number 8, Edinburgh: Centre for Law and Society, University of Edinburgh (www.law.ed.ac.uk/cls/esytc/findings/digest8.pdf).

Smith, L. and Foxcroft, D. (2009) *Drinking in the UK: An exploration of trends*, York: Joseph Rowntree Foundation.

Smith, R.P., Larkin, G.L. and Southwick, S.M. (2008) 'Trends in US emergency department visits for anxiety-related mental health conditions, 1992-2001', *Journal of Clinical Psychiatry*, vol 69, no 2, pp 286-94.

Sonkin, B., Edwards, P., Roberts, I. and Green, J. (2006) 'Walking, cycling and transport safety: an analysis of child road deaths', *Journal of the Royal Society of Medicine*, vol 99, pp 402-5.

Sourander, A., Niemela, S., Santalahti, P., Helenius, H. and Piha, J. (2008) 'Changes in psychiatric problems and service use among 8-year old children: a 16-year population-based time-trend study', *Journal of the American Academy of Child and Adolescent Psychiatry*, vol 47, no 3, pp 317-27.

Sourander, A., Santalahti, P., Haavisto, A., Piha, J., Ikaheimo, K. and Helenius, H. (2004) 'Have there been changes in children's psychiatric symptoms and mental health service use? A ten-year comparison from Finland', *Journal of the American Academy of Child and Adolescent Psychiatry*, vol 43, no 9, pp 1134-45.

Sourander, A., Ronning, J., Brunstein-Klomek, A., Gyllenbert, D., Kumpulainen, K., Niemela, S., Helenius, H., Sillanmaki, L., Ristkari, T., Tamminen, T., Molanen, I., Piha, J. and Almqvist, F. (2009) 'Childhood bullying behavior and later psychiatric hospital and psychopharmacologic treatment findings from the Finnish 1981 Birth Cohort Study', *Archives of General Psychiatry*, vol 66, no 9, pp 1005-12.

Spear, L. (2002) 'The adolescent brain and the college drinker: biological basis of propensity to use and misuse alcohol', *Journal of Studies on Alcohol and Drugs*, Suppl no 14, pp 71-81.

Spear, L. (2009) 'Heightened stress responsivity and emotional reactivity during pubertal maturation: implications for psychopathology', *Developmental Psychopathology*, vol 21, no 1, pp 87-97.

Spear, L. and Varlinskaya, E. (2005) 'Adolescence: alcohol sensitivity, tolerance and intake', *Recent Developments in Alcoholism*, vol 17, pp 143-59.

Stansfeld, S.A., Berglund, B., Clark, C., Lopez-Barrio, I., Fischer, P., Ohrstrom, E., Haines, M.M., Head, J., Hygge, S., van Kamp, I., Berry, B.F. and RANCH Study Team (2005) 'Aircraft and road traffic noise and children's cognition and health: a cross-national study', *Lancet*, vol 365, no 9475, pp 1943-9.

Stattin, H. and Kerr, M. (2000) 'Parent monitoring: a reinterpretation', *Child Development*, vol 71, no 4, pp 1072-85.

Steffensmeier, D., Schwartz, J., Zhong, H. and Ackerman, J. (2005) 'An assessment of recent trends in girls' violence using diverse longitudinal sources: is the gender gap closing?', *Criminology*, vol 43, no 2, pp 355-405.

Steinberg, L. and Silk, J. (2002) 'Parenting adolescents', in M.J. Bornstein (ed) *Handbook of parenting*, Mahwah, NJ: Lawrence Erlbaum Associates, Inc, pp 103-35.

Steinhausen, H.C. and Winkler-Metzler, C. (2003) 'Prevalence of affective disorders in children and adolescents: findings from the Zurich epidemiological studies', *Acta Psychiatrica Scandinavica Supplementum*, vol 418, no 1, pp 20-3.

Stroud, L., Foster, E., Handwerger, K., Papandonatos, G.D., Granger, D., Kivlighan, K.T. and Niaura, R. (2009) 'Stress response and the adolescent transition: performance versus peer rejection stress', *Development and Psychopathology*, vol 21, no 1, pp 47-68.

Sullivan, O. (2010) 'Changing differences by educational attainment in men and women's domestic work and child care', Paper presented to the British Sociological Association Annual Conference, Glasgow, 7-9 April.

Susman, E., Dorn, L. and Schiefelbein, V. (2003) 'Puberty, sexuality and health', in L. Lerner, M. Easterbrooks and J. Mistry (eds) *Handbook of psychology: Developmental psychology* (vol 6), Hoboken, NJ: John Wiley, pp 293-324.

Sweeting, H., Young, R. and Der, G. (2006) 'Peer victimization and depression in early mid-adolescence: a longitudinal study', *British Journal of Educational Psychology*, vol 76, no 3, pp 577-94.

Sweeting, H., Young, R. and West, P. (2009) 'GHQ increases among Scottish 15 year olds 1987-2006', *Social Psychiatry and Psychiatric Epidemiology*, vol 44, no 7, pp 579-86.

Sweeting, H., West, P., Young, R. and Der, G. (2010) 'Can we explain increases in young people's psychological distress over time?', *Social Science & Medicine*, vol 71, pp 1819-30.

Symonds, J. and Hagell, A. (2011) 'Adolescents and the organisation of their school time: changes over recent decades in England', *Educational Review*, vol 63, no 3, pp 291-312.

Thapar, A., Collishaw, S., Potter, R. and Thapar, A.K. (2010) 'Managing and preventing depression in adolescents', *British Medical Journal*, vol 340, c209.

Tick, N.T., van der Ende, J. and Verhulst, F.C. (2007a) 'Twenty-year trends in emotional and behavioural problems in Dutch children in a changing society', *Acta Psychiatrica Scandinavica*, vol 116, no 6, pp 473-82.

Tick, N.T., van der Ende, J. and Verhulst, F.C. (2008) 'Ten-year trends in self-reported emotional and behavioural problems of Dutch adolescents', *Social Psychiatry and Psychiatric Epidemiology*, vol 43, no 5, pp 349-55.

Tick, N.T., van der Ende, M.S., Koot H.S. and Verhulst, F.C. (2007b) '14-year changes in emotional and behavioral problems of very young Dutch children', *Journal of the American Academy of Child and Adolescent Psychiatry*, vol 46, no 10, pp 1333-40.

Timberlake, J.M. (2003) *Racial and ethnic inequality in exposure to neighborhood poverty and affluence*, University of Chicago Population Research Center Discussion Paper 2002-01, Chicago, IL: University of Chicago.

Toh, S. (2006) 'Trends in ADHD and stimulant use among children, 1993-2003', *Psychiatric Services*, vol 57, no 8, p 1091.

Tolley, E., Girma, M., Stanton-Wharmby, A., Spate, A. and Milbern, J. (1998) *Young opinions, great ideas*, London: National Children's Bureau.

Trainor, S., Delfabbro, P. Anderson, S. and Winefield, A. (2009) 'Leisure activities and adolescent psychological well-being', *Journal of Adolescence*, vol 33, no 1, pp 173-86.

Tremblay, R.E. (2010) 'Developmental origins of disruptive behaviour problems: the "original sin" hypothesis, epigenetics and their consequences for prevention', *Journal of Child Psychology and Psychiatry*, vol 51, no 4, pp 341-67.

Tymms, P., Bolden, D. and Merrell, C. (2008) 'Science in English primary schools: trends in attainment, attitude and approaches', *Perspectives on Education* 1, London: Welcome Foundation, pp 19-42 (www.welcome.ac.uk/perspectives).

UNICEF (United Nations Children's Fund) (2007) *Child poverty in perspective: An overview of child well-being in rich countries. A comprehensive assessment of the lives and well-being of children and adolescents in the economically advanced nations*, Florence: UNICEF Innocenti Research Centre.

UNODC (2011) 'Global Study on Homicide', United Nations Office on Drugs and Crime: Geneva. (www.unodc.org/documents/data-and-analysis/statistics/Homicide/Globa_study_on_homicide_2011_web.pdf).

van Dijk, J.J.M., van Kesteren, J.N. and Smit, P. (2008) *Criminal victimisation in international perspective, Key findings from the 2004-2005 ICVS and EU ICS*, The Hague: Boom Legal Publishers.

van Hoof, A., Raaijmakers, Q.A., van Beek, Y., Hale, W. and Aleva, L. (2008) 'A multi-mediation model on the relations of bullying, victimization, identity, and family with adolescent depressive symptoms', *Journal of Youth and Adolescence*, vol 37, no 7, pp 772-82.

van Jaarsveld, C.H.M., Fidler, J.A., Simon, A.E. and Wardle, J. (2007) 'Persistent impact of pubertal timing on trends in smoking, food choice, activity and stress in adolescence', *Psychosomatic Medicine*, vol 69, no 8, pp 798-806.

Verhulst, F.C., van der Ende, J. and Rietbergen, A. (1997) 'Ten-year time trends of psychopathology in Dutch children and adolescents: no evidence for strong trends', *Acta Psychiatrica Scandinavica*, vol 96, pp 7-13.

Vitiello, B., Zuvekas, S.H. and Norquist, G.S. (2006) 'National estimates of antidepressant medication use among US children, 1997-2002', *Journal of the American Academy of Child and Adolescent Psychiatry*, vol 45, no 3, pp 271-9.

Wangby, M., Magnusson, D. and Stattin, H. (2005) 'Time trends in the adjustment of Swedish teenage girls: a 26-year comparison of 15-year-olds', *Scandinavian Journal of Psychology*, vol 46, no 2, pp 145-56.

Webster, C., Simpson, D., MacDonald, R., Abbas, A., Cieslik, M., Shildrick, T. and Simpson, M. (2004) *Poor transitions: Social exclusion and young adults*, Bristol: The Policy Press.

Weinberg, N.Z., Rahdert, E., Colliver, J.D. and Glantz, M.D. (1998) 'Adolescent substance abuse: a review of the past 10 years', *Journal of American Academy of Child and Adolescent Psychiatry*, vol 37, no 3, pp 252-61.

Wellings, K., Nanchahal, K., Macdowall, W., McManus, S., Erens, B., Mercer, C.H., Johnson, A.M., Copas, A.J., Korovessis, C., Fenton, K.A. and Field, J. (2001) 'Sexual behaviour in Britain: early heterosexual experience', *Lancet*, vol **358**, no 9296, pp 1843-50.

Werner, E.E. and Smith, R.S. (1992) *Overcoming the odds: High risk children from birth to adulthood*, Ithaca, NY: Cornell University Press.

West, P. and Sweeting, H. (2003) 'Fifteen, female and stressed: changing patterns of psychological distress over time', *Journal of Child Psychology and Psychiatry*, vol 44, no 3, pp 399-411.

West, P., Sweeting, H. and Young, R. (2008) 'Transition matters: pupils' experiences of the primary–secondary school transition in the West of Scotland and consequences for well-being and attainment', *Research Papers in Education*, vol 25, no 1, pp 21-50.

Wheaton, B. and Clarke, P. (2003) 'Space meets time: integrating temporal and contextual influences on mental health in early adulthood', *American Sociological Review*, vol 68, no 5, pp 680-706.

Whincup, P.H., Gilg, J.A., Odoki, K., Taylor, S.J.C. and Cook, D.G. (2001) 'Age of menarche in contemporary British teenagers: survey of girls born between 1982 and 1986', *British Medical Journal*, vol 322, no 7294, pp 1095-6.

White, H.R., Loeber, R., Stouthamer-Loeber, M. and Farrington, D.P. (1999) 'Developmental associations between substance use and violence', *Development and Psychopathology*, vol 11, no 4, pp 785-803.

Whitlock, J. (2003) *Fostering school connectedness: Research facts and findings*, ACT for Youth, Upstate Centre of Excellence, Ithaca, NY: Cornell University.

Whittington, C.J., Kendall, T., Fonagy, P., Cottrell, D., Cotgrove, A. and Boddington, E. (2004) 'Selective serotonin reuptake inhibitors in childhood depression: systematic review of published versus unpublished data', *Lancet*, vol 363, no 9418, pp 1341-5.

Wigfield, A., Eccles, J.S., MacIver, D., Reuman, D.A. and Midgley, C. (1991) 'Transitions during early adolescents: changes in children's domain-specific self-perceptions and general self-esteem across the transition to junior high school', *Developmental Psychology*, vol 27, pp 552-65.

Wilens, T.E. (2004) 'Attention-deficit/hyperactivity disorder and the substance use disorders: the nature of the relationship, subtypes at risk, and treatment issues', *Psychiatrics Clinics of North America*, vol 27, no 2, pp 283-301.

Williamson, D.E., Birmaher, B., Anderson, B.P., Al-Shabbout, M. and Ryan, N. (1995) 'Stressful life events in depressed adolescents: the role of dependent events during the depressive episode', *Journal of the American Academy of Child and Adolescent Psychiatry*, vol 34, no 5, pp 591-8.

Williamson, D.E., Birmaher, B., Frank, E., Anderson, B.P., Matty, M.K. and Kupfer, D.J. (1998) 'Nature of life events and difficulties in depressed adolescents', *Journal of the American Academy of Child and Adolescent Psychiatry*, vol 37, no 10, pp 1049-57.

Williamson, D.E., Birmaher, B., Ryan, N., Shiffrin, T., Lusky, J., Protopapa, J., Dahl, R. and Brent, D. (2003) 'The stressful life events schedule for children and adolescents: development and validation', *Psychiatry Research*, vol 119, no 3, pp 225–41.

Wilson, D., Sharp, C. and Patterson, A. (2006) *Young people and crime: Findings from the 2005 Offending, Crime, and Justice Survey*, Home Office Statistical Bulletin, London: Research, Development and Statistics Directorate, Home Office.

Windle, M., Miller-Tutzauer, C. and Dominico, D. (1992) 'Alcohol use, suicidal behaviour, and risky activities among adolescents', *Journal of Research on Adolescence*, vol 2, no 4, pp 317–30.

Windle, M., Spear, P., Fuligni, A., Angold, A., Brown, J., Pine, D., Smith, G., Giedd, J. and Dahl, R. (2008) 'Transitions into underage and problem drinking: developmental processes and mechanisms between 10 and 15 years of age', *Pediatrics*, vol 121, Suppl, pp S273–S289.

Winnail, S.F., Valois, R.F. and Dowda, M. (1997) 'Athletics and substance use among public high school students in a Southern state', *American Journal of Health Studies*, vol 13, no 4, pp 187–94.

Winograd, G., Cohen, P. and Chen, H. (2008) 'Adolescent borderline symptoms in the community: prognosis for functioning over 20 years', *Journal of Child Psychology and Psychiatry*, vol 49, no 9, pp 933–41.

Wolke, D., Woods, S., Bloomfield, L. and Karstadt, L. (2000) 'The association between direct and relational bullying and behaviour problems among primary schoolchildren', *Journal of Child Psychology and Psychiatry*, vol 41, no 8, pp 989–1002.

Wong, I.C.K., Murray, M.L., Novak-Camilleri, D. and Stephens, P. (2004) 'Increased prescribing trends of paediatric psychotropic medications', *Archives of Disease in Childhood*, vol 89, no 12, pp 1131–2.

Wright, S. (2005) *Young people's decision-making in 14-19 education and training: A review of the literature*, Nuffield Review of 14-19 Education and Training Briefing Paper 4, Oxford: Department of Educational Studies, University of Oxford.

Xue, Y., Leventhal, T., Brooks-Gunn, J. and Earls, F. (2005) 'Neighborhood residence and mental health problems of 5–11 year olds', *Archives of General Psychiatry*, vol 62, no 5, pp 554–63.

Yin, Z., Katims, D. and Zapata, J.T. (1999) 'Participation in leisure activities and involvement in delinquency by Mexican American adolescents', *Hispanic Journal of Behavioral Sciences*, vol 21, no 2, pp 170–85.

Youngman, M. (1978) 'Six reactions to school transfer', *British Journal of Educational Psychology*, vol 48, no 4, pp 282–9.

Youniss, J., McLellan, J.A., Su, Y. and Yates, M. (1999) 'The role of community service in identity development: normative, unconventional, and deviant orientations', *Journal of Adolescent Research*, vol 14, no 2, pp 248-61.

Yule, W. and Smith, P. (2008) 'Post-traumatic stress disorder', in M. Rutter, D. Bishop, D. Pine, S. Scott, J. Stevenson, E. Taylor and A. Thapar (eds) *Rutter's child and adolescent psychiatry*, Oxford: Blackwell Publishing, pp 686-97.

Zaff, J.F., Moore, K.A., Papillo, A.R. and Williams, S. (2003) 'Implications of extracurricular activity participation during adolescence on positive outcomes', *Journal of Adolescent Research*, vol 18, no 6, pp 599-630.

Zarrett, N.R. (2007) 'The dynamic relation between out-of-school activities and adolescent development', PhD dissertation, University of Michigan.

Zarrett, N., Peck, S.C. and Eccles, J.S. (2007) 'What does it take to get youth involved? A pattern-centered approach for studying youth, family, and community predictors of youth out-of-school activity participation', Society for Research on Child Development, 'Innovative approaches for assessing adolescents' experiences in organized activities', Biennial meeting of the Society for Research on Child Development, 29 March-1 April 2005, Boston, MA.

Zuzanek, J. and Mannell, R. (2003) 'Trends in adolescent time use: Canada 1986 to 1998', Paper presented at the International Association for Time Use Research Conference, Brussels, Belgium, 17-19 September.

The Nuffield Foundation's Changing Adolescence Programme

The **Changing Adolescence Programme** (originally called the Adolescent Mental Health Initiative) was established in 2005 in response to research findings that showed a significant increase in young people's emotional and behavioural problems between 1975 and 1999. The aim of the programme was to examine the reasons for this increase and to understand better how the lives of young people have changed over the last 30 or so years.

The programme consisted of a series of commissioned research reviews to look at various aspects of teenage life, to evaluate evidence of emerging trends over time, and to assess the research literature on possible causes of those trends. The work of the programme also included seminars and workshops to bring together researchers, policy makers and practitioners in strategic discussions. The research programme was chaired for the Foundation by Professor Sir Michael Rutter, and co-ordinated by Dr Ann Hagell. Further information on the programme is available at www.nuffieldfoundation.org/changing-adolescence.

Six new research reviews were funded, and other Nuffield Foundation grants also fed into the work of the programme. The key grants on which this book is based included:

Professor Barbara Maughan, King's College London: *Secular trends in child and adolescent mental health* (grants awarded 2001 and 2004)

Dr Stephan Collishaw, Cardiff University: *Testing causes of time trends in adolescent mental health* (Nuffield Foundation New Career Development Fellowship 2005)

Dr Leon Feinstein, Professor Jacqueline Eccles, Dr Karen Robson, Institute of Education and University of Michigan: *Time trends in young people's time use and implications for mental health* (awarded 2007)

Dr Michael Donmall, Dr Tim Millar, Dr Judith Aldridge and Dr Petra Meier, University of Manchester: *Trends in adolescent substance use: social, behavioural and mental health perspectives* (awarded 2007).

Professor Frances Gardner, Dr Stephan Collishaw, Professor Barbara Maughan and Professor Jackie Scott, University of Oxford, Cardiff University, King's College London and University of Cambridge: *Time trends in parenting and in adolescent problem behaviour. Can one help explain the other?* (awarded 2007)

Professor Sarah Curtis, Professor Stephan Stansfield, Durham University and University of London: *Mapping links between young people, neighbourhoods, schools and families with respect to mental health* (awarded 2007)

Dr Seija Sandberg and Professor Robert MacDonald, University College London and University of Teesside: *Review of adolescent stress* (awarded 2008)

Professor John Gray, Professor Maurice Galton and Dr Colleen McLaughlin University of Cambridge: *School experiences and mental health outcomes amongst 10-14 year olds: A review of the effects of school transfers, transitions and other potentially relevant school-related factors* (awarded 2008).

Dr Ann Hagell, Dr Jennifer Symonds, Dr Nacho Gimenez-Nadal and Dr Stephen Peck: *Preliminary analyses of UK adolescent time trends in the Multinational Time Use Study* (funded through the main CAP support funds, 2010)

Reference list for primary data sources for graph data in Chapter Seven

HBSC, Health Behaviour of School-aged Children survey

Currie, C., Hurrelmann, K., Settertobulte, W., Smith, R. and Todd, J. (2000) *Health and health behaviour among young people*, Copenhagen: World Health Organization (WHO) Regional Office for Europe.

Currie, C., Roberts, C., Morgan, A., Smith, R., Settertobulte, W., Samdal, O. and Barnekow Rasmussen, V. (2004) *Young people's health in context*, Copenhagen: World Health Organization (WHO) Regional Office for Europe.

Currie, C., Gabhainn, S.N., Godeau, E., Roberts, C., Smith, R., Currie, D., Picket, W., Richter, M., Morgan, A. and Barnekow, V. (2008) *Inequalities in young people's health*, Copenhagen: World Health Organization.

ESPAD, European School Survey Project on Alcohol and Other Drugs

Hibell, B., Andersson, B., Bjarnason, T. and Koch, G.G. (2007) *The 1995 ESPAD report: Alcohol and other drug use among students in 26 European countries*, Stockholm: The Swedish Council for Information on Alcohol and Other Drugs (CAN) and The Pompidou Group at the Council of Europe.

Hibell, B., Andersson, B., Ahlström, S., Balakireva, O., Bjarnason, T., Kokkevi, A. and Morgan, M. (2000) *The 1999 ESPAD report: Alcohol and other drug use among students in 30 European countries*, Stockholm: The Swedish Council for Information on Alcohol and Other Drugs (CAN) and The Pompidou Group at the Council of Europe.

Hibell, B., Andersson, B., Bjarnason, T., Ahlström, S., Balakireva, O., Kokkevi, A. and Morgan, M. (2004) *The ESPAD report 2003: Alcohol and other drug use among students in 35 European countries*, Stockholm: The Swedish Council for Information on Alcohol and Other Drugs (CAN) and The Pompidou Group at the Council of Europe.

Hibell, B., Guttormsson, U., Ahlström, S., Balakireva, O., Bjarnason, T., Kokkevi, A. and Kraus, L. (2009) *The 2007 ESPAD report: Substance use among students in 35 European countries*, Stockholm: The Swedish Council for Information on Alcohol and Other Drugs (CAN) and The Pompidou Group at the Council of Europe.

SDDU, Smoking, Drinking and Drug Use survey
Fuller, E. (ed) (2009) *Smoking, drinking and drug use among young people in England 2008*, London: NHS Information Centre for Health and Social Care (www.ic.nhs.uk/pubs/sdd08fullreport).

SHEU, Schools Health Education Unit
Schools Health Education Unit (2010) *Young people into 2010*, Exeter: SHEU (for an overview of the surveys). SHEU data for these graphs were provided by SHEU to Dr Jennifer Symonds (personal communication, 16 February 2010). We are very grateful to David McGeorge, SHEU Publications Manager, for his assistance.

Index

Note: page numbers in *italic* type refer to figures.